MIDTERM MADNESS

THE ELECTIONS OF 2002

EDITED BY
LARRY J. SABATO

ROWMAN & LITTLEFIELD PUBLISHERS, INC.
Lanham • Boulder • New York • Oxford

ROWMAN & LITTLEFIELD PUBLISHERS, INC.

Published in the United States of America
by Rowman & Littlefield Publishers, Inc.
A Member of the Rowman & Littlefield Publishing Group
4501 Forbes Boulevard, Suite 200, Lanham, Maryland 20706
www.rowmanlittlefield.com

P.O. Box 317, Oxford OX2 9RU, United Kingdom

British Library Cataloguing in Publication Information Available

Library of Congress Cataloging-in-Publication Data

Midterm madness : the elections of 2002 / edited by Larry J. Sabato.
    p.   cm.—(Center for Politics series)
    Includes bibliographical references and index.
    ISBN 0-7425-2685-2 (cloth : alk. paper)—ISBN 0-7425-2686-0 (pbk. :
alk. paper)
    1. United States. Congress—Elections, 2002.   2. Elections—United
States.   I. Sabato, Larry.   II. Series.
JK19682002 .M53   2003
324.973′0931—dc21   2003001964

Printed in the United States of America

∞ ™ The paper used in this publication meets the minimum requirements of
American National Standard for Information Sciences—Permanence of Paper for
Printed Library Materials, ANSI/NISO Z39.48–1992.

MIDTERM MADNESS

Contents

Acknowledgments   vii

List of Tables and Figures   ix

Preface   xi

1 The George W. Bush Midterm: From Popular-Vote Loser to Political Colossus in Two Not-So-Easy Election Steps
Larry J. Sabato, University of Virginia Center for Politics   1

2 Air Force Won
Chuck Todd, The Hotline   35

3 Playing Second Fiddle: Political Ads, International Newsmakers Bury Election Coverage
Mark Jurkowitz, Boston Globe *Media Writer*   47

4 Starting to Click: Online Campaigning in the 2002 Elections
Michael Cornfield, Institute for Politics, Democracy, and the Internet at The George Washington University   57

5 U. S. House Races: Republican Resurgence after Eight Lean Years
Maureen Schweers, The House Race Hotline   67

6 Iowa Senate: Harkin's Best Yet
Mike Glover, Associated Press   77

7 Minnesota Senate: Tragedy and Triumph in a National Headline Contest
Daniel J.B. Hofrenning, St. Olaf College   85

8 Missouri Senate: Sympathy's Time Limit for Jean Carnahan
Steve Kraske, Kansas City Star   95

9 New Jersey Senate: Back to the Future as Torricelli Yields to Lautenberg
Bruce A. Larson, Fairleigh Dickinson University   105

10 New Hampshire Senate: Down to the Wire in New
   Hampshire
      Linda L. Fowler, Dartmouth College   125

11 North Carolina Senate: Dole Finally Beats Clinton (Sort Of)
      Ryan Thornburg, washingtonpost.com   137

12 South Dakota Senate: George Bush vs. Tom Daschle, Once
   Removed
      David Kranz, Sioux Falls Argus Leader   145

13 Tennessee Senate: The Resurrection of Lamar Alexander
      James W. Brosnan, The Memphis Commercial Appeal   155

14 Texas Senate: A Race about Race
      Jay Root, Fort Worth Star-Telegram   167

15 It's a Sonny Day in Georgia
      Charles S. Bullock III, University of Georgia   177

16 California Governor: Don't Vote, It Will Only Encourage
   Them
      Mark Z. Barabak, Los Angeles Times   187

17 Florida Governor: Three Elections in One
      Susan A. MacManus, University of South Florida   195

18 Illinois Governor: It Was More Than the Ryan Name
      Paul Green, Roosevelt University   209

19 Iowa Governor: Vilsack Gets an Encore
      David Yepsen, Des Moines Register   219

20 Maryland Governor: The Close of Camelot
      Daniel LeDuc, The Washington Post   225

21 Minnesota Governor: The End of the Ventura Interlude
      Holly A. Heyser, St. Paul Pioneer Press   233

22 Pennsylvania Governor: Philadelphia Gets a Governor
      Thomas Fitzgerald, Philadelphia Inquirer   247

23 Texas Governor: The Democratic "Dream Team" Bites the
   Dust
      Peggy Fikac, San Antonio Express-News   255

24 A Final Look in the Rearview Mirror for 2002: The Midterm
   Map of America
      Larry J. Sabato, University of Virginia Center for Politics 263

Index   267

About the Contributors   279

Acknowledgments

The indispensable man in organizing and assembling this book was Joshua J. Scott, director of communications at the University of Virginia Center for Politics. The editor cannot thank him enough for his careful work and untiring dedication to this project. Assisting Joshua was Emily Roper, whose remarkable organizational and editorial abilities made this book possible. Finally, the editor wishes to acknowledge the editing and graphic support of two of the Center for Politics's most talented and hardest working staffers, Rakesh Gopalan and Adam Blumenkrantz, as well as the fine professionals at Rowman & Littlefield, especially our wonderfully talented editor, Jennifer Knerr, and her marvelously able assistant, Renee Legatt.

Tables and Figures

TABLES

Table 1.1	Gain or Loss for President's Party: Presidential Election Years	4
Table 1.2	Gain or Loss for President's Party: Midterm Election Years	4
Table 1.3	Party Identification Among Voters Who Cast a Ballot, 1998–2002	12
Table 1.4	Voter Turnout in Midterm Elections	13
Table 1.5	Senate Races, 2002	16
Table 1.6	Defeated Senate Incumbents, 1980–2002	20
Table 1.7	Defeated House Incumbents, 1980–2002	21
Table 1.8	Gubernatorial Races, 2002	22
Table 1.9	Total Votes by Party, 2002	32
Table 5.1	House Incumbents Defeated in General Election, 2002	73
Table 9.1	Election-Eve Poll of New Jersey Voters, 2002	116
Table 15.1	Selected Results from Georgia's General Election, 2002	182

FIGURES

Figure 1.1	Political Divisions of the U.S. Senate on Opening Day, 80th–108th Congresses	6
Figure 1.2	Political Divisions of the U.S. House of Representatives on Opening Day, 80th–108th Congresses	7
Figure 1.3	Number of Governors by Party, 1947–2003	8

ix

Figure 1.4   Voter Turnout in Midterm Elections   13

Figure 1.5   Senate Races, 2002 (map)   18

Figure 1.6   Gubernatorial Races, 2002 (map)   25

Figure 1.7   Partisan Make-up of State Legislatures, 2003 (map)   30

Figure 21.1   Polling in Minnesota Governor Race, 2002   241

Figure 24.1   The Midterm Map of America, 2002 (map)   265

Preface

There are midterms and then there are MIDTERMS. The 2002 election at the middle of President George W. Bush's first term was a capital-letter MIDTERM. The Senate, House, and governor contests produced drama aplenty. A tragic plane crash killed a U.S. senator just ten days before the election, casting his state into mourning and political confusion. Another senator, losing in his reelection bid because of corruption, chose to withdraw in midcampaign, throwing his race into chaos. The president's own brother was involved in a knockdown, drag-out campaign for reelection in the state that installed the current White House occupant by a grand total of 537 votes.

And there was so much more, besides. A vicious redistricting cycle paired up incumbents versus incumbents around the country, and forced many other members of Congress to scramble or change residency to survive—or to throw in the towel and retire. An orgy of campaign spending by the parties and interest groups, unmatched in all of American history, flooded most states and districts with highly negative television advertisements and mailers. Famous names like Thurmond took their final bow, and others, including two Kennedys, lost elections where they had been favored.

Most of all, 2002 featured a titanic struggle between the political parties for control of Congress. Both houses were narrowly divided in the so-called 50–50 America produced by the split 2000 presidential election. Which party, if either, would emerge with the spoils of war? The battle between the partisans seesawed, fed by a key defection in the U.S. Senate, then the September 11 disaster, followed by a deluge of corporate scandals, the build-up to confrontation with Iraq, and a killing spree by deranged snipers in the Washington area. In the end, there was no landslide as in 1974 or 1994, but there was a clear victor: the Republicans. And the colossus of 2002 was Bush, the driving force behind the GOP triumph who made history by becoming the first chief executive since Franklin D. Roosevelt to add seats to his party's contingent in both the U.S. Senate and U.S. House in his first midterm election. Firmly securing the House and recapturing the Senate gave Bush an unusual opportunity in American politics—to be stronger in the second half than the first half of his term.

The rich stew of the 2002 midterm elections will be painstakingly analyzed and dissected, as befits any prize recipe, in this book. We have gathered together a superb team of academics and journalists to examine 2002 both from the macro level (the election as a national event with profound meaning for the nation) and from the micro level (the individual key contests for Senate, Governor, and House).

Naturally, with 34 Senate, 36 governor, and 435 House contests in 2002, we needed to be selective, lest this volume resemble *War and Peace* in length. As the reader can see, the editor has attempted to mix and match races that were won by Republicans or Democrats in each of the "big three" categories of the houses of Congress and the statehouses. Mostly, highly competitive elections were chosen, but a few less competitive but still instructive contests were included. And clearly, it was vital for the reader to get a good flavor of the regional differences in 2002, so every section of the United States finds representation in this book.

First, this volume's editor, Dr. Larry J. Sabato, director of the University of Virginia Center for Politics, sets the scene, providing a historical perspective by briefly reviewing post–World War II midterm history. Then Sabato examines all the key parts of the 2002 election, analyzing the voting returns and demographics in detail. In the following chapter Chuck Todd, editor-in-chief of *The Hotline*, Washington's premier daily briefing on American politics, gives his perspective, noting what both major parties did right and wrong.

Next, *Boston Globe* media writer Mark Jurkowitz analyzes the media's influence—or lack thereof—in the 2002 elections, followed by a discussion of politics on the Internet by Michael Cornfield, professor and director of the Institute for Politics, Democracy, and the Internet at The George Washington University. Next, Maureen Schweers of *The House Race Hotline* offers a thorough roundup of House races that resulted in a Republican resurgence in the "more numerous body" of Congress.

Turning next to the Senate, well-known Associated Press writer Mike Glover kicks off the series by looking at the Iowa contest where Democrats used extensive get-out-the-vote (GOTV) efforts to return Senator Tom Harkin to Capitol Hill. Nationally, the GOP had the better 2002 GOTV program, which Republicans dubbed the "72-Hour Project," referring to the three days before the election. In 2000, it was the Democrats who triumphed in the GOTV. Every year is different, and as Glover shows with Iowa, every state does not follow the national trend in any given year—a principle worth remembering as we wade through generalizations about our elections! Continuing the focus on the Senate, professor Daniel Hofrenning of St. Olaf College chronicles the tragedy of Senator Paul Wellstone's death and the circus atmosphere that ensued in Minnesota for Wellstone's seat. Steve Kraske, political writer for the *Kansas City Star*, examines Missouri Senator Jean Carnahan's failed bid to finish the remainder of her deceased husband's term.

Bruce Larson of Fairleigh Dickinson University looks at another wild ride and investigates the strange turn of events in the New Jersey Senate race as Senator Robert Torricelli stepped out of the running just five weeks before Election Day due to corruption accusations. Dartmouth College professor Linda Fowler examines Republican Congressman John Sununu's close and crucial Senate victory in New Hampshire. The next two chapters look at the North Carolina and South Dakota Senate races, respectively, which offered variations on a theme: proxy match-ups. Ryan Thornburg of washingtonpost.com analyzes the Tar Heel battle that pitted a Dole against a representative of the Clinton era, while the *Sioux Falls Argus Leader*'s David Kranz examines the South Dakota Senate race that many perceived as a once-removed war between President George W. Bush and then–Senate Majority Leader Tom Daschle. James W. Brosnan, veteran reporter for the *Memphis Commercial Appeal*, chronicles the rise of former Tennessee governor and two-time Republican presidential candidate Lamar Alexander, while Jay Root of the *Fort Worth Star-Telegram* analyzes the fascinating issue of race in the intriguing, historic contest for U.S. senator from Texas.

No state in 2002 surprised the experts more than Georgia. University of Georgia Professor Charles S. Bullock III takes an in-depth look at the many-faceted shocker in the Peach State. Bullock analyzes the gubernatorial and Senate elections that brought Republicans to power and turned Georgia politics upside down.

The remaining chapters focus on selected gubernatorial elections throughout the country, beginning with California Governor Gray Davis's successful reelection. *Los Angeles Times* reporter Mark Z. Barabak evaluates voter apathy in a depressing contest between two unpopular candidates. Susan MacManus of the University of South Florida analyzes the Florida governor's race that saw first the previously unknown Bill McBride defeat former U.S. Attorney General Janet Reno in the Democratic primary, and then McBride lose in a landslide to incumbent Governor (and presidential brother) Jeb Bush. Paul Green of Roosevelt University looks at the so-sad-it's-funny battle of the Ryans in the Illinois governor election, while veteran *Des Moines Register* reporter David Yepsen analyzes Democrat Tom Vilsack's reelection as governor of Iowa.

Daniel LeDuc of *The Washington Post* ably chronicles the unexpected rise of the moribund Republican Party in Maryland, as the GOP's Robert Ehrlich defeated Camelot's own Kathleen Kennedy Townsend for the governorship. The next chapter, by Holly Heyser of the *St. Paul Pioneer Press*, records the end of the Independence Party interlude in Minnesota, as the often outrageous Governor (and former professional wrestler) Jesse Venture steps aside; Heyser analyzes the three-way race to fill "The Body's" large, if clownish, shoes. Thomas Fitzgerald of the *Philadelphia Inquirer* looks at the election that put a Philadelphian in the Pennsylvania governor's mansion for the first time in 88 years, while Peggy Fikac of the *San Antonio Express-News* looks at the fall of the diverse, ahead-of-its-time Democratic ticket in Texas.

We hope you enjoy the special combination of topics and talents brought together for this project on an especially important American election. The chapters vary considerably in style and format. We decided that it was best to let this skilled mix of academics and journalists to speak in their individual voices. After all, as we note in chapter 1, a midterm election is a collection of local contests, and that aspect of federalism must be reflected here.

Most midterms are forgettable, even in the short term. The 2002 midterm already has made it into the history books, and it has the potential for reordering the normal, downhill flow of a presidency. More importantly, if President Bush and his guru Karl Rove have their way, this fascinating election could possibly, just possibly, mark the beginning of the end of 50–50 America—and the opening of a new era of GOP tilt.

Larry J. Sabato

1

The George W. Bush Midterm

From Popular-Vote Loser to Political Colossus in Two Not-So-Easy Election Steps

LARRY J. SABATO

University of Virginia Center for Politics

Rarely have a president's fortunes changed as rapidly as George W. Bush's. Elected in 2000 by the skin of a controversial Supreme Court decision's teeth, Bush began his term as an exceptionally weak chief executive, dependent on a fickle electorate's tolerance for a popular-vote loser and with only paper-thin control of Congress. The loss of the U.S. Senate, with the defection of Jim Jeffords (I-VT) in May 2001, appeared to foreshadow a difficult four years at the helm, as did the onset of a recession in March 2001. On September 10, 2001, Bush's short honeymoon with Congress and the public was over, his popularity was close to falling below 50 percent, and the Democrats were increasingly optimistic about taking control of the House of Representatives and extending a Senate majority in November 2002. And then came September 11. The president's deft handling of a massive national tragedy, and the war that followed, transformed his image. The American citizenry rallied around their leader, partly of necessity and fear, but also out of gratitude for a job professionally and skillfully handled.

Unlike many previous crises, however, the war on terrorism would be a lengthy one, and thus the boost in Bush's ratings was similarly sustained. To the considerable surprise of most longtime election observers, national security—which had been placed on the backburner or off the stove entirely after the fall of Communism in the late 1980s—dominated the 2002 midterm elections, trumping a bad economy and other domestic concerns. The continued threat posed by al Qaeda, a looming confrontation with Iraq, and Bush's popularity and dominant persona enabled Republicans to move up rather than down in the Senate and the House. For President Bush, who figuratively bet his ranch on the 2002 outcome, the pleasing results delivered the popular mandate that eluded him in 2000. A second honeymoon seemed in store, as the GOP Congress prepared to do the chief executive's bidding—at least for a little while, and within the legislature's structural, limited ability to act quickly on a broad agenda of any type.

A SHORT HISTORY OF POST–WORLD WAR II MIDTERM ELECTIONS

Every four years, at the midterm of the incumbent president, the elections for U.S. Senate, House, and state governorships take on supreme importance. Cosmic interpretations of the various campaigns and the election results dominate television and print news, and political journalists, academics, and junkies read the tea leaves with such enthusiasm that even Miss Cleo is probably impressed.

But is all the attention and crystal ball-gazing justified? A good case can be made that the midterms deserve most of their hype, because the governors and congressmen elected then have an enormous impact on policy during their terms. A few will even be elected president or vice president eventually, having been shaped by the events that propelled them to their first offices.

But the predictions flowing from the midterms are another matter. To cite just two examples: When the Republicans took over both congressional chambers and many key governorships in 1994, premature obituaries of President Bill Clinton dominated the news for months; he won an easy reelection in 1996, partly because of those GOP victories, which led the Republicans to overreach in the government shutdown of 1995. Clinton's next midterm, in 1998, led to equally erroneous conclusions. Despite the Monica Lewinsky scandal, Democrats actually picked up House seats, a feat not accomplished since 1934 in the heydey of Franklin Delano Roosevelt's New Deal. The impeachment-bound Republicans seemed to be digging another presidential grave for their party, and Vice President Al Gore appeared to be the inevitable beneficiary. Yet history records a win by George W. Bush in 2000—a technical knockout, to be sure, but a win nonetheless.

So if midterm elections are not terribly predictive, what do they teach us? Let's take a brief trip through midterm history since World War II to find out.

Chronological Countdown to 2002

Just for starters, let's take a glance at the midterm results from 1946 to 1998 (also see tables 1.1 and 1.2, as well as figures 1.1, 1.2, and 1.3 for reference). It is all so easy to analyze after the fact, and every bit of it falls neatly into a sentence or two:

- 1946: After fourteen years of solid Democratic control under FDR and Truman, voters want change. The end of World War II and post-war economic dislocation encourage the "time for a change" theme. Truman doesn't seem up to the job—who would after Franklin Roosevelt?—and the mantra becomes, "To err is Truman." So Republicans captured both houses of Congress, grabbing 55 House seats and 12 Senate seats, plus 2 more governorships (for a total of 25 out of 48).
- 1950: Truman's come-from-behind presidential victory in 1948 had restored Democratic rule by adding 76 House and 9 Senate seats. But eighteen straight years of Democratic presidencies took its toll again in the midterm, as Democrats gave back 29 House and 6 Senate seats.
- 1954: Eisenhower's triumph two years earlier gave the GOP narrow majorities in Congress, even though his coattails were not particularly long. By the time of the midterm, a slight swing away from the Republicans cost 18 of the party's 24 newly gained House seats and one Senate seat.
- 1958: This is the first modern example of the so-called "sixth-year itch," when voters decide to give the other party sizeable congressional majorities after the first six years of a two-term presidency. While Democrats had already won back control of Congress in 1956, despite Eisenhower's landslide reelection, the additional 48 House and 13 Senate berths for Democrats insured that Ike's legislative influence would be minimal in his final two years in office.
- 1962: Like Eisenhower before him, John F. Kennedy had almost no coattails in his 1960 presidential squeaker; Democrats actually lost 20 House seats and 2 Senate seats. JFK feared more losses in his 1962 midterm, but the Cuban Missile Crisis—the "Missiles of October"—boosted support for his administration just before the balloting. The result was a wash, with Democrats losing 4 House

Table 1.1   Gain or Loss for President's Party: Presidential Election Years

Year	President	House	Senate	Governor
1948	Truman (D)	+76	+9	+6
1952	Eisenhower (R)	+24	+2	+5
1956	Eisenhower (R)	−2	0	−2
1960	Kennedy (D)	−20	−2	0
1964	Johnson (D)	+38	+2	−1
1968	Nixon (R)	+7	+5	+4
1972	Nixon (R)	+13	−2	−1
1976	Carter (D)	+2	0	+1
1980	Reagan (R)	+33	+12	+4
1984	Reagan (R)	+15	−2	+1
1988	Bush (R)	−3	−1	−1
1992	Clinton (D)	−10	0	+2
1996	Clinton (D)	+9	−2	−1
2000	Bush (R)	−2	−5	−1

Table 1.2   Gain or Loss for President's Party: Midterm Election Years

Year	President	House	Senate	Governor
1946	Truman (D)	−55	−12	+2
1950	Truman (D)	−29	−6	−6
1954	Eisenhower (R)	−18	−1	−9
1958	Eisenhower (R)	−48	−13	−5
1962	Kennedy (D)	−4	+3	0
1966	Johnson (D)	−47	−4	−8
1970	Nixon (R)	−12	+2	−11
1974	Ford (R)	−48	−5	−5
1978	Carter (D)	−15	−3	−5
1982	Reagan (R)	−26	+1	−7
1986	Reagan (R)	−5	−8	+8
1990	Bush (R)	−9	−1	−2
1994	Clinton (D)	−52	−9	−10
1998	Clinton (D)	+5	0	0
2002	Bush (R)	+6	+2	−1

seats but picking up 3 Senate seats. "October Surprises" can affect congressional elections every bit as much as presidential contests.

- 1966: Lyndon Johnson's historic 61 percent landslide in 1964 appeared to presage a new era of Democratic rule, as he carried in 38 House freshmen and 2 additional senators to an already heavily Democratic Congress. But that was before Vietnam began to devour

LBJ. Already by 1966, voters were turning against the president's conduct of the war, and it cost the Democrats 47 House seats and 2 Senate seats—though not overall control of Congress.

- 1970: Richard Nixon's close 43 percent victory in 1968 didn't stop him from dreaming of a "silent majority" of Republicans and conservative Southern Democrats, and he made a major effort to improve the GOP's weak position in Congress. (Nixon had added but 7 House members and 5 senators to the Republican minority in 1968.) His efforts paid off to a certain degree, as the GOP added 2 Senate seats in 1970, while holding House losses to a relatively small 12 seats. Democrats still ruled the Capitol Hill roost, though.

- 1974: Oddly, Nixon's 61 percent reelection landslide in 1972 almost precisely returned his party to its paltry 1968 levels in both houses. The Republicans could ill afford a coattail-less election, given what was soon to happen: Nixon's resignation in disgrace, a recession, and an unelected successor GOP president (Gerald Ford) who squandered his initial popularity by pardoning Nixon—all just in time for November 1974. Democrats picked up 48 House seats and 5 Senate seats; Ford was left mainly with his veto power for his remaining two years in office.

- 1978: Jimmy Carter's narrow 1976 election left Congress virtually unchanged, though still heavily Democratic. And Carter's fall from grace had barely started in 1978. A quiet midterm before the storm of 1980 nonetheless subtracted 15 House and 3 Senate seats from the Democratic totals.

- 1982: Ronald Reagan's ten-point slaughter of Carter in 1980 was a now-rare coattail election, as the GOP also won 33 House seats and 12 Senate seats. That was enough to take over the Senate outright and obtain a working majority on some issues with conservative House Democrats. But this tumultuous period in American politics continued through 1982, when a serious recession deprived the GOP of 26 House seats. The Senate stayed Republican, however, and the GOP actually added a seat.

- 1986: After yet another coattail-less reelection of a president—Reagan's massive 59 percent win in 1984—the sixth-year itch returned in 1986. Voters turned over 8 Senate seats to the Democrats, and thus control of that body. The GOP lost only 5 House seats, but the Democrats were solidly in charge of the House in any event.

- 1990: Vice President Bush had won Reagan's "third term" in 1988 by a solid 54 percent margin, but the Republicans suffered from no

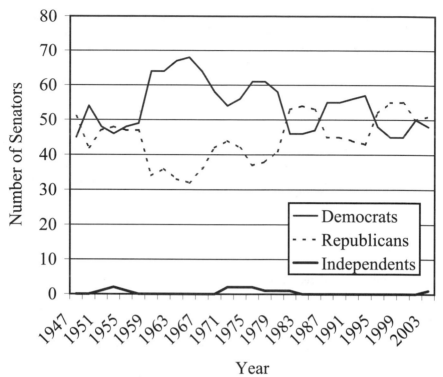

Figure 1.1   Political Divisions of the U.S. Senate on Opening Day, 80th–108th Congresses

coattails again, losing 3 House seats and one Senate seat. With partisan politics somewhat at abeyance due to the pre–Persian Gulf War military buildup, a quiet midterm saw Republicans lose 9 House seats and one Senate berth. Much like Carter in 1978, Bush did not see the gathering storm clouds in this eerie calm.

- 1994: A recession and a disengaged administration took George H. W. Bush from the all-time heights of 90 percent popularity to a humiliating 38 percent finish in the 1992 election. With Ross Perot securing 19 percent, Bill Clinton's 43 percent victory was not impressive, and Democrats lost 10 House seats and kept even in the Senate. A disastrous overreaching by new President Clinton on health care reform, gays in the military, and other issues, coupled with a slow economy, produced a sixth-year itch in the second year. In 1994 Republicans gained an eye-popping 52 House seats and 9 Senate seats to win control of both houses.

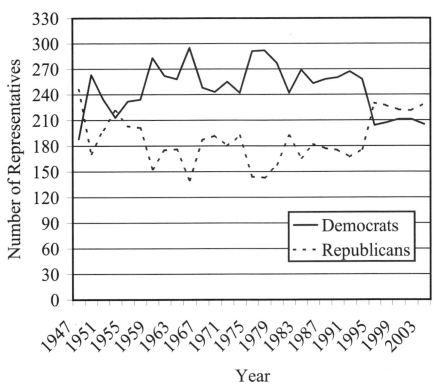

Figure 1.2 Political Divisions of the U.S. House of Representatives on Opening Day, 80th–108th Congresses

- 1998: Proving that every defeat can yield the seeds of victory, Clinton let Republicans overreach just as he had. Running against both ex–Senate Majority Leader Bob Dole (the GOP nominee) and Speaker Newt Gingrich (the unpopular foil), Clinton won a 49 percent reelection. But Democrats captured only 9 House seats and actually lost 2 more Senate seats, leaving Republicans in charge of Congress. Would Clinton have another catastrophic midterm election? It certainly looked that way as the Monica Lewinsky scandal unfolded. But Republicans again overplayed their hand, beginning unpopular impeachment proceedings that produced a Democratic gain of 5 House seats (with the Senate unchanged).

And now, this historical review leads us to the subject of this volume. In capsule, the 2002 midterm could be summarized in this way:

- 2002: The George W. Bush Midterm, plain and simple. In an election dominated by terrorism, Iraq, and the president himself, the Republicans defied conventional wisdom by gaining seats in both houses of Congress, making Bush the first president since Franklin D. Roosevelt in 1934 to pick up seats in both houses in his first term. The Democrats were unable to link the poor economy to Bush, and the media's extensive coverage of the impending confrontation with Iraq and the Washington, D.C.–area sniper incidents overshadowed the somewhat fuzzy Democratic election agenda. In the final two weeks of the general election, key White House adviser Karl Rove sent Bush on a whirlwind campaign tour of the battleground states, which ended up reaping rich rewards for the GOP. The Republicans gained 2 seats in the Senate and 6 House seats. The only positive note for the Democrats was a net gain of 3 governorships, but the GOP maintained a narrow overall statehouse majority (26 to 24).

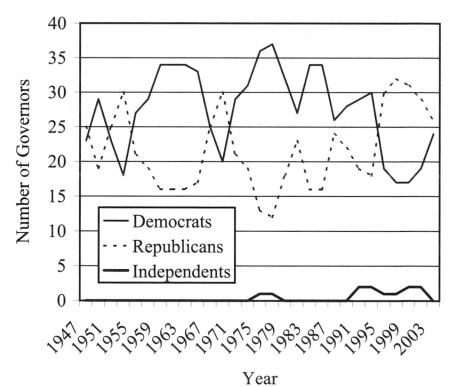

Figure 1.3   Number of Governors by Party, 1947–2003

HOW "AIR FORCE ONE" WON

Many years ago in his seminal book, *Presidential Power*, political scientist Richard Neustadt famously wrote that the power of the president is "the power to persuade."[1] With due respect to Neustadt, after the 2002 elections, a strong case can be made for a new formulation: "The power of the president is the power to set the agenda."

By nature, agenda-setting is a prerequisite to persuasion, so my axiom may be no more than a preface to Neustadt's. Still, in 2002 we all saw the enormous ability of a skillful and daring president to set the table for an election. George W. Bush ran roughshod over all Democratic attempts to make domestic concerns such as health care and Social Security the central issues of the Senate and House contests. Beginning in late August, he and his administration changed the subject from the CEO scandals (Enron, ImClone, Tyco, WorldCom, Global Crossing, Qwest, Arthur Anderson, Halliburton, Merrill Lynch, Rite-Aid, Adelphia, and Martha Stewart) to the possibility of war with Iraq. Whatever the Constitution may say about shared war-making authority, the president, and not the Congress, possesses most war powers today, and war is "the big story," trumping even a bad economy as a headline grabber. While both parties were culpable in having taken large sums of money from corporate thieves, the issue was mainly a goldmine for the Democrats, who continue to benefit from the longtime Republican image as the party of big business. By contrast, the GOP almost always gains when the subject at hand is foreign policy. At least since the Vietnam War era, Republican presidents have been viewed as more competent in international relations—a conclusion reinforced by the foreign policy successes of Nixon, Reagan, and both Bushes and the failures of LBJ, Carter, and Clinton. So transforming the top of the news from a Democratic plus to a Republican advantage was no small achievement during election season.

This factor alone would not have delivered a victory to the Republicans. President Bush himself needed to put his considerable store of post–September 11 chips on the line. It is never an easy decision for a president to spend his capital, because capital is not easily accumulated nor quickly restored once lost. Most presidents revel in popularity and hesitate to do anything to lose it. Most presidents have learned to be extremely cautious, and not to take unnecessary risks. Thus, the usual behavior of a president in midterm elections is to raise money for party candidates early in the year, then make occasional appearances in September and October for favored nominees, avoiding too close identification with candidates who may lose. George Bush decided to set a new precedent, however. He campaigned extensively for party candidates from Labor Day onwards, braving criticism that he was "spending too much time on politics." He criss-crossed the country over and over, appearing a half-dozen times or more in the states with key races. He barnstormed for House candidates, not just Senate and gubernatorial contenders. In the last ten days he never left the trail, spending long days and nights jetting to contests that the latest tracking polls showed he could influence.

And this extraordinary effort, preparation, planning, and expenditure of money yielded a result no president since FDR had been able to savor. The risks were dangerously high, but the rewards were magnificent. The opposition party was plunged into a deep depression, Bush's party was in position to make the second half of the president's term even more productive than the first, and Bush was on the mountaintop, clearly in command, seemingly a strong early favorite to become the first Bush reelected to the nation's highest office.

As always, other factors besides the president played a role in the November results. For example, the tragic and frightening sniper shootings in the Washington, D.C., area transfixed the national media from late September through the election. Between Iraq and the snipers, it was almost impossible for campaigns to get much notice. In a few cases, candidates tried to make political hay out of the shootings; Democratic gubernatorial nominee Kathleen Kennedy Townsend of Maryland criticized GOP candidate Robert Erhlich on his anti–gun control stance, for instance. But in the Free State example, the effort appeared to backfire, and for the most part, candidates wisely avoided the tragedy. Retrospectively, the snipers—who had no discernible political agenda—were a curse for Democrats. Their unfolding story became a black hole into which all available media light was sucked, leaving little for anything other than Iraq. Of course, Democrats did little to help their cause since they never developed a compelling story line for their election agenda, though one doubts anything could have competed with Iraq and the snipers.

PIECING TOGETHER THE 2002 JIGSAW PUZZLE: VOTING PATTERNS IN THE ELECTORATE

The exit polling operation of the Voter News Service (VNS), a vote-counting consortium used by major news organizations, imploded on Election Day,[2] making it impossible to say with precision how Americans had voted by race, gender, income, and so on. Coming on the heels of the VNS's humiliation in Florida in 2000,[3] the 2002 breakdown left the networks in the lurch on election night, and political scientists high and dry for post-election demographic analysis. However, there were numerous random-sample telephone surveys taken on election evening and in the days following the election.[4] While these surveys are a poor substitute for polls taken at the ballot locations themselves (because surveys taken at the ballot locations guarantee a pure sample of real voters as they exit the booths), they will have to do for our purposes. Even exit polls are an approximation of the results, after all, so the post-election surveys can still suggest the basic voting patterns as they occurred on November 5.

It should not surprise anyone that the American electorate was not turned on its head in 2002. The same fundamental alignments visible in 2000 (and many years before that) were apparent in 2002. Drawing upon several post-election sources referenced above, we can estimate the following divisions among the voters in 2002 congressional contests:

- Whites voted Republican by about 57 percent to 43 percent; African Americans chose Democrats by close to 90 percent to 10 percent, and Hispanics/Latinos picked Democrats by perhaps 64 percent to 36 percent.
- White males voted Republican by about 64 percent to 36 percent, while white females chose the GOP narrowly, 53 percent to 47 percent.
- Republicans appeared to carry both baby boomers and senior citizens by a few percentage points. In 2000, the Democrats tied among boomers and won seniors by four points.
- Rural areas were once again GOP country, with suburban localities tied overall, and central cities strongly Democratic.
- While Protestants stayed Republican (about 58 percent to 42 percent), Roman Catholics edged into the GOP column as well by a point or two. In 2000, Catholics had voted Democratic by three points.

And on it goes, with the overall pattern essentially this: Republicans did 2–5 percent better in most demographic categories than in 2000, with Democrats faring worse by about the same margins.[5] Individual states varied from the national average, of course, and the state chapters that follow in this volume will show how and why.

The key question here is, which particular demographic was driving these marginal changes in voter preferences across the board? The most sensible, reasonable answer is perfectly logical, given our earlier analysis of the 2002 midterm election. Since President Bush dominated the campaign and undoubtedly energized the Republican base around the nation, surely simple partisan identification among those who turned up at the polls must explain a great deal of the election results. Sure enough, several post-election surveys revealed a modest but significant change in the composition of the 2002 electorate, when compared with the previous two national elections. For example, the Ayres, McHenry and Associates poll for the American Association of Health Plans, surveying 1,000 self-reported voters immediately after the election[6] showed that Republicans comprised fully 40 percent of the 2002 electorate, compared to just a third in both 1998 and 2000. As seen in table 1.3, the Democratic and Independent proportions of the electorate were down considerably from the earlier years.

Therefore, relative partisan turnout was very likely the key to the 2002 midterm election. The standard analyst and journalist refrain, "It all depends on turnout," was never more accurate.

Not incidentally, other aspects of voter turnout reinforced the polarized, partisan nature of the 2002 vote. Based on the same post-election surveys as well as state-by-state analyses, it appears that white (pro-Republican) turnout was generally up, while African-American and Hispanic/Latino (pro-Democratic) turnout was down in most places—not dramatically, but enough to affect the outcome in close contests.

Overall, national voter turnout was on the high side of normal, about 39.3 percent of the voting age population. As table 1.4 indicates, and figure 1.4 shows, the 2002 turnout is the best since 1982, and the second-best in three decades. No doubt the tens of millions of dollars spent by both major parties on voter identification and get-out-the-vote efforts in 2002 had a positive effect on turnout. Yet it is important to keep in mind that the 39.3 percent participation is only marginally better than most recent years, and that the three midterms from 1962 to 1970 averaged a far higher 47.4 percent turnout.

As usual, certain states with cultures encouraging civic participation, as well as some states with especially competitive elections, produced voter

Table 1.3   Party Identification Among Voters Who Cast a Ballot, 1998–2002

| | *Percent of the Electorate* | | |
Party Identification	*2002*	*2000*	*1998*
Republican	40	32	33
Democratic	31	37	34
Independent	23	27	30

Source: Conducted November 6–7 and released on November 18, by Ayres, McHenry and Associates (R) for the American Association of Health Plans. The poll surveyed 1,000 voters and had a margin of error +/–3 percent.

Table 1.4 Voter Turnout in Midterm Elections

Year	Turnout of Voting Age Population (VAP)
1962	47.3
1966	48.4
1970	46.6
1974	38.2
1978	37.2
1982	39.8
1986	36.4
1990	36.5
1994	38.8
1998	36.4
2002	39.3

Source: Federal Election Commission, www.fec.gov. Voting age population (VAP) means adults age 21 and over from 1962 to 1970, and age 18 and over from 1974 to 2002.

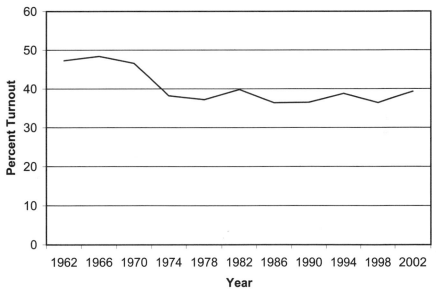

Figure 1.4 Voter Turnout in Midterm Elections

turnouts much above the national average, including Minnesota, 61.4 percent; South Dakota, 61.3 percent; Maine, 50.6 percent; and Vermont, 50 percent. Other states had less to brag about, especially Arizona, California, Virginia, Washington, and the District of Columbia. Especially noteworthy in this bottom category was California. Despite intense and expensive contests for governor and all statewide executive offices, among other races, the Golden State yielded the lowest turnout in its recorded gubernatorial history, about 30 percent. Highly negative campaigns and two especially unpopular party candidates for governor, Democrat Gray Davis and Republican Bill Simon, were mainly responsible for this dismal showing. Democratic minority groups in California showed the sharpest declines. Compared to the previous gubernatorial election in 1998, the Hispanic percentage of the total electorate dropped from 13 percent to 10 percent, and the African-American share of the electorate collapsed from 13 percent in 1998 to 4 percent in 2002.

THE GENERAL ELECTIONS OF 2002: SENATE, HOUSE, GOVERNORS, AND STATE LEGISLATURES

All divisions of the 2002 midterms contained surprises. Republicans defeated Democrats to retake the U.S. Senate. The GOP surged ahead in the House, coming just one seat short of the party's 230-seat high watermark achieved in the 1994 midterm. Democrats captured key state governorships, while both parties traded control of twenty statehouses. And mirroring the congressional results, Republicans secured 8 additional houses of state legislatures and about 180 extra berths in state senates and houses around the country.

U.S. Senate Contests

What began with the defection of Republican Jim Jeffords in May 2001 ended with a clear-cut GOP victory in the 2002 elections. Eighteen months of 51 to 49 Democratic domination in the U.S. Senate were transformed by a net Republican pick-up of two seats (see table 1.5 for results). The most stunning upset came in Georgia, where a GOP sweep of major offices elevated U.S. Representative Saxby Chambliss to the Senate, defeating one-term Senator Max Cleland (D). In Minnesota, the tragic death of Democratic Senator Paul Wellstone in the crash of a small plane ten days before the election led to a dramatic series of events. First, Democrats quickly settled upon former Vice President Walter F. Mondale as their substitute candidate against Republican Norm Coleman, former mayor of St. Paul. Much as a similar plane crash had elected a Democrat in Missouri's 2000 Senate race,[7] public sympathy generated an early lead for Mondale of about a half-dozen percentage points. Then the Democrats threw it all away with an ill-advised "memorial service" that became a rude political pep rally just a week before Election Day. Republican senators, in town to pay their respects to Wellstone, were booed, as was Independent Governor Jesse Ventura. Mondale lost by two percentage points on Election Day, and the GOP won the governorship and an extra U.S. House seat, too. Finally, in Missouri, Senator Jean Carnahan—appointed to fill the seat won by her deceased husband in a 2000 sympathy vote—lost the contest for the remaining four years of that term to former Congressman Jim Talent (R). Democrats added a single Senate seat by defeating one-term Republican Tim Hutchinson of Arkansas. Son of a former U.S. senator, state Attorney General Mark Pryor (D) won the seat, but Hutchinson actually defeated himself. Elected as a Christian conservative candidate, the senator divorced his wife of 29 years and married a young staffer during his term. This did not play well in a state still tarred by tales of Bill Clinton's sexual misdeeds while governor.

The GOP had the tougher Senate road to travel in 2002, defending twenty seats to the Democrats' fourteen, and having five open seats (North Carolina, New Hampshire, South Carolina, Tennessee, and Texas) to the Democrats' two (Minnesota and New Jersey). (See figure 1.5 on page 18.) Remarkably, Republicans held every one of their open seats,[8] recruiting strong candidates such as former presidential contenders Elizabeth Dole in North Carolina and Lamar Alexander in Tennessee. While losing Minnesota, as noted earlier, Democrats did manage to hold an open seat in the Garden State—though only with a highly unusual maneuver. One-term, scandal-drenched Senator Robert Torricelli (D) dropped out of his reelection race in late September, with polls showing him losing handily to GOP nominee Doug Forrester. The New Jersey Supreme Court had to approve a candidate substitution, since the ballot deadline had passed. The Court infuriated Republicans with a unanimous ruling in the Democrats' favor, and the Democrats placed on the ballot 78-year-old former Senator Frank Lautenberg, who had previously served from 1983 to 2001. New Jersey's solid Democratic majority prevailed in November, and Lautenberg won easily.

The closest Senate match-up in the nation was conducted in South Dakota, where Democratic U.S. Senator Tim Johnson eked out a 524-vote victory over U.S. Representative John Thune, the Republican recruited by the White House. Johnson's prime backer was Senate Majority Leader Tom Daschle, and Thune's was obviously President Bush. In South Dakota, though not the nation, hometown boy Daschle trumped Bush, barely, thanks to an overwhelming Democratic vote among Native Americans on

Table 1.5   Senate Races, 2002

State	Candidate	Percent	Total
Alabama	Jeff Sessions (R)*	59	790,757
	Susan Parker (D)	40	537,882
Alaska	Ted Stevens (R)*	79	155,054
	Frank Vondersaar (D)	10	20,466
Arkansas	Mark Pryor (D)	54	435,355
	Tim Hutchinson (R)*	46	372,909
Colorado	Wayne Allard (R)*	51	707,349
	Tom Strickland (D)	46	634,227
Delaware	Joseph Biden (D)*	58	135,170
	Ray Clatworthy (R)	41	94,716
Georgia	Saxby Chambliss (R)	53	1,068,902
	Max Cleland (D)*	46	928,905
Idaho	Larry Craig (R)*	65	265,849
	Alan Blinken (D)	33	132,845
Illinois	Richard Durbin (D)*	60	2,075,476
	Jim Durkin (R)	38	1,317,196
Iowa	Tom Harkin (D)*	54	550,156
	Greg Ganske (R)	44	446,209
Kansas	Pat Roberts (R)*	83	632,134
Kentucky	Mitch McConnell (R)*	64	726,396
	Lois Weinberg (D)	36	400,818
Louisiana[a]	Mary Landrieu (D)*	52	642,974
	Suzanne Haik Terrell (R)	48	603,160
Maine	Susan Collins (R)*	59	290,266
	Chellie Pingree (D)	41	205,901
Massachusetts	John Kerry (D)*	81	1,596,793
Michigan	Carl Levin (D)*	61	1,893,788
	Andrew Raczkowski (R)	38	1,184,548
Minnesota	Norm Coleman (R)	50	1,084,512
	Walter Mondale (D)	47	1,025,498
Mississippi	Thad Cochran (R)*	85	521,482
Missouri	Jim Talent (R)	50	934,093
	Jean Carnahan (D)*	49	911,507
Montana	Max Baucus (D)*	63	202,908
	Mike Taylor (R)	32	102,766
Nebraska	Chuck Hagel (R)*	83	391,648
	Charles Matulka (D)	14	68,657
New Hampshire	John Sununu (R)	51	225,506
	Jeanne Shaheen (D)	47	206,689
New Jersey	Frank Lautenberg (D)	54	1,112,499
	Doug Forrester (R)	44	909,383
New Mexico	Pete Domenici (R)*	66	323,923
	Gloria Tristani (D)	34	170,199
North Carolina	Elizabeth Dole (R)	54	1,229,822
	Erskine Bowles (D)	45	1,029,539

State	Candidate	Percent	Total
Oklahoma	James Inhofe (R)*	57	578,579
	David Walters (D)	37	369,789
Oregon	Gordon Smith (R)*	56	688,050
	Bill Bradbury (D)	40	483,235
Rhode Island	Jack Reed (D)*	78	241,315
	Bob Tingle (R)	22	66,613
South Carolina	Lindsay Graham (R)	54	597,158
	Alex Sanders (D)	44	483,598
South Dakota	Tim Johnson (D)*	50	167,481
	John Thune (R)	49	166,954
Tennessee	Lamar Alexander (R)	55	901,019
	Bob Clement (D)	44	731,735
Texas	John Cornyn (R)	55	2,480,991
	Ron Kirk (D)	43	1,946,681
Virginia	John Warner (R)*	84	1,298,843
West Virginia	Jay Rockefeller (D)*	63	269,621
	Jay Wolfe (R)	37	157,032
Wyoming	Mike Enzi (R)*	73	133,554
	Joyce Jansa Corcoran (D)	27	49,578

Source: ABC News 2002: The Vote. abcnews.go.com/sections/politics/election2002/congress.html.
* Indicates incumbent.

a In the Louisiana Senate race, incumbent Senator Mary Landrieu (D) defeated Republican Suzanne Haik Terrell in a December 7 runoff election. The results from the November 5 election are as follows: Landrieu (D): 46 percent; Terrell (R): 27 percent; John Cooksey (R): 14 percent; Tony Perkins (R): 10 percent; five other candidates split the remaining votes.

reservations. (Thousands of Indians were registered for the first time prior to November 2002.) Johnson's triumph was historically significant since incumbent House members in South Dakota had won five consecutive battles to defeat incumbent senators since 1972. Most recently, Johnson had defeated Senator Larry Pressler in 1996. The last U.S. senator from South Dakota to survive a challenge from the state's sole U.S. representative was Republican Karl Mundt in 1960.

In addition to South Dakota, Democrats also took cheer from Louisiana, where incumbent Senator Mary Landrieu was narrowly reelected (52 percent to 48 percent) over Republican Suzanne Haik Terrell. Landrieu's second term came to her only a little easier than her first, which she won by less than 6,000 votes in 1996. Under the Bayou State's unique "free for all" primary, all candidates for the Senate had to run simultaneously on November 5, with a winner declared only if one candidate topped 50 percent of the vote. Landrieu came close, with 46 percent, but she was forced into a December 7 run-off with second-place finisher Terrell, who garnered 27 per-

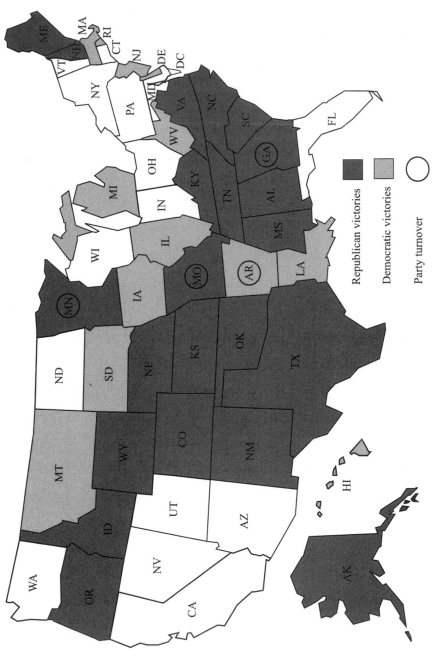

Figure 1.5　Senate Races, 2002

Republican victories

Democratic victories

Party turnover

cent. Since all GOP candidates together received 51 percent of the November 5 ballots, Landrieu was in real trouble. She had a cool relationship with several key African-American leaders, yet was viewed by many whites as being "too liberal." But on December 7, the Democrat was rescued by GOP dissension. The Republican governor, Mike Foster, and the GOP Senate also-rans were less than enthusiastic about Terrell, partly because of sour grapes, and partly because they viewed her as too moderate—hand picked by the White House and forced upon them by party outsiders.

The White House, too, contributed to Terrell's undoing. After a full-court press of personal appearances in Louisiana by President Bush, Vice President Cheney, former President Bush, and many others, the president fired his economic team of Treasury Secretary Paul O'Neill and adviser Larry Lindsey on the day before the election. Reportedly, the firings were not supposed to be announced until December 9, but Secretary O'Neill was so angry he released the news himself on Friday, thus securing a bit of revenge against President Bush. Coupled with a stunning rise in unemployment to 6 percent on the same day, the big news created disastrous headlines about the poor economy, just as citizens began to go to the polls. (Imagine what could have happened if such a scenario had unfolded on November 4: The Democrats might well have retained control of the Senate.) Landrieu had already been emphasizing economic issues, such as the administration's alleged preference for Mexican sugar over the Bayou State's own—a charge hotly denied by the White House. Popular U.S. Senator John Breaux clearly assisted Landrieu as well. Considerably more conservative than his colleague, he vouched for her to the voters who trusted him far more. Like Tom Daschle in South Dakota, Breaux bested Bush, embarrassing the president in a state (like South Dakota) Bush had easily carried in 2000.

Landrieu was one of 24 incumbent senators out of 28 running in 2002 to be successfully reelected—a return rate of 85.7 percent. One of the four defeated senators, Republican Bob Smith of New Hampshire, lost in a primary to Congressman John Sununu (who won the seat in November), while the other three senators (Carnahan, Cleland, and Hutchinson) fell in the general election. As table 1.6 suggests, 2002 was neither a toxic environment nor an especially rewarding time for incumbent senators, with about half the recent election years yielding more incumbent defeats, and half less. As we shall see, incumbent House members running for reelection were much safer in 2002.

U.S. House of Representatives

Later in this volume, Chuck Todd and Maureen Schweers of *The Hotline* will examine the U.S. House elections in considerable detail, but for now, it

Table 1.6 Defeated Senate Incumbents, 1980–2002

Year	Primary	General
1980	4	9
1982	0	2
1984	0	3
1986	0	7
1988	0	4
1990	0	1
1992	1	4
1994	0	2
1996	1	1
1998	0	3
2000	0	6
2002	1	3

will suffice to point out several controlling factors. First, the population-based transfer of House seats took place mainly from areas of Democratic strength (Northern states and central cities) to geographic regions of GOP dominance (the South and West, plus suburbs and rural locales). Naturally, this tended to benefit Republicans. In the ten states that *lost* House seats in the 2000 Census (Connecticut, Illinois, Indiana, Michigan, Mississippi, New York, Ohio, Oklahoma, Pennsylvania, and Wisconsin), the Republicans actually picked up a House seat in the 2002 elections, while the Democrats lost a net *thirteen* seats! Now, looking just at the eight states that gained seats in the 2000 Census (Arizona, California, Colorado, Florida, Georgia, Nevada, North Carolina, and Texas), Democrats captured four new seats in the 2002 elections but Republicans won double that, *eight* new seats.[9] Second, Republicans had enough control of governorships and state legislative bodies throughout the country to hold their own, perhaps more, in the tug-of-war partisan redistrictings that took place in some states. So for every Maryland or Georgia, where the Democratic governor and legislature redrew district boundaries to elect more Democrats to the U.S. House, there was a Michigan or Pennsylvania, where the GOP governor and legislature helped their own partisans. (Georgia's partisan redistricting backfired on the Democrats, but that is a story for a later chapter.) Third, most redistrictings in 2001–2002 were incumbent-protection devices, benefiting both parties. But since there were slightly more GOP than Democratic incumbents, Republicans gained a bit from this widespread tactic. Finally, the Republicans outspent the Democrats in House elections by a massive margin of $494 million to $307 million—more than one and a half times the amount. Obviously, the money edge mattered greatly in the relative handful of seats, no more than forty, which were highly competitive between the parties.

In the end, 98 percent of incumbents who sought another House term were reelected—relatively high even by House standards. (Since World War II, about 92 percent of all House members who ran again won again.) As table 1.7 shows, just eight House incumbents lost in the primaries, and another eight in the general election; this total of 16 was far below the number losing in the last two redistricting years, 1982 (39) and 1992 (43). Furthermore, fully half of 2002's "sad sixteen" lost because they were running against another House incumbent—and thus an incumbent *had* to lose.[10]

Gubernatorial Contests

The history of midterm elections for state governors is about as depressing for the incumbent White House party as midterms for the U.S. House and Senate. In the fifteen midterm elections since World War II (refer back to table 1.2), the president's party has lost statehouses in eleven of them. In two cases, 1962 and 1998, the gubernatorial elections were a wash between the parties, and in just two other elections (1946 and 1986) did the president's party *gain* governorships.[11] The latter case was especially odd, since the Republicans under President Reagan lost the U.S. Senate by dropping eight Senate seats net in 1986, yet at the same time the GOP picked up eight governorships net.[12]

Even with an electoral breeze at his back, President Bush in 2002 would not be as fortunate as President Reagan was in 1986. However, the

Table 1.7   Defeated House Incumbents, 1980–2002

Year	Primary	General
1980	6	31
1982	10	29
1984	3	16
1986	3	6
1988	1	6
1990	1	15
1992	19	24
1994	4	34
1996	2	21
1998	1	6
2000	3	6
2002	8	8

Table 1.8 Gubernatorial Races, 2002

State	Candidate	Percent votes	Total votes
Alabama	Bob Riley (R)	49	674,052
	Don Siegleman (D)*	49	670,913
Alaska	Frank Murkowski (R)	56	111,311
	Fran Ulmer (D)	41	81,434
Arizona	Janet Napolitano (D)	47	472,197
	Matt Salmon (R)	44	446,913
	Dick Mahoney (I)	7	1,242
Arkansas	Mike Huckabee (R)*	53	429,450
	Jimmie Lou Fisher (D)	47	375,412
California	Gray Davis (D)*	48	3,127,588
	Bill Simon (R)	42	2,754,247
Colorado	Bill Owens (R)*	63	840,331
	Rollie Heath (D)	34	449,067
Connecticut	John Rowland (R)*	56	573,134
	Bill Curry (D)	44	448,441
Florida	Jeb Bush (R)*	56	2,828,288
	Bill McBride (D)	43	2,172,696
Georgia	Sonny Perdue (R)	52	1,039,493
	Roy Barnes (D)*	46	933,594
Hawaii	Linda Lingle (R)	52	193,794
	Mazie Hirono (D)	47	176,619
Idaho	Dirk Kempthorne (R)*	56	231,270
	Jerry Brady (D)	42	171,495
Illinois	Rod Blagojevich (D)	52	1,820,059
	Jim Ryan (R)	45	1,584,684
Iowa	Tom Vilsack (D)*	53	536,541
	Doug Gross (R)	45	454,272
Kansas	Kathleen Sebelius (D)	53	435,462
	Tim Shallenburger (R)	45	371,325
Maine	John Baldacci (D)	47	233,543
	Peter Cianchette (R)	42	205,335
Maryland	Bob Ehrlich (R)	51	842,075
	Kathleen Kennedy Townsend (D)	48	784,454
Massachusetts	Mitt Romney (R)	50	1,088,141
	Shannon O'Brien (D)	45	980,839
Michigan	Jennifer Granholm (D)	51	1,631,276
	Dick Posthumus (R)	48	1,504,755
Minnesota	Tim Pawlenty (R)	44	997,907
	Roger Moe (D)	37	819,428
	Tim Penny (I)	16	364,069
Nebraska	Mike Johanns (R)*	69	325,453
	Stormy Dean (D)	27	129,691
Nevada	Kenny Guinn (R)*	68	343,859
	Joe Neal (D)	22	110,930

State	Candidate	Percent votes	Total votes
New Hampshire	Craig Benson (R)	59	257,386
	Mark Fernald (D)	38	167,458
New Mexico	Bill Richardson (D)	56	253,594
	John Sanchez (R)	39	174,514
New York	George Pataki (R)*	49	2,152,194
	Carl McCall (D)	33	1,448,810
	Tom Golisano (I)	15	632,574
Ohio	Bob Taft (R)*	58	1,837,428
	Tim Hagan (D)	38	1,214,959
Oklahoma	Brad Henry (D)	43	448,133
	Steve Largent (R)	43	441,776
	Gary Richardson (I)	14	146,206
Oregon	Ted Kulongoski (D)	49	595,446
	Kevin Mannix (R)	46	561,803
Pennsylvania	Ed Rendell (D)	53	1,898,214
	Mike Fisher (R)	45	1,584,566
Rhode Island	Don Carcieri (R)	55	173,545
	Myrth York (D)	45	143,750
South Carolina	Mark Sanford (R)	53	582,736
	Jim Hodges (D)*	47	517,740
South Dakota	Mike Rounds (R)	57	189,899
	Jim Abbot (D)	53	140,260
Tennessee	Phil Bredesen (D)	51	843,476
	Van Hilleary (R)	48	796,943
Texas	Rick Perry (R)*	58	2,617,106
	Tony Sanchez (D)	40	1,809,915
Vermont	Jim Douglas (R)	45	101,912
	Douglas Racine (D)	42	95,599
	Con Hogan (I)	10	21,875
Wisconsin	Jim Doyle (D)	45	800,958
	Scott McCallum (R)*	41	732,781
	Ed Thompson (I)	11	185,085
Wyoming	Dave Freudenthal (D)	50	92,545
	Eli Bebout (R)	48	88,741

Source: ABC News 2002: The Vote. abcnews.go.com/sections/politics/election2002/governor/html.
* Indicates incumbent.

Republican Party's net loss of a single statehouse in 2002 (from 27 down to 26 governors) was remarkable (see table 1.8). First, the GOP had been expected to lose their outright majority of governorships since so many of their executive posts were at risk. Some of the GOP governors elected in the landslide Republican year of 1994 were retiring or being forced out by term limits, giving the Democrats a golden opportunity for open-seat takeovers on the "time for a change" theme. Second, bad economic times and squeezed state budgets created conditions conducive to party turnovers. Third, the Democrats had done an impressive job of gubernatorial candidate recruitment, for the most part—far better, one could argue, than their congressional recruitment efforts. So the stage was set for Democrats to secure their first statehouse majority since the 1992 elections.

It was not to be, of course, despite some important Democratic pickups. Fully twenty states changed gubernatorial parties, an unusually large number, as figure 1.6 indicates. The Democrats snatched the vital industrial states of Illinois, Michigan, Pennsylvania, and Wisconsin—probably their biggest triumphs of election 2002, while capturing a group of states not often closely associated with the Democratic Party (Arizona, Kansas, Maine, New Mexico, Oklahoma, Tennessee, and Wyoming). The party also held Iowa and California with one-term incumbents Tom Vilsack and Gray Davis, as well as Oregon with non-incumbent Ted Kulongoski, who succeeded two-term Governor John Kitzhaber (D). In an odd similarity, the Republicans also took over states rarely dominated by the GOP: Hawaii, Maryland, Minnesota, and Vermont. Non-incumbent GOP candidates Mitt Romney and Don Carcieri enabled the Republicans to hold onto the two most Democratic states in the Union, Massachusetts and Rhode Island, while entrenched GOP governors were reelected in Arkansas (Mike Huckabee), Colorado (Bill Owens), Connecticut (John Rowland), Florida (the president's brother, Jeb Bush), Idaho (Dirk Kempthorne), Nebraska (Mike Johanns), Nevada (Kenny Guinn), New York (George Pataki), Ohio (Bob Taft), and Texas (Rick Perry). They also recaptured friendly states out of their possession for four to eight years: Alabama, Alaska, New Hampshire, and South Carolina, defeating incumbents Don Siegelman (D-AL) and Jim Hodges (D-SC) in the two Southern states. A third Southern state provided the GOP's most stunning upset, as former state senator Sonny Perdue denied Democratic Governor Roy Barnes a second term. Not a single public poll forecast the result, and Perdue became the first GOP governor of the Peach State since Reconstruction. Georgia, alone among the states of the Old Confederacy, elected no Republican governor in the twentieth century. Finally, the Republicans extended their long lease on the governorship of South Dakota (since 1979) with the election of Mike Rounds to succeed four-term Governor Bill Janklow, who was term-limited and elected to the U.S. House in 2002.[13]

Despite all the change, just three elected incumbents (Siegelman of Alabama, Barnes of Georgia, and Hodges of South Carolina, all Democrats) were defeated for reelection. It is fair to say that all three lost primarily because the Bush-led GOP surged in the conservative South in 2002. Siegelman lost by a mere 5,000 votes out of over 1.3 million cast to Congressman

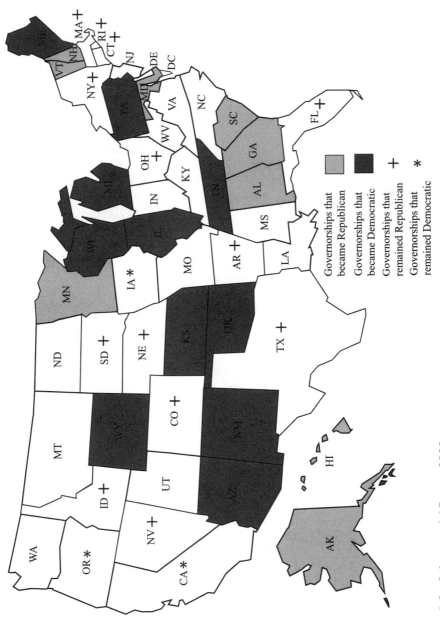

Figure 1.6   Gubernatorial Races, 2002

Governorships that became Republican

Governorships that became Democratic

+ Governorships that remained Republican

* Governorships that remained Democratic

Bob Riley. Hodges and Barnes came up short by large margins to former Congressman Mark Sanford and Sonny Perdue. One non-elected incumbent, Republican Scott McCallum of Wisconsin, also lost in 2002; McCallum had become governor when fourteen-year incumbent Tommy Thompson resigned in January 2001 to take the Health and Human Services secretariat in President Bush's cabinet. With a very bad economy in the Badger State, as well as a yearning for change after sixteen years of GOP control, McCallum never led his opponent, Democratic state attorney general Jim Doyle, throughout the general election—though the final result was reasonably tight (three percentage points). Former Governor Thompson's brother, Ed, running as a Libertarian, may have drained some crucial votes from McCallum. While Tommy Thompson officially supported McCallum, the two had never been close, despite McCallum's fourteen years of service to Thompson as lieutenant governor.

As mentioned above, the Democratic Party found solace in the election of big-state governors in the North. Representative Rod Blagojevich of Illinois beat the ill-named state attorney general Jim Ryan, who—despite no familial relationship to incumbent GOP Governor George Ryan—was held responsible by the voters for George Ryan's serious corruption in office. Thus ended a remarkable run of twenty-six uninterrupted years of Republican gubernatorial rule in the Land of Lincoln. In Michigan, another bright, young Democratic star was born when state attorney general Jennifer Granholm defeated Republican lieutenant governor Dick Posthumus to succeed three-term Governor John Engler (R). In Pennsylvania, former Philadelphia mayor and Democratic National Committee chairman Ed Rendell easily defeated state attorney general Mike Fisher (R) to become the first Democratic governor of Pennsylvania since 1994 and the first "Philly" mayor to serve as state governor since 1914.

With ten women on the 2002 ballot as major-party nominees for governor, the expectation for female victories had been high. While a new record was set—four women elected governor simultaneously, eclipsing the 1990 record of three—there were fewer wins than expected. A woman had to win in Hawaii, since both Republicans and Democrats had nominated women, Linda Lingle and Mazie Hirono, respectively. Lingle avenged her 5,000-vote loss of 1998 to Democratic Governor Benjamin Cayetano by defeating Lieutenant Governor Hirono substantially, thereby becoming only the second GOP governor of Hawaii and the first one in forty years.[14] The other three women winners in 2002 were Democrats: Janet Napolitano of Arizona, Kathleen Sebelius of Kansas, and Jennifer Granholm of Michigan. The six losing women, all Democrats, were: Fran Ulmer of Alaska, Jimmie Lou Fisher of Arkansas, Mazie Hirono of Hawaii, Kathleen Kennedy Townsend of Maryland, Shannon O'Brien of Massachusetts, and Myrth York of

Rhode Island, who also lost as the Democratic nominee for governor in 1994 and 1998. Without question, the biggest surprise on the list of defeated women was Lieutenant Governor Kathleen Kennedy Townsend, daughter of Robert and Ethel Kennedy. In heavily Democratic Maryland, Townsend had been expected to win handily, but her own inept campaigning, combined with the deep unpopularity of the governor she had served, Democrat Parris Glendening, enabled GOP Representative Bob Erhlich to pull an upset. With the four newly elected women governors, a total of 23 women have served as state governor in American history; over 2,000 men have also done so.

There was one minority governor added to the short list of such state chief executives in 2002. Former Congressman, United Nations Ambassador, and Clinton Cabinet Energy Secretary Bill Richardson was elected governor of New Mexico. Richardson is Hispanic, as was his unsuccessful GOP opponent, John Sanchez. Another Hispanic Democratic nominee, Tony Sanchez of Texas, was not as fortunate as Richardson, with GOP Governor Rick Perry, George Bush's lieutenant governor and 2000 successor, capturing a massive 58 percent to 40 percent majority. Both African-American candidates for governor, Democrats Carl McCall of New York and Joe O'Neal of Nevada, lost, overwhelmingly defeated by Republican incumbents George Pataki and Kenny Guinn. There has been only one elected black governor in all of American history, L. Douglas Wilder of Virginia, who served from 1990 to 1994. Counting Richardson, there have been nine Hispanic or Latino governors, three Republicans and six Democrats, including five from New Mexico.[15]

While figure 1.6 and table 1.8 show all the 2002 gubernatorial elections, and subsequent chapters discuss some of them in considerable detail, several not yet mentioned should be stressed in any wrap-up account. The contest with the most national significance may well have been held in Florida, where President Bush's sibling, Jeb, sought a second term. After the close call George W. Bush endured in the Sunshine State in 2000, the White House wanted to insure a strong finish for the brother Bush on the 2002 ballot. Their hopes were fully realized. Moderate Democrat Bill McBride, a wealthy attorney, had managed to narrowly beat former U.S. attorney general Janet Reno in the September Democratic primary. Bush had hoped for Reno, a liberal, but instead he faced a surging, upset winner in McBride. Luckily for Bush, McBride proved less adept than expected on the stump and in debate, and Governor Bush—generally quite popular during his first term—was reelected in a landslide, 56 percent to 43 percent.

Florida's political significance notwithstanding, the biggest prize of 2002 was control of the largest state, California, which would be the world's sixth greatest economy were it an independent nation (as it often

seems to be). The Golden State had a less-than-golden, dramatically unsatis-
fying election. One-term Democratic incumbent Gray Davis was highly
unpopular, with exceptionally low personal ratings. The Republicans nominated a former federal prosecutor, Bill Simon, who was politically maladroit
and too far to the right for this liberal state's preferences. "None of the
Above" might well had won the governorship, had this choice been on the
ballot. It wasn't, and the state's Democratic tilt enabled Davis to win a 48
percent to 42 percent victory, with all other statewide Democratic nominees
also in the winner's circle.

Occasionally, capturing a governorship enables a candidate to win
twice—assuming the new governor is a U.S. senator. Alaska's junior Republican senator, Frank Murkowski, was elected governor in a landslide, 56
percent to 41 percent, over Democratic Lieutenant Governor Fran Ulmer.
Murkowski resigned his Senate seat and took office on December 2, 2002,
and then on December 20, he chose his own daughter, Lisa Murkowski, a
45-year-old Republican state legislator, to serve in the Senate until 2004.
Charges of nepotism naturally greeted this historically unprecedented
appointment.

Independents played a role in a handful of the gubernatorial contests,
even though both Independent governors, one-term Jesse Ventura of Minnesota and two-term Angus King of Maine, left office (Ventura by choice, King
via term limits). Ventura backed former Democratic congressman and
newly minted Independent Tim Penny to succeed him. Penny was in a three-
way tie for much of the campaign, but a strong backlash to the memorial
service-cum-pep-rally for the late U.S. Senator Paul Wellstone sent Penny
tumbling in the polls, and elected GOP nominee Tim Pawlenty (45 percent)
over both Penny (16 percent) and Democrat Roger Moe (36 percent). In
Oklahoma, meanwhile, a Republican-turned-Independent, Gary Richardson, may have drained just enough votes from Republican Steve Largent (a
former congressman and pro-football Hall of Famer) to deliver the statehouse to Democrat Brad Henry, who won by less than a percentage point,
with Richardson taking about 14 percent. And in Vermont, an Independent
and third-party candidate collected about 13 percent of the vote, with
Republican state Treasurer Jim Douglas edging Democratic Lieutenant
Governor Doug Racine, 45 percent to 42 percent. However, under the Vermont constitution, the state legislature gets to choose the governor when no
candidate receives a majority. The secret-ballot election would have been
controversial, but Racine graciously conceded to Douglas, averting the need
for the legislative conclave. While all these states, as well as Arizona, Wisconsin, and a few others, featured electorally significant Independent candidates, there is now no Independent governor in any state for the first time
in twelve years. In modern times there have never been more than two Inde-

pendents serving as governor simultaneously (refer back to figure 1.3). Combined with the lack of any pure Independents in either house of Congress, the Independent-less governorship suggests again the durability of the two major parties in America.[16]

State Legislative Elections

One of the hidden gems of American politics, and a true test of the existence—or not—of partisan election "waves," is the contest for control of state legislatures. These fascinating elections receive little coverage on midterm or presidential election nights, but as down-ballot, relatively hidden public offices, they reveal the underlying trends of any election year.

And so it was in 2002. Any doubt that the midterm election had a Republican flavor disappeared when the National Conference of State Legislatures tallied up the nationwide results. For the first time since 1952, Republicans had secured more state legislative berths than the Democrats; of 7,382 total state legislators in the fifty states, 49.6 percent were Republican and 49.4 percent were Democratic. (The nonpartisan, unicameral Nebraska legislature and a handful of independents, such as one Green Party candidate elected from Portland, Maine, accounted for the remaining 1 percent.) Subsequent party switches from Democratic to Republican, especially in the Georgia state senate, expanded the GOP majority slightly. Put in historical context, this Republican achievement was even more significant. The average loss for the president's party in post–World War II midterm elections for state legislatures has been approximately 350 seats. In 2002 Republicans *gained* 180 seats, before party switches, in the 49 partisan legislatures.[17]

In addition to the overall seat gain, the GOP took control of eight state legislative houses: the state senates of Arizona, Colorado, Georgia, Missouri, Washington, and Wisconsin, and the House of Representatives in North Carolina and Texas (see figure 1.7). By contrast, the Democrats seized only the Illinois Senate (plus attained a tie in the previously Republican Oregon Senate). Before the election, Democrats were in charge of both houses in 18 states, Republicans in 17 states, with the rest split. After the 2002 midterm, the GOP was running 21 state legislatures, the Democrats only 16.

Not surprisingly, given the South's increasing tilt to the Republicans, a disproportionate share of the GOP state legislative pick-ups came in the South—59 seats out of the 180 total. Republicans gained 16 seats (net) just in the Texas House, and the Lone Star's lower house went from 78D-72R to 88R-62D in a single election. (The Texas Senate was already Republican, but narrowly so; in 2002, it changed to firm GOP control, from 16R-15D

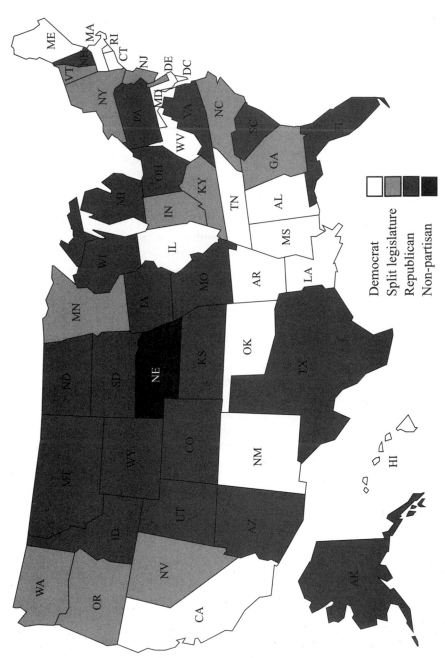

Figure 1.7 Partisan Make-up of State Legislatures, 2003

Source: National Conference of State Legislatures, "Republican Gains Bring Parties to Legislative Parity," December 9, 2002. www.ncsl.org.

to 19R-12D.)[18] And there is much room for further Republican growth in the South. Even after the expansion of the party's state legislative contingent in recent elections, Republicans are the majority legislative party in only four states (Florida, South Carolina, Texas, and Virginia). Three states (Kentucky, North Carolina, and Georgia) have split-party control of their state legislatures, while fully *six* Southern state legislatures are still controlled entirely by the Democrats: Alabama, Arkansas, Louisiana, Mississippi, Oklahoma, and Tennessee. Already, the GOP is within striking distance of a majority in the North Carolina Senate, the Oklahoma House and Senate, and the Tennessee House and Senate. While the South will never be as one-party Republican as it was one-party Democratic from the 1870s to the 1960s, the region is now reasonably designated as two-party competitive but Republican-tilting in most elections, most years.

CONCLUSION:
IS MIDTERM HISTORY CHANGING?

Some observers have sought to downplay the Republican triumph of 2002, noting that a "mere" 41,000 votes in two states (Missouri and New Hampshire) gave the Senate to the GOP, and about 100,000 votes out of 71 million cast nationwide created a sizeable Republican majority in the House of Representatives. But such a minimization of the results does a disservice both to the election process and the winning party.

Big things come in small packages, and major electoral events can turn on a relative handful of votes. (Remember a certain 537 ballots in Florida in 2000?) No one contends that 2002 was another 1994, though it is notable that Republicans have almost returned to that earlier year's seat level in the House, their modern record. Moreover, all the trends at every level were in the GOP's direction. The toss-ups in the House and the Senate broke substantially for the Republicans; the Democrats failed to gain a majority of the governorships, as had once seemed quite likely; and the GOP gained an exceptional number of state legislative seats against the historical odds.

Take a final glance at the overall tallies (see table 1.9). Republican candidates for governor secured 49.7 percent of all votes cast for the statehouses to 44.6 percent for Democrats. The GOP did even better in Senate races, with 51.2 percent to the Democrats' 46 percent, and better still in the House: 51.6 percent to 45.5 percent for the Democrats. That is not a mere drift—it is a clear election trend.

In fact, two midterms in a row have rewritten history. Democrats gained five U.S. House seats in Bill Clinton's second midterm (1998), and now we have 2002's even more dramatic results. Are the old rules that dic-

Table 1.9 Total Votes by Party, 2002

Party	Number of Votes	Percentage
Governors		
Republicans	30,130,280	49.7
Democrats	27,035,675	44.6
Independents/Others	3,412,098	5.6
Total	60,578,053	
Senate		
Republicans	21,823,998	51.2
Democrats	19,605,164	46.0
Independents/Others	1,165,692	2.7
Total	42,594,854	
House		
Republicans	36,838,455	51.6
Democrats	32,466,172	45.5
Independents/Others	2,124,380	3.0
Total	71,429,007	

Source: Calculations by author. Percentages may not total 100 because of rounding.

tated a midterm loss of seats for the president's party changing? Perhaps the presidential electronic throne of television, combined with massive "in" party spending, modest and easily manipulated voter turnout, and a chief executive's extensive campaigning, are tipping the electoral odds in favor of the White House party, instead of against it. Maybe this is happening, but a mere two elections do not a trend make. The backfiring of the Clinton impeachment issue in 1998 and Bush's national security card in 2002 are enough reason, for now, to explain these consecutive anomalies. Moreover, the rapid Democratic comeback in Louisiana on December 7, 2002, is a cautionary tale about how quickly electoral conditions can change.

Still, the possibility of a new midterm paradigm is intriguing, and only time—and more midterms—will reveal whether the "Bush midterm" of 2002 becomes the new political standard of the 21st century.

NOTES

1. Neustadt, Richard. *Presidential Power: The Politics of Leadership*. New York: Science Editions, 1962.

2. For more information, see "The 2002 Elections: The Exit Polls," *The New York Times*, Nov. 6, 2002, and "Networks to examine future of VNS after election night failures," The Associated Press, Nov. 6, 2002.

3. Sabato, Larry J. *Overtime: The Election 2000 Thriller*. New York: Longman, 2000, pp. 143–144.

4. Between Nov. 6 and Nov. 12, 2002, *The Hotline* (www.nationaljournal.com/pubs/hotline) reported polls such as the Fox News/Opinion Dynamic: State by State, 11/11/02.

5. For comparative purposes, see the presidential exit poll table in Larry J. Sabato, *Overtime: The Election 2000 Thriller*. New York: Longman, pp. 108–109.

6. Nov. 6–7, margin of error + or − 3 percent.

7. Senator Jean Carnahan's husband, Mel, ran in 2000 for the Senate seat against Republican Senator John Ashcroft. Just weeks before the election, Mel Carnahan was killed in a plane crash. Since the state's ballots had already been printed, Mel Carnahan remained on the ballot, and posthumously won the November contest. Missouri Governor Roger Wilson (D) nominated Jean Carnahan to fill her deceased husband's Senate seat.

8. Results from the Republican open-seat contests: New Hampshire: John Sununu (R) replacing Robert Smith (R); North Carolina: Elizabeth Dole (R) replacing Jesse Helms (R); South Carolina: Lindsay Graham (R) replacing Strom Thurmond (R); Tennessee: Lamar Alexander (R) replacing Fred Thompson (R); Texas: John Cornyn (R) replacing Phil Gramm (R). In the Democratic open seats, the results were as follows: Minnesota: Norm Coleman (R) took the seat away from the Democrats by defeating Walter Mondale (D); and New Jersey: Frank Lautenberg (D) held the seat of Senator Robert Torricelli (D).

9. Cohen, Richard E. "New Lines, Republican Gains," *National Journal*. Vol. 34, no. 45 (Nov. 9, 2002): p. 3285.

10. Brian Kerns R-IN, 7th District; Frank Mascara D-PA, 20th District; Lynn Rivers D-MI, 13th District; Bob Barr R-GA, 7th District; Ronnie Shows D-MS, 4th District; George Gekas R-PA, 17th District; David Phelps D-IL, 19th District; Jim Maloney D-CT, 5th District. Of the four pairs of incumbents running against one another in the general election, the Republicans won three (Nancy Johnson, John Shimkus, and Chip Pickering) while the Democrats won just one, and barely (Tim Holden). About half of the 51 were incumbents (26) and the others non-incumbent winners (25).

11. By comparison, since the close of World War II, the president's party gained seats in House elections only twice, in 1998 and 2002, and the White House party has added Senate seats four times, in 1962, 1970, 1982, and 2002. In 1998 the U.S. Senate elections were a net wash.

12. Of course, only about a third of the states—not a random sample—feature Senate elections in any midterm year, and not all states have a gubernatorial election, either—currently 36 out of the 50 states. These mixed sets of states can result in unusual and incompatible election outcomes, from time to time.

13. Janklow served as governor from 1979 to 1987, and again from 1995 to 2003. Two other Republicans, George Mickelson (1987–1993) and Walter Dale Miller (1993–1995) filled in the gap between Janklow's separated terms.

14. Republican William F. Quinn was the first elected governor of the nation's fiftieth state, serving from 1959 to 1962.

15. Martin, Mart. *The Almanac of Women and Minorities in American Politics, 2002.* Colorado: Westview Press, 2000. Pp. 225–228.

16. The only official Independents in Congress, Senator Jim Jeffords and Congressman Bernie Sanders of Vermont, actually caucus with the Democrats. See also Larry J. Sabato and Bruce Larson, *The Party's Just Begun: Shaping Political Parties for America's Future.* 2nd Ed. New York: Longman, 2002.

17. My thanks to Tim Storey of the National Conference of State Legislatures in Denver, Colorado, for this information.

18. See SouthNow Update, November 27, 2002, tables 1–2, http://www.south now.org.

2

Air Force Won

CHUCK TODD
The Hotline

Every election fits into a pattern, the problem is that sometimes we don't know if the election that just took place is a morphing of an old pattern or the start of a new one. This defensive analysis can easily be applied to the 2002 elections.

Like the last three Congressional elections—1996, 1998, 2000—Campaign 2002 was another tight election nationally that saw one party nab the advantage and win every close election at the very end.

In 1996, it was the GOP with a late surge saving the party from seeing Bob Dole's doomed presidential campaign landslide them out of power. In 1998, it was Clinton's pending impeachment, which gave the Democrats the small wind they needed to make history and deny the six-year-itch phenomenon from claiming the Democrats and Bill Clinton as another victim. In 2000, whether it was the late disclosure of George W. Bush's D.U.I. or the mere fact that the party in power at the time (the Democrats) had used its political advantages very adroitly, giving the party its best get-out-the-vote effort in decades, Democrats got the very late boost in every close race.

As for 2002, the pattern held, with the Republicans benefiting from a last-minute surge, boosted some by the reality of the times—i.e., a country at war—and more so by the popularity and power of its leader, President George W. Bush.

But here is where we get a bit defensive in the analysis of Campaign 2002: Some Republicans are trying to make the claim that the 2002 election is the beginning of a new realignment, a new grab at electoral power not seen since the '80s and really not realized by the Republican Party since the early twentieth century.

If Campaign 2002 is the latter and not the former then we won't know it for another decade. For now, it seems all the more correct to view the 2002 campaign as another in the lengthening line of close campaigns all shifting ever-so-slightly in one direction.

So how did the GOP do it?

HOW THE REPUBLICANS WON

Let's start with the GOP's biggest asset in 2002—geography. We go back to the very first National Republican Senatorial Committee PowerPoint presentation to which the media was privy, apparently prepared in December of 2000. The spin from the Republicans was that while the party was defending more seats (20) than the Democrats (14), 17 of the 20 GOP Senate seats up for reelection were states Bush carried, while 6 of the 14 Democratic defenses were in states Bush carried. Put it another way, the Republicans only had to defend 3 Senate seats in the blue states (i.e., states Gore carried in 2000), while Democrats had twice as many seats to defend in the red states.

Fast forward to what were the ten in-play Senate seats going into the final week of Campaign 2002: Arkansas, Colorado, Georgia, Louisiana, Minnesota, Missouri, New Hampshire, North Carolina, South Dakota, and Texas.

Nine of the final ten in-play Senate races were in states Bush carried (Minnesota was the lone exception). Because 2000 was such a divisive election, it gave strategists a truer sense of each party's base states. And this was the opening the Republicans were able to exploit with the president's popularity.

What this list of Senate states illustrates well is that this was not a case of Republicans somehow successfully wooing a slew of swing voters their way in order to win back control of the Senate. This was actually a much more simple campaign for the Republicans to win—all they had to do was convince as many Bush 2000–voting Republicans as possible to vote in these Bush states in order to win. Strategists call these individuals "marginal voters."

In this case, the only swing voter the Republican Senate campaigns in each of these states were trying to woo was the voter who "swings" between voting and not voting, not the overly hyped (and mostly nonexistent) voter that somehow switches between the two parties every election year. Republicans knew that *their* swing voters, when they vote, vote Republican. The trick was getting them to show—something that hadn't happened for the Republican Party in a midterm since 1994. In 2002, a lot of them showed.

It was in fact this phenomenon that helped boost turnout from the all-time low of 1998. Prior to the election, few Democratic strategists worth his or her salt would have believed that an increased voter turnout from 1998 would help Republicans win a lion's share of the close races. There was a running assumption that if turnout somehow went up in 2002, it would benefit Democrats. Wrong!

In fact, what is more disconcerting for Democrats is that there is very little evidence that turnout was down among their base. In fact, there's evidence that Democratic base turnout was actually up in *some* key races. But the story of this election was about more marginal Republicans showing up to the polls, not about a depression of Democratic turnout. No race illustrates this better than the North Carolina Senate race.

In 1998, a year that was deemed as a very good Democratic turnout cycle, the Democrat's successful Senate candidate in North Carolina—John Edwards—received 1,029,237 votes. That was just under one hundred thousand votes more than the Republican he defeated, former Senator Lauch Faircloth. In terms of percentage, Edwards won 51 to 47 percent.

In 2002, Democrat Erskine Bowles received nearly 20,000 *more* votes than Edwards got in 1998. Bowles, however, was blown out in his bid for the Senate by Elizabeth Dole, 54 to 45 percent, illustrating how dramatically higher GOP turnout was in just North Carolina between this midterm and the '98 midterm. Overall, Republicans got nearly 300,000 more voters to the polls in the Tar Heel State.

Elections are about cobbling together enough votes to garner a majority (or plurality) in a contest and in 2002, Republicans had a bigger pool of voters to come up with their majorities in most of these competitive Senate states than the Democrats.

This geographical and base Republican vote advantage does as much to explain how Republicans won back the Senate than any other dynamic. Of course, geography alone couldn't win it all—the landscape needed a little issue fertilization from the White House.

The president's popularity and his control of the issue environment was crucial in putting many of these Republicans in these individual races over the top. The durability of Bush's job approval rating is proving to be one of the more remarkable political achievements in the last fifty years. And this is following a president (Bill Clinton) whose approval ratings regularly boggled the minds of political analysts.

Undoubtedly, Bush's handling of the aftermath of the September 11 attacks has had a lot to do with a large majority of Americans giving him the benefit of the doubt, but the White House still deserves credit with the sustaining power of the job approval rating. That's where the bully pulpit proved to be so key in the 2002 midterms.

Think back to July and August of 2002. Corporate America was reeling from scandal and the economy was as unstable as it has been in a decade. It was the only period since September 11, 2001, where Bush looked politically vulnerable. After all, the poster child company of corporate wrongdoing, Enron, had tons of political connections to his White House. Moreover, the administration's Vice President, Dick Cheney, was seeing his corporate career come under scrutiny to the point where the media actually kept a running tally (over 50 days) of how long it had been since Cheney had allowed himself to be queried by the press on any topic, and more specifically, his days at Halliburton.

But that was August, the country's vacation month. Things would change drastically in just a few short days of the president returning from vacation at his ranch in Crawford, Texas. The moment Congress and the president returned from vacation was the seminal point in the Republicans' drive to turn the country's focus away from Wall Street and back to Baghdad. Most of September was dominated by the debate between the unilateralists and the multilateralists—i.e., debating whether to go it alone in a potential war with Iraq or campaign for United Nations approval. This debate led to the push on both sides of the issue for a congressional resolution to approve any use of force against Iraq.

The negotiation of the use of force resolution, of course, was not something that was done overnight. Democrats in many swing or lean-Republican states were sidelined while the political fallout of the impending confrontation with Iraq was being debated on the front pages of their local papers. Although candidates continued to buy airtime through political advertising, the free media covering the most competitive campaigns allowed Iraq and terrorism to dominate the debate.

This lasting coverage of the Iraq debate only served to postpone and nearly erase the public's focus on the domestic front, particularly the corporate scandals and the weakness of the economy as political issues. Polls showed that those two issues bothered voters, but not in a partisan way. They had somehow put distance in their heads between these domestic issues and the White House.

There are plenty of reasons as to why the economy never became a partisan issue in the federal races. One theory simply states that the country blamed September 11 as much if not more than the White House for the nation's economic problems. A second theory is that the public wasn't as economically depressed as the Democrats would have had them believe. Thanks to very low interest rates and no dip in the housing market, the security blanket of the value of our homes may help explain why there was not a great outrage over the economy. A concern? Yes. A crisis? Not yet.

Now, let's revisit where we are on the political calendar at this point. The congressional debate on the use of force resolution against Iraq took us well into October, essentially delaying the start of the final national focus on the elections. Still, at the time, Democrats were convinced there was still enough time for the country to focus back on domestic issues, giving the party out of power a chance to build some momentum heading into November. But then an unexpected story crept into the national headlines—the sniper attacks on the Washington, D.C., suburbs. These trying days for the political capital of the country became compelling television for every market in the country, even leading to the issue of ballistics fingerprinting of guns to make it into several political campaigns. The focus on this story, which did not come to an end until late October, ate into precious time for Democrats to galvanize voters nationally for a very short sprint to the November 5 finish line.

Just as the media (and the rest of the nation) was finally ready to focus on the midterm elections, the president embarked on his now famous two-week barnstorming trek across the country on Air Force One. The media and analysts picked up anecdote after anecdote to support the theory that Bush's targeted stops across the country created the final winning margins for the GOP in several important races. There is little doubt that Bush pulled Colorado's Wayne Allard and New Hampshire's John Sununu from the GOP trash pile of losers; these were two Senate seats most Republicans were beginning to write off in the final ten days of the campaign. But Bush, and possibly Bush alone, was the difference.

And it wasn't just the Senate. In fact, much of Bush's final schedule had as much to do with making sure the GOP held its House majority than it did with Bush's obsession with winning back Senate control. He spent more than half of his final campaign time in key House races. One notable example is Iowa, where the White House had long given up its ambitions of winning either of the state's key statewide races. The National Republican Congressional Committee asked for a final Bush swing into Cedar Rapids on behalf of GOP Representative Jim Leach who, like the two Senate examples in Colorado and New Hampshire, was thought by many to be on political life support. On Election Day, Leach won by a surprisingly comfortable margin, especially in the county Bush stumped in just hours before the vote.

Bush may not have had coattails in any election where his name was actually on the ballot (as Democrats gleefully pointed out in 1998 and 2000), but in 2002, Bush had some of the longest coattails in political history.

THE BLAME GAME

In the aftermath of the election, many Democrats strategists have been beating themselves up over the fact that they could not dominate (much less even participate effectively in) the issue environment. Some have argued that the party didn't stand up loud enough in opposition to the pending war with Iraq. Some argued that the party didn't stand up loud enough for repealing the Bush tax cut.

Elections are not like the movie *War Games,* where one could program a computer with a scenario and get a result of what would have happened. But if a computer program could be created to do this, and a scenario was entered where Democrats were campaigning nationally against the White House on its tax cut and its use-of-force request in Iraq, many observers would have bet that the Republicans would have seen electoral gains rivaling 1994. It's too easy of an excuse to blame the message. The Democrats appeared to lack a message not because they had nothing to say, but because the Republicans, led by the White House, articulated their message of security so effectively.

This Democratic blame game is amusing for political junkies, especially considering that a shift of less than one-half of 1 percent of votes in Senate races nationally would have kept Democrats in control of the Senate. A similar percentage shift in House votes in approximately ten close House races would have at least given the Democrats a net gain in seats and might have actually put the party in a position to win back control of that chamber too.

But what's the fun in that, right? Every election has to be treated as a referendum on somebody, and in the Democratic Party, the rank-and-file chose to make it a referendum on its congressional leaders. Surprisingly, most of the early blame game centered on the Democrats' House leader, Representative Dick Gephardt (D-MO); "surprisingly" because if it was not for Gephardt, the party could have seen Iraq become a much bigger political problem. Remember the "Baghdad 3"? Three Democratic members of Congress—David Bonior of Michigan, Jim McDermott of Washington, and Mike Thompson of California—chose to criticize Bush's Iraq policy while on the soil of that controversial country.

In retrospect, it's shocking that the "Baghdad 3" never once appeared in a paid political commercial. Credit for that phenomenon has to go to Gephardt, who negotiated a passable Iraq resolution with the White House within hours of the "Baghdad 3"'s first appearances on television. Did one of Gephardt's demands of the White House in exchange for public support on Iraq include making sure the "Baghdad 3" were not used for political gain? Inquiring political junkie minds want to know.

On strategy, there's no question Democrats deserve some blame for the performance in House races. The party wasn't just out-gunned on money (something they are always out-gunned on) but they were overwhelmed on the strategy front.

On paper, Democrats should not have lost House seats. Maybe winning control of the lower chamber was out of reach, but winning seats sure wasn't. Looking at the results, it is clear Democrats lost ground in the House on bad strategy, bad candidate recruiting, and bad luck. Later in this book, there will be a more detailed account of how the Democrats just blew it on the House front (see chapter 7). Needless to say, there's plenty of evidence that on tactics alone, Democrats could have avoided much of their House losses.

When it comes to the blame game, one person who has not gotten much attention is then-Senate Majority Leader Tom Daschle. One reason he's escaped the political blame game is that on tactics, Daschle was very sound. He was a champion fundraiser for the party, going to great lengths to keep the Senate committee competitive financially with its GOP counterpart. And he went to great political lengths to ensure the viability of the New Jersey and Minnesota seats—Daschle was intimately involved in the reshaping of both races. But while Daschle played a large role on the political mechanics front, his role as party messenger is still in doubt. This is an area where Daschle needs to improve if he does harbor future national ambitions, or if he simply wants to remain the titular head of his party.

In hindsight, one has to wonder how the outcomes in the Georgia and Missouri Senate races might have been altered had Daschle negotiated a quicker end to the debate over the creation of the Homeland Security Department. What if Republicans didn't have that "obstructionist" charge to use against the now ex-Senators from those two key states—Max Cleland and Jean Carnahan? Yet another scenario to plug into our fantasy elections war game computer.

And speaking of election scenarios, here's one more: What if Jim Jeffords didn't hand control of the Senate to the Democrats? Some GOP strategists believe the Jeffords party switch did as much to change the dynamic of the campaign as any other single political event in the last two years. How successful would Bush have been on the "obstructionist" charge if Republicans held the Senate the whole time? Would the word "obstructionist" even have been part of the 2002 vocabulary?

One glaring void the 2002 midterm elections exposed was that there is no obvious leader of the Democrat Party. Both Daschle and Gephardt were possible candidates for that unofficial post, but failing to have the "majority" or "speaker" titles in front of their names eliminated them for now. So who is the leader?

The political calendar will provide a titular head of the party soon enough as whoever ends up as the next nominee for president in 2004 will become the head of the party. Whether that post is temporary for that person or more permanent, of course, depends on the outcome in November 2004. But until then, the party is going to be viewed as a ship without a captain.

On the House side, the rise of Nancy Pelosi of California as the Democratic leader doesn't necessarily elevate her to national party leader just yet—Daschle as Senate Minority Leader will still hold a bigger sway. And then there are the Clintons. The power couple is still a fundraising machine for the party, but politically Democrats still are not sure how to handle the two, especially the former president. Do they embrace him or ignore him? For the last two years, the party has tried to find a middle ground but one wonders if that's the most effective strategy. Finding the Clinton middle ground, one could argue, has only assured the party two defeats in the last two election cycles.

Another weakness the GOP exposed in the 2002 midterms in the Democratic Party is its problems in connecting with rural America. Despite an unprecedented effort by the party to embrace the rural culture in the South, Democrats came up short in a number of races. But one election cycle of being on the side of the gun owner doesn't necessarily build up a permanent trust. It is going to take Democrats a few election cycles to assure rural America that they are with them. A sponsorship on the NASCAR truck circuit can only go so far in one year.

But clearly, the Democratic Party has to grow beyond the African-American–urban reliance if they are going to win close races in the South. As our North Carolina example showed, just maximizing turnout in the Democratic base constituencies isn't going to be enough in the South. The party has to appeal to "Bubba." Remember, the party's last two successful White House candidates were when the Democratic nominee made an open appeal to rural America. Jimmy Carter was the first country music president and Bill Clinton was Bubba with an Ivy League education. The country music set is now much more comfortable in the GOP tent and that may do more to explain why a Democratic presidential candidate has not received 50 percent of the vote since Carter in 1976.

As for President Bush's future and the future of the GOP, things haven't been this good for them in a while. But don't expect the honeymoon to last. One-party rule of the trifecta (the White House, Senate, and the House of Representatives) never seems to last very long. The Republicans had it for about six months in 2001 until Jim Jeffords' switch. The last time Democrats controlled the trifecta was after the 1992 elections—voters ousted the party from two (the Senate and House) of those three slots in just two short years. Prior to 1992, the last time one party held the trifecta was during Jimmy Carter's lone presidential term.

The bottom line is that it is not easy holding on to power when one is the party in power. That said, Bush is in a much stronger position politically in terms of dealing with Congress than he was in the first six months his party controlled Congress. And Bush is much stronger politically than either Clinton or Carter during their brief stints of trifecta control. That political strength is key for Bush because the last thing he needs is a Congress run by his own party that drags down his reelection chances in 2004. History has proven that running *against* Congress is a good strategy for reelection for a president whose party doesn't control Congress. It's not as easy to win reelection when there isn't a political foil.

Massive reorganizing of government is not always a means to holding power for a long time. It eventually caught up with the Democrats the both times they had presidents seeking to massively reorganize the structure of government. Don't be surprised if Bush's remaking of the government with the addition of the Homeland Security Department doesn't come with its share of political landmines.

IN THE STATEHOUSES

No analysis of a midterm election is complete without a discussion of the battles for control of the statehouses. In 2002, 36 governor seats were up for reelection. At any given point in the election cycle, approximately 30 of those 36 were in play. There were two reasons for the tumultuous nature of the gubernatorial elections. One was cyclical, as a number of the GOP governors elected in 1994 were term-limited in 2002. But the bigger reason may have been financial. The fiscal problems facing the federal government were tenfold on the state level because in many of these states (unlike the feds) governors *have* to balance their budgets. And when budgets have to be balanced in tough economic times, one of two things has to occur and neither is politically popular: taxes have to go up, or services have to be cut (or worse, both simultaneously).

One could argue that the voter revolt over the economy and other domestic issues that Democrats thought would propel them in the federal elections ended up playing itself out on the governors' front. While just a small handful of Senate seats actually changed party hands, 20 of the 36 governor seats up for reelection saw a party out of power win. In this era where incumbents get reelected at an extremely high clip, a 50 percent or more partisan turnover in any election season is remarkable.

Going into the cycle, Democrats were expecting to make big gains, primarily for the reasons noted above. The fact that Republicans still hold a slight lead in governor's seats (26 to 24) was something for the GOP to boast about. When population is taken into account, Democrats can technically claim that a slight majority of the population has a Democratic governor, but that's not much of a mandate to cling to. Sure, Democrats have more governorships now than they did before—but only three more.

The Democrats' biggest victories came in the industrial states (Michigan, Wisconsin, Illinois, and Pennsylvania). In some ways, it was a political shift whose time had come, foretold by presidential politics: Democrats have carried all four states in the last three presidential races. It is naïve to read the Democratic wins in these three states as some sort of precursor to problems for Bush's reelection. Remember, all four of these states had GOP governors in 2000 and Bush did not carry any of them.

The GOP's biggest wins came in predominantly Democratic states, including Maryland, Massachusetts, and Hawaii. The Maryland win is the most intriguing for GOP strategists to study. One wonders if the Maryland GOP model can be applied to Republicans pining for hope in states like California and Washington.

And fitting the theme of gubernatorial turnover in the absence of turnover on the federal level was each of the two party's biggest upsets of 2002. For the Democrats, it was their shocking victory over celebrity-athlete-turned-politician Steve Largent in the Oklahoma governor race. Largent's loss should serve as a lesson to any future celebrities seeking office (this means you, Mr. Schwarzenegger) that fame alone doesn't win elections. Campaigns matter and in this case, Democrat Brad Henry ran a much better campaign than Largent. (For those keeping football score in Oklahoma, you know that Largent is the second high-profile football star to lose statewide. In 1964, legendary Sooner football coach Bud Wilkinson lost a bid for the Senate. But we digress.)

For the GOP, their biggest upset was in Georgia, where Republican Sonny Perdue inexplicably ousted incumbent Democratic Governor Roy Barnes. For those assuming the Barnes and Cleland oustings in Georgia were proof of some sort of GOP tide in the state, they should realize that Democrats won a majority of the down-ballot statewide contests in Georgia, specifically for lieutenant governor, attorney general, and secretary of state. Students of campaigns know that when there is a tide favoring one party, especially on the state level, the down-ballot offices usually go the same way as the top of the ticket. This was *not* the case in Georgia. There were at least 60,000 voters in the state that saw fit to reelect the state's African-American Democratic attorney general but oust Barnes; at least 100,000 voters reelected the Democratic lieutenant governor but ousted Barnes. Some Georgia Democrats want to blame Barnes' defeat on the Confederate flag issue (see chapter 17). But why would those voters motivated to oust Barnes over the issue also reelect Democrats down the ballot? It's an interesting riddle, one that could have been solved a lot more easily at the exit poll had the Voter News Service consortium worked. In a state like Georgia in 2002, the absence of trustworthy post-election data really hampers our ability to understand the mind of the electorate. The lack of exit polling is a real tragedy for political scientists and historians, but this loss of data also hampers strategists in future races.

While the victories were on the margins in the micro-sense, the macroperspective of the 2002 midterms was historical. A party in the White House actually winning control of a chamber is indeed historic. The mood in which these midterms were held—a time when the fear of terrorist attacks still grips many in the country—makes these elections historic. The impact these elections will have on the fate of current political players in 2004 and beyond is still to be seen. For these reasons and many others, the 2002 elections have to be studied and examined for their greater meaning.

3

Playing Second Fiddle

Political Ads, International Newsmakers Bury Election Coverage

MARK JURKOWITZ
Boston Globe *Media Writer*

Arguably, the biggest news story to emerge during the hotly contested 2002 Massachusetts gubernatorial campaign involved a single word—"unbecoming."

During the crucial final debate in what was then viewed as a tossup race between Republican Mitt Romney and Democrat Shannon O'Brien, the GOP candidate used that word to criticize his rival's aggressive tactics. The next day, the implications of a male candidate referring to a female candidate as "unbecoming" became the hot topic of discussion. O'Brien, who campaigned with New York Senator Hillary Clinton, suggested it was a throwback to an earlier era of gender inequality. Romney, who hit the stump with Arizona Senator John McCain, took umbrage at the idea that there were sexist overtones to the remark.

Whatever the case, it made for some of the campaign's biggest headlines. "Camps spar over Romney word choice," declared the *Boston Globe*'s page-one headline. The *Boston Herald*'s screaming front-page headline was considerably less restrained. "O'Brien plays gender card," it declared, disapprovingly. When the results were tallied five days later and Romney won a surprisingly easy victory, it seemed that most late-breaking voters agreed with that assessment. But in a state with a major budget deficit, a slumping economy, and palpable voter distaste for business as usual at the State House, it's not likely that most citizens wanted the campaign to hinge on a debate over semantics.

The "unbecoming" front-page furor was a symbol of a 2002 midterm campaign that history will not regard as one of the media's finest hours. The issues that made headlines were unremarkable, if not trivial. Political journalism itself appeared to be a nonfactor in the campaigns. Most pundits and pollsters failed to detect the significant late movement toward the GOP that became the Election Day story. Unprecedented torrents of TV advertising swamped actual campaign coverage. And had it not been for the tragic death of Minnesota Senator Paul Wellstone, the entire campaign might well have slipped under the radar screen of a national press corps consumed with the Washington sniper and the confrontation with Iraq.

Fittingly, election night offered one final unpleasant surprise for the media. The Voter News Service (VNS), the media consortium that provides the exit poll data that allow networks to predict election-night victors (the 2000 Florida presidential fiasco notwithstanding), was crippled by computer problems, leaving frustrated anchors with much time to kill and not much to say.

If there was one overarching theme that summed up the role of the media in campaign 2002, it was that reporters played second fiddle to the image-makers and ad buyers.

"I was stunned by the abandonment of covering the campaign," said Craig Crawford, executive publisher of *The Hotline* political newsletter who traveled to a number of battleground states. "There was some horse race coverage, but none of it influential. So much of the coverage was about the television ads. The ads drove the print coverage."

"Up until the last week, I would have said the media's main role was not to have a role," added S. Robert Lichter, president of the Center for Media and Public Affairs (CMPA), which monitored broadcast network coverage of the campaign.

Wellstone's tragic death in a small plane crash, and the emergence of former Vice President Walter Mondale as his replacement, provided a surprising story line that did generate a dramatic spike in national press attention during that final week. It also created perhaps the only media moment that swayed the outcome of a critical race.

According to the CMPA survey, the ABC, CBS, and NBC evening newscasts devoted more minutes (141 minutes) to campaign coverage during the last eight days before the balloting than it did during the prior eight weeks (130 minutes). "It's like they flipped a page on their appointment calendar and it said 'cover election,'" noted Lichter, with more than a hint of sarcasm. A primary catalyst for the dramatically increased eleventh-hour coverage was the Wellstone/Minnesota Senate race story, which according to the CMPA, generated a full 61 minutes of network news airtime in the final days of the election season.

It also created a pivotal moment when Wellstone's memorial service was transformed into a partisan pep rally before the eyes of Minnesota voters watching on live television. Hy Berman, a University of Minnesota history professor who was commentating on that event for KARE-TV in Minneapolis, saw the switchboard light up and the angry e-mails pour into the station and knew instantly "that this was a defining moment." According to Berman, Wellstone had about a nine-point lead against Republican Norm Coleman on the day he died and Mondale seemed likely to maintain that edge. But Berman is convinced that the televised images of that memorial service swung the election to Coleman.

But the unusual events in Minnesota were the exception. In a column for *The Hartford Courant* a few days before the voting, Quinnipiac University journalism professor Paul Janensch mocked the level of media attention by quoting one "reader" saying: "I heard a rumor that there is an election next Tuesday. Is this true?"

On the network news level, the campaign was overwhelmed by what appeared to be more urgent and dramatic stories. According to the *Tyndall Report,* which also monitors the big three national nightly newscasts, the Washington sniper saga was the leading story in each of the four weeks leading up to Election Day—from October 7 to November 1. And the cable news networks—CNN, Fox News Channel, and MSNBC—were giving it even bigger play, treating the sniper tale as one of those breathless, relentless 24/7 sagas like the O. J. Simpson case, the anthrax scare, or the death of Princess Diana.

During the same time span, the looming confrontation with Iraq, the war on terror—including the deadly Bali bombing—and the Moscow theater siege also dominated airtime, pushing the election deeper onto the back burner. But even so, several experts say the flagging national media interest was less a function of the unique circumstances surrounding this election than part of a broader trend.

"The amount of coverage of midterm elections was thoroughly normal," said analyst Andrew Tyndall. "It was ignored, but that is par for the course. The national news media have an awful time covering Congressional elections. They can't work out how to make a critical swing district in Kentucky interesting to people who don't live in Kentucky."

Lichter has noticed a steady decline in campaign coverage since the three-way 1992 presidential race and the 1994 Congressional elections that ushered in the conservative Gingrich Revolution. "The longer term trend

since 1996 is that coverage has diminished sharply and it can't be attributed
to the nature of the race anymore," he said. "The network news has become
more social and lifestyle" oriented. "It's clear that something has happened."

While levels of coverage are much harder to quantify in local elections,
some indicators confirmed the national trend. In early November, the Lear
Center Local News Archive—a collaboration of the USC Annenberg School
and the University of Wisconsin—released the results of an ongoing survey
examining campaign news on 122 television stations in the top 50 media
markets. That study, which covered the period from September 18 to October 24, found that for every one election-related story on local television,
viewers were exposed to four political ads. In fact, only 37 percent of the
broadcasts viewed by the Lear researchers contained any kind of news coverage of the campaign.

It has become an article of faith that in recent years, consultants hired
by local stations to boost ratings in competitive markets have advised their
clients that viewers are bored silly by stories about government or politics.
And in releasing the Lear survey, associate dean of the USC Annenberg
School Martin Kaplan echoed that sentiment by noting that "many station
managers feel that putting political news on their airwaves would be ratings
poison for their broadcasts."

Perhaps the lack of sustained, aggressive coverage helps explain
another 2002 election media phenomenon—the fact that many journalists
failed to detect the Republican surge that returned control of the Senate and
widened the party's majority in the House of Representatives.

"The story frame was an assumption that it was going to be a rerun
of 2000, that it was going to be too close to call," said Tyndall. "And they
were wrong."

One key element of the story that the media missed was the ballot box
power of President George W. Bush, who went on a last-minute barnstorming tour of key states that attracted considerable attention from local television cameras. As the Center for the Study of Elections and Democracy
(CSED) at Brigham Young University pointed out in its analysis of the 2002
midterm races, the president enjoyed strong and widespread public
approval. In its survey, the CSED questioned a national sample of voters as
well as voters in four battleground states: Colorado, Connecticut, Arkansas,
and Missouri. In each sample, Bush's approval ratings registered in the mid
60's, a lofty number for a midterm president and a factor he clearly used in
rallying support for Republican candidates.

"Bush's trips were galvanizing," said Crawford. "His coverage, particularly on television, was extensive and all favorable and there was no effort
to get alternative views. Bush would land somewhere and the Democrats

would go into hiding. I just hadn't seen a president roll through every venue like Caesar."

Perhaps the most pungent post-mortem on the failure of the media prognosticators was offered up by well-known *Washington Post* media critic Howard Kurtz, in a November 7 story aptly headlined "The Losers' Circle."

"They said the Democrats were a solid bet to hang on to the Senate. They said many of the races were tight as a tick. They said these were primarily local contests in which a president couldn't have much impact," Kurtz wrote, regurgitating the words of many media commentators. "So what do journalists have to say for themselves now?"

In Georgia, another state where Bush made a last-minute appearance, Republican gubernatorial challenger Sonny Perdue upset incumbent Roy Barnes, and GOP Senate hopeful Saxby Chambliss upended favored incumbent Max Cleland. Yet in a poll conducted by WSB-TV and *The Atlanta Journal-Constitution* that ran in the *Journal-Constitution* two days before the election, Cleland was shown with a five-point lead among likely voters and Barnes appeared to have an insurmountable eleven-point lead over Perdue. "Barnes's comfortable lead allows Democrats to focus most of their attention on the Senate showdown," the story reported.

"All the polls were wrong," commented Michael Adams, the president of the University of Georgia. "It was the worst performance by pollsters I've ever seen."

As was the case in other states featuring competitive races, the verdict in Georgia is that the Bush factor and an intense Republican get-out-the-vote effort trumped anything the journalists could write or say. "My own view, is that the journalistic impact this time was minimal," said Adams. "Particularly in the governor's race, it was more style and process than it was particular issues."

It was also an onslaught of television advertising. A week after Election Day, the Alliance for Better Campaigns—a coalition of groups pushing broadcasters to donate free airtime during campaigns—released its accounting of the TV political ad dollars spent in 2002. With a total of 28,340 ads aired, the Atlanta market finished second in the nation, behind only Boston. And the only station that topped WTOC-TV in Savannah in number of ads broadcast was WMUR-TV in Manchester, New Hampshire.

The most powerful media outlet in the Granite State, WMUR has raked in so many ad dollars—particularly during the quadrennial New Hampshire presidential primary season—that it has jokingly been called "the house that Steve Forbes built," in recognition of the former GOP presidential hopeful's heavy spending habits. In 2002, with an open seat in the governor's race, a Republican Senate primary and a very competitive Senate final pitting popular Democratic Governor Jean Shaheen against Congressman John Sununu, it was windfall time at WMUR. According to the alliance numbers, the station aired an incredible 17,328 campaign ads from January 1 to November 5.

"It was an unusual year in terms of the number of candidates who had a lot of money and started spending early," said the station's general manager Jeff Bartlett, in a serious bit of understatement.

Andrew Smith, the director of the University of New Hampshire Survey Center, said WMUR made a serious and solid effort to cover the campaign season. He also cites the impact of the conservative newspaper, the (Manchester) *Union Leader*, which pounded away at the losing Shaheen campaign and may have helped cut into her vote total in that city. Once considered a political kingmaker in New Hampshire, the *Union Leader* has been eclipsed in recent years by the growing power of WMUR, another piece in a mounting body of evidence that television has far surpassed print in election-year clout. That is largely a reflection of the power of TV ads.

Like so many other election observers, Smith said the decisive factors were advertising and an intense get-out-the-vote effort. "There were some journalists that mattered, but I didn't see any particular stories or particular issues that people had to pay attention to," he said. "The amount of money spent on advertising dwarfed everything."

In Massachusetts, a state famous for its love of politics and energetic corps of political reporters, the story was much the same. Advertising dollars spent by Romney and O'Brien—but also spent by New Hampshire candidates in the Boston market—poured in at a near obscene pace. The alliance numbers revealed that Boston TV stations led the nation with 41,154 political ads sold. And the total amount of estimated 2002 ad revenue in the Boston market, which several observers pegged as conservative, was put at $37.1 million.

In the Bay State, much of the media's energy was consumed in organizing what eventually turned out to be five televised gubernatorial debates. Several featured three minor party candidates and became confusing cacophonies of shouting and interruption. The final face-off, which included only Romney and O'Brien and was moderated by NBC's Tim Russert, may have proved crucial since voters seemed put off by O'Brien's attack-oriented "unbecoming" performance. The next day's *Globe* published an intriguing story that featured five Marlborough, Massachusetts, residents who had all proclaimed themselves undecided going into that last debate. "All five said [O'Brien] turned them off," the story concluded. "All five said Romney had won their votes."

The article proved prescient, but Romney's five-point margin of victory still caught the savvy Massachusetts press crew by surprise.

In a way, the biggest media story to come out of the 2002 campaign had nothing to do with the many hard-fought political races. Instead it was an internal journalism battle—waged with dueling polls and surveys—about the quality and quantity of political reporting itself. At its core, it raises the question of whether dramatic reform is needed in order to keep America's voters informed and interested.

Less than a week before Election Day, the National Association of Broadcasters (NAB) released a survey headlined "Nationwide poll finds broad voter approval of broadcast election coverage." The poll of 800 registered voters found that 43 percent thought local stations were spending "too much time" on election coverage; 40 percent said the quantity was just about right; and only 15 percent thought broadcasters were under-covering the election campaign. At the same time, 44 percent said local broadcast coverage was the most crucial tool for helping voters select a candidate compared to only 18 percent who primarily relied on newspapers for that function.

"We find many stations out there doing a good job of trying to serve their communities with good political coverage," said Barbara Cochran, president of the Radio-Television News Directors Association (RTNDA).

Contrast that cheery assessment with the headline on the November 1 release of the Lear Center Local News Archive survey: "Political Ads Dominate Local TV News Coverage: Stations Air Over Four Times as Many Political Ads as Campaign Stories; Devote Almost Twice As Much Time to Advertising as to News."

Or try this blunter headline on the November 13 CSED study: "Election Day Voters Say Quality of Campaigns Declining: Too Many Ads, Too Much Mail; Most Voters Tuned Out."

Who's telling the truth here? Alex Jones, director of the Harvard's Shorenstein Center on the Press, Politics, and Public Policy, seems to side with the critics. "Television is still the vehicle for political communication but it's all in the advertising," he said. Stations "don't want to get in the way of that by giving anything away for free."

But giving airtime away for free during election cycles is exactly the goal of the Alliance for Better Campaigns, an umbrella group trying to reform the electoral system by changing the rules for broadcasters. The alliance, for example, is supporting a proposed Senate bill requiring TV and radio stations to provide at least two hours a week of "candidate-centered" or "issue-centered" programming before elections as part of a basic public service obligation. The measure would also let candidates purchase ads through a voucher system funded by fees on broadcasters.

The alliance released numbers indicating that during the 2002 campaign, television stations collected more than a cool billion in political ad revenue, a record that marked roughly a 25 percent spending increase over the 2000 presidential campaign. "The problem is that most Americans get their political information from broadcast television and what they are getting now is the worst of the political process," said alliance president Paul Taylor. "As a rule, local stations are retreating from substantive coverage."

The Lear Center Local News Archive's analysis of the 2002 campaign found that to the extent that local television news covered the election, gubernatorial races dominated the news while U.S. Senate and House races were practically ignored. It reported that coverage of campaign strategy and the "horserace" comprised a full 51 percent of election stories while only 37 percent of those stories focused on the issues.

"By and large it's depressing," said Martin Kaplan. "Stations are happy to run ads, but squeamish about running coverage."

Like the Lear Center, the CSED analysis found voters being inundated with political ads during the election season. In the final week of the campaign, voters in three states featuring tight battles—Colorado, Arkansas, and Missouri—said they saw 12 to 13 television campaign ads per day. "In three out of the four battleground races studied, respondents saw the 2002 campaign as more negative in tone than other recent races," the CSED noted. That sense was captured by venerable *Washington Post* writer David Broder in a column headlined "Death by Negative Ads."

"What I have heard, this year in particular, has been a chorus of complaints about the trivialization and avoidance of serious issues and the proliferation of personal attacks," Broder wrote.

Paul Taylor and his allies feel the remedy to this distorting imbalance of ads and serious news coverage is the adoption of free airtime provisions, something broadcasters are clearly resisting, thus far successfully.

"Our position is that whatever stations want to do voluntarily is fine," said the RTNDA's Cochran, summing up the industry view. "We'd be very concerned about any proposal that would have the government mandating a particular type of content for news coverage."

In fact, the alliance reports that seven TV station groups—Capitol Broadcasting, Cox Television, Granite Broadcasting, Hearst-Argyle Television, Liberty Corporation, E. W. Scripps, and New York Times Broadcasting—did commit to providing extensive free airtime in 2002 for everything from debate coverage to candidate issue statements. Those 83 stations, however, represented a small percentage of local TV outlets.

In an interesting twist to the debate over mandated free airtime, the National Association of Broadcasters (NAB) survey asked respondents what would happen if candidates were guaranteed free airtime. According to the poll, 64 percent said they would use the time to air attack ads against their opponents while only 32 percent predicted they would seize the opportunity to inform the public on issues.

"It's clear that voters . . . have little confidence that a free airtime mandate would be used wisely by the candidates," said a research executive at the firm that conducted the poll.

All of which could mean that while voters may be dissatisfied with what they see on their television screens during a campaign season, they feel candidates are incorrigible enough to resist any well-intentioned remedies. And then again, maybe it really depends on whose survey you believe.

The question of how to make political journalism more meaty and relevant is not exactly a new one. After what many observers saw as a desultory 1988 presidential campaign that represented the nadir of modern political journalism, Harvard's Shorenstein Center proposed a much-publicized "Nine Sundays" plan. The idea was that on the nine Sunday evenings prior to Election Day, broadcasters would devote a 90-minute program to the campaign—featuring debates, conversations with the nominees, and even candidates' speeches. A decade and a half later, the idea seems like a fanciful pipe dream, even as the problem it was intended to solve continues to fester.

Another traditional problem with campaign coverage—the networks' feverish race to predict the outcome of tight races on election night—was remedied thanks to a technical snafu. The VNS had desperately tried to fix the bugs in the system and make amends for its role in the 2000 election-night Florida fiasco in which the networks first called the state for Gore, then pulled it back, then called it for Bush, and then pulled it back again. But on election night, a problem with the VNS's new computer system prevented it from providing the exit polls analyses networks needed to call the victors in tight races shortly after the polls close. (Or in some cases, even before all the polls close.)

So those watching on election night got a taste of "old-fashioned" coverage as significant numbers of votes actually had to be counted before winners could be announced. Network commentators and anchors professed to be enjoying this nostalgic journey back to bygone election nights, but their body language seemed to belie those sentiments. When Fox News Channel anchor Brit Hume told viewers "we're not able yet to make a call" in the Georgia Senate race shortly after the polls closed there, it seemed like you could almost see his jaw clench.

Still, the night did not exactly drag on interminably. Shortly before 9 p.m., CNN—which was still aggressive about projections—called Elizabeth Dole the winner in the crucial North Carolina Senate race that seemed to have been tightening dramatically. For those paying close attention, that was the first real sign that the Republicans were headed for a big night, a trend that had escaped most of the nation's distracted journalists in the final days of a campaign on which they never really got much of a handle.

4

Starting to Click

Online Campaigning in the 2002 Elections

MICHAEL CORNFIELD

*Institute for Politics, Democracy, and the Internet
at The George Washington University*

CAMPAIGN 4.0

The extravagant predictions that the Internet would revolutionize American politics, or, at the least, come into its own as a major technological force comparable to television, have thus far proven almost as embarrassing as the Ponzi-scheme promises of dot-com entrepreneurs. But where the business prophets have a lot to account for, in every sense of the word "account," the political and civic evangelists of the Internet have no need to hang their heads and settle debts. The Internet is, indeed, a growing force in campaigns for elective office.

It is also an evolving force. The Internet is not an easy medium to use, especially for people who are switching to it instead of growing up with it. Imagine if you had to change the way you turned on your TV every six months, because "Friends" was now viewable only through NBC 7.0 or higher. Annoying, but doable. Now imagine that you had to change the way you produced and bought time for a television ad every two years, in order to get your spots before the voters. Frustrating, to the point of a turnoff. No other medium makes this kind of learn-as-you-go demand on citizens and campaigners.

The pay-offs in learning how to use the Internet on a regular basis lie in its breathtaking economies, reach, and versatility. Campaigns that put out some money and put in some learning time can then rappel down the slope that represents marginal costs for online communication. They can use the Internet like a television, radio, telephone, fax, mail service, newspaper, magazine, book, meeting hall, storefront, plaza, and library. They can use it to conduct research, recruit and mobilize volunteers, raise money, keep pace with a breaking news story, get a message to a targeted audience—and monitor the success of all these functionalities, the better to make quick adjustments.

Multiple capabilities at shrinking costs are one thing; political effectiveness is another. A campaign cannot do everything at once, not with Election Day bearing down on it. What works, and what doesn't?

BEHAVIORAL PATTERNS AND CAMPAIGN EFFECTIVENESS

The 2002 election was only the fourth of the digital era, so generalizations must be tentative.[1] However, patterns are emerging. We can see a consensus forming among political professionals on how best to deploy the Net to win an election. That consensus depends in part on how citizens are using the Net to get informed and get involved, and we can see some patterns in their usages, too. (Usages, as in plural, because not all citizens behave the same way online.) The same phenomenon may be discerned among the third party to the campaign communication process, the news media.

The scholars behind www.politicalweb.info have provided an overview of what was going on at campaign Web sites in 2002. They report that more than three-quarters of sites for House, Senate, and gubernatorial office had biographical and issues sections, as well as information on how to give the campaign money. This is the campaign Web site as virtual brochure, a minimalist, one-to-many use of a many-to-many medium. More than 60 percent solicited volunteer sign-ups, a stab at interactivity. There is no telling how much campaigns followed through in communicating with the recruits. Only 12 percent of the 2002 campaign Web sites had "forward this to friends" forms, which encourage visitors to spread the word such that the campaign can keep track and acquire more e-mail addresses. Less than 10 percent developed multimedia content expressly for the Web site: games, videos, databases. In short, while campaigners are fond of intoning that "the future is now," as far as online campaigning is concerned, the future is tomorrow at the earliest—coming soon, perhaps, in campaign 5.0 for the 2004 elections.

And how did the voters respond to what the campaigns tried? Poll data show that more Americans are turning to the Internet for news or information about politics or the campaign. What we may label the "online public," an intersecting subset of the online and adult populations, continues to expand. More Americans are going online, and more of those online and eligible to vote are looking at political information. In November 2000, the population of the online public stood at approximately 33 million Americans. In November 2002, it was at 46 million.

However, most of the online public slights campaign Web sites. Although access to Web sites run by parties and candidates is as easy as access to news sites (a fact unique to this medium), only 12 percent of Net users have ever visited a campaign Web site. Public trust levels for information from party, candidate, and other campaign Web sites are low: 32 percent of visitors to such sites said they "almost never" or "never" trust partisan information.[2] Campaigners need to pour more energy into advertising their sites, and improving the contents of their Web pages so that they are of comparable quality to what Net users see when they look for business, health, financial, and even entertainment information.

What about the press? The Internet has loosened the definition of a news mediator; although brand names such as CNN.com and NewYork Times.com dominate the traffic numbers, the Web is host to a mélange of little-known yet often highly sophisticated news and commentary sites. These serve as feeders to the brand names, hungrier for material thanks to the ever-faster news cycle. They also develop their own followings, if not sustaining subscribers. For an example, one need look no further than the editor of this volume. Professor Larry Sabato is now an online publisher ("The Crystal Ball" at www.centerforpolitics.org) as well as a news media source of campaign analysis and predictions. In effect, his regular postings to his Web site and e-mail list made him a journalist as well as a scholar during the 2002 campaign season.

The online source the campaign press liked the most was www.opensecrets.org. Its sponsor, the Center for Responsive Politics, netted over 3,000 mentions in the Nexis news database in 2001, and was well past 4,000 for 2002 before the general campaigns got underway in the fall.[3] Opensecrets.org takes campaign financial disclosure information filed with the government and organizes it for journalists to use in horserace and investigative stories. A zip code entry box on the home page yields local angles for individual donors and recipients. The Center's e-mail newsletters and alerts suggest analytic pieces by outlining the money-in-politics angle on current issues (i.e., homeland security, prescription drugs, trade promotion authority). Most impressively, the Web site has a database that sorts ten years of PAC and individual contributions into 122 categorical blocks that suit the headlines: "Abortion: Pro-Choice," "Abortion: Pro-Life," "Accountants," and so forth. The ideological tilt behind opensecrets.org is most visible in its issue briefs, grouped under the header "Tracking the Payback." It's not so much a partisan as a populist/progressive tilt. The Center for Responsive Politics believes that elected officials respond mainly to those who shovel them money. That's a common belief among journalists, too.

Web site traits and traffic just scratch the surface of online campaigning. E-mail, database integration, cybernetic analysis of real-time feedback, online advertising, viral publicity ("word of mouse"), and text messaging have all come into play. The George Washington University Institute for Politics, Democracy, and the Internet surveyed online campaigning in fifty of the most contested races of 2002. Respondents were asked to assess the effectiveness of the new technology in nine possible applications. The campaigners gave the highest marks to using the Net to conduct research and to communicate with the press. Online advertising and GOTV operations received the lowest marks.

Many respondents said their campaigns attempted online volunteer recruitment and fund-raising. Campaigners undoubtedly took note of the huge and sudden influxes of support to John McCain's presidential bid after he won the New Hampshire primary in 2000. However, the 2002 data show a disjunction between actual results and the perceived effectiveness. There seems to have been confusion among campaigners about what constitutes reasonable goals in recruitment and fundraising, and about the best ways to achieve them.

The answer to the reasonable goals question varies with a campaign's situation and resources. McCain benefited from the sequential structure of presidential primaries (every week, there was a fresh and legitimate challenge to tell Net supporters about), his great fame (how many 2002 candidates went on a national book tour?), and same-day registration in New Hampshire. The answer to the best ways question is more uniform. As McCain showed, it doesn't take much money. The amounts the surveyed campaigns spent, roughly 1–5 percent of their budgets, was probably sufficient in most cases. But it does take continuous effort at massaging lists and databases and keeping content up to date. The McCain campaign devoted almost a year before the New Hampshire primary to planning, constructing, publicizing, experimenting, and tweaking its Internet operations. MoveOn.org, the pioneering online PAC which made its name in the 2000 cycle, has never stopped. It was able to raise over $1 million in a 48-hour span in October 2002 for a handful of candidates who voted against the Iraq war resolution.

By contrast, a study of 168 campaign Web sites on Election Day found that barely a quarter of them were current to that day, and less than a tenth of the campaigns sent out e-mail reminders to vote and help turnout the vote.[4] In Minnesota, the DFL party sent out an emergency appeal for cash on behalf of the Mondale campaign on November 1, beseeching Net readers of the message to go to the party Web site, yet the action alert left out the link to the site. It would have been fascinating to see how the Wellstone campaign, with its 30,000 online volunteers and its innovative volunteer "miles" rewards program, would have used the Internet to get out the vote in Minnesota, also a state with same-day registration.

In the area of campaign research, we learned that the Internet not only facilitates the mining of data about candidates and policies, but about voters as well, in an unexpected manner. Forays into online polling continue, hampered by the statistical manipulations necessary to convert the population reachable through the Net into one that approximates an electorate. The new wrinkle involves the tracking of Web traffic. We know that growing numbers of Web searchers visited the Fox News and Rush Limbaugh sites near Election Day. Traffic doubled at these conservative news sites, while remaining steady at such liberal news sites as ABC and CNN. Meanwhile, search requests for Bill McBride, the Democratic nominee for governor of Florida, dropped even as it increased for his opponent, Republican incumbent Jeb Bush. Traffic also soared for arguably the biggest upset winner in the country, Republican Sonny Perdue, who took the Georgia governorship away from Roy Barnes.[5]

This Web activity correlates with the apparent late break in for Republican candidates across the nation. It could be a leading indicator, and a contributing cause to Republican turnout and victories. Alternately, the traffic could be a lagging indicator, a byproduct or associated consequence of the turnout. Either way, what matters at this stage of the development of online politics is that a correlation exists between Web traffic and voter movement. Web traffic is an indicator of active interest by the public. Polls, by contrast, measure intentions and opinions extracted from a passive sample of the public by questioners. You can be sure that entrepreneurial political consultants will develop Web traffic data into another diagnostic tool in the professional kit.

FLASH! ONLINE HUMOR WORKS!

It was a campaign cycle marked more by proliferation than innovation, but one form caught attention in a distinctive way. Humorous parodies and other satirical material have been circulating on the Net for years, but 2002 brought a sparkling assortment to the virtual trail. Bill Simon and Tim

Hagan, gubernatorial challengers in California and Ohio, respectively, won news coverage and site traffic by riffing off corporate advertising campaigns. AFLAC sought a restraining order against Hagan's attack site taftquack. com, which featured a quacking duck. An Ohio lower court ruled that Taftquack qualified as protected political speech. Simon's campaign let it be known that E-Bay was concerned about its attack site, e-gray.org, which mimicked the auction pages of the Web giant to lance Grey Davis as a governor who sold out to special interests.

The elementary lesson was that humor cuts through the cyber-clutter; a funny Web page is just the sort of message people like to pass along to friends and co-workers. The advanced lesson was that when the humor provokes its target or a prominent company or celebrity to respond publicly, the news media will carry the message over the largest obstacle online publicity entails, which is getting people to go to the site. The extra credit lesson was that when the humor comes with documentation, as in these two cases, it raises the quality of the public discourse—even though it may be negative.

The standout example of humorous campaigning was a flash animation video entitled "Social Insecurity." Shipped the night of October 2 to Democratic National Committee (DNC) e-mail subscribers, and posted on the party Web site hours later, this online cartoon found an edgy way to make the point that privatization would have sent Social Security retirement accounts tumbling: a caricatured President Bush pushes an elderly woman in a wheelchair down a graph line symbolizing stock market declines in the last few years.

The look and sound of the cartoon was vintage Road Runner. Its argument was almost as old, considering that in 1964 a Lyndon Johnson ad featured a pair of scissors snipping a Social Security card in half as a portent of what Barry Goldwater would do as president. The video mischief succeeded mainly because, once again, it got its target to cry foul. Republican National Committee (RNC) Chair Mark Racicot called the cartoon "beyond offensive." Perhaps it was—but when someone complains like that, who among us doesn't want to see for themselves? The news media ate up the controversy. Matt Drudge linked to the video under the headline "Dems Depict Bush Murdering Senior." Over the next two days, half a million people visited the DNC Web site to rubberneck, as it were. The traffic might have been higher had the Internet as a whole and the DNC site in particular not suffered technical difficulties. It might have been much lower had the RNC issued no comment.

The traffic spike and capital buzz lasted a week. For that time, the election was about Social Security, not just the war on terrorism. The RNC tried to fight fire with fire, posting a cartoon with Bush as Superman flying to the rescue of the elderly woman. Whereupon the DNC released a sequel it had commissioned, in which the woman arises from her crash to chide Bush about prescription drugs. But the RNC generated (and had) the last laugh. Members of its e-mail list, estimated at five million addresses, received a "personalized interactive greeting card" on Election Day, addressed from RNC Deputy Chairman Jack Oliver to the individual subscriber. To the strains of "Yankee Doodle Dandy," the video asked Net viewers to mark a mock ballot Republican or Democrat, and then saw a happy or sad ending, accordingly.

This is not as big a breakthrough in campaign communication as the 1993 television ad series starring "Harry and Louise." Nevertheless, the cartoon wars mark a significant and promising development in online campaigning. Cartoons can grab attention from the online public, many of whom are at work or study, and are thus receptive to a humorous break. Cartoons can also convey complex and abstract information quite well—is there a more intelligent television series on the commercial networks than "The Simpsons"?—and what cartoons depict can be documented and explained a link away. I trust the national parties and other campaigners will continue to amuse and expand their lists and battle for news media attention through animated videos. I also trust more of the news media will assess the truth claims of these productions.

HOPE YET GLIMMERS FOR SUBSTANTIVE DISCOURSE

Meanwhile, pragmatism aside, whatever happened to the revolutionary potential for online democracy? The forces of reaction used the Internet to stamp the 2002 elections before the campaigns began, circulating computer-generated redistricting plans which, upon enactment, kept contested House races to a minimum. But the forces of enlightened progress had their online moments as well.

Substantive exchanges among campaigns are one of the things civic idealists continue to hope for on the Internet. So long as neither the government nor a commercial oligopoly exacts a steep fee for access to the Net, campaigns face no external barriers to conducting serious research and incorporating the findings into detailed postings which accompany public messages. The Net makes it possible for campaigns to move beyond drive-by attack spots and sound bite competitions. (Please note: I'm not calling for an end to attacks, but to gratuitous, empty, distorting attacks, which documentation and, even better, the public expectation of documentation, deters.)

One of the four U.S. House races in which two incumbents faced each other featured an exemplary Web battle of substantive charges. Representatives Nancy Johnson (R) and Jim Maloney (D) locked horns to win the newly drawn 5th District of Connecticut. Early in October, Johnson turned a large part of her campaign Web site home page over to a chart that compared the number of bills signed into law that she and her opponent had introduced since 1997 (when he joined her in Congress). The count, also featured in a television ad, was Johnson 23, Maloney 1.

Strategists often counsel campaigns to ignore a contrast if it doesn't favor their side. But a contrast about legislative effectiveness can't be safely ignored. The proven ability to get bills passed into law transcends that staple of campaign rhetoric, taking positions on the issues. It also transcends most other candidate qualifications for office (the autobiography/résumé being another rhetorical staple). Legislative effectiveness speaks to the essence of what elective office is all about.

Maloney responded with a similar bar chart on his home page. It disputed Johnson's 23–1 count by citing bill status reports from Thomas, the online database of congressional votes, to show that only 2 of the 23 bills Johnson listed had actually become law. Meanwhile, according to the Maloney campaign, its candidate/incumbent had crafted 9 bills which had become law. The Web site described each one. The Johnson campaign defended its number, contending that the other 21 bills were folded into legislation enacted under another name. This could have been true. It was said by the Johnson campaign to be true of several of the 9 bills in the Maloney column. But here the online battle died down.

With a bit of simple programming, either campaign could have gone further and made it easy for site visitors to drill down according to the issues and localities that mattered to them. Then the online public could have seen customized examples about how legislative effectiveness affected their lives. As good as this exchange was, its rarity and limits suggest that a civic organization (working with *Congressional Quarterly* data, perhaps) needs to develop a systematic and nonpartisan database of Congressional track records. Then more citizens could move beyond interest group ratings and sound bite interpretations in judging the legislative effectiveness of their federal representatives.

Pitched battles over public policies and public character traits (such as legislative effectiveness) are rare in our two-party, winner-take-all, partisan-redistricted system. Candidates and consultants take the blame for avoiding such battles, but the structure suggests the strategy. The great exception in contemporary campaigning, the one structural feature that demands candidates address the same topic at the same time, is of course the debate. But civic-minded members of the public can use the Internet, with or without an accompanying debate, to spur such battles as well.

The Pennsylvania Economy League, a nonprofit, nonpartisan research organization with a 65-year history and a sterling reputation for civic improvement, developed a Net-based strategy to push the two major-party candidates for governor of Pennsylvania into addressing issues of economic performance, education quality, and community vitality. They set up a Web site, IssuesPA.net, and encouraged local leaders, media, educators, and interested voters to consult it, and then go on to prod the campaigns of Democrat Ed Rendell and Republican Mike Fisher to fill out a detailed questionnaire. More than 80,000 unique visitors passed through IssuesPA.net and came away with downloads, questions, and agenda items. Their informed pressure—over 200 op-eds in local newspapers being a popular venue to express it—elevated the quality of three candidate forums also sponsored by the League.

This initiative was expensive by civic standards (over $500,000), and it lasted more than a year. But, as columnist Neal Peirce noted, it succeeded in "creating a single conversation in a megastate divided into localized—and often very parochial—media markets."[6] The lesson: the decentralized structure of the Internet makes it possible for public agendas to be set from the outside-in, a twist of the classic two-step flow of influence long confirmed by political communications scholars. The customary flow goes from politicians through opinion leaders to the electorate. In this instance, it flowed from opinion leaders through politicians to the electorate; the campaigns were the target of IssuesPA.net's campaign.

CONCLUSION

The breakthrough moment for online politics, analogous to FDR's fireside chats on radio and Eisenhower's television ads, has not yet occurred. The list of stand-out moments in online politics to date—the release of the Starr Report, Jesse Ventura's victory, John McCain's prolonged candidacy—remains short, and historic only within the category of online politics itself. Nothing that happened in 2002 makes that list, not yet anyway (if, say, "Social Insecurity" and IssuesPA.net spur imitators, then they might).

Even so, the Internet is on its way to being an essential component of electoral politicking, as a behind-the-scenes and incrementally valuable tool comparable to the telephone. It will be essential to smart campaigning because it will enable a campaign to draw work, money, and knowledge more effectively out of its principals and supporters. The Internet may not increase voter turnout and political participation generally. Ironically, however, the lower the participation rate, the more power that goes to the minority who do participate, and the Internet will empower them. Such empowerment will not accrue automatically; to succeed, an online campaigner must adopt a trial-and-error, constant-learning attitude at odds with the message-control mind-set of professional campaigners of the mass communications era. But more people are getting it, and getting with it.

As Net politics starts to click, there will be tensions between what works and what is best for democracy. Raising the level of campaign dialogue, for example, can be readily done through the Internet, as we have seen. It is something idealists yearn for, but something that campaigners regard as a luxury, or even a liability in certain circumstances. There is a similar divergence of civic and political interest concerning the role of big money. Yet the effect of incorporating the Internet into both the vocation of winning elections and the structure of a healthy democratic politics may turn on a third factor, one where interests converge, and that is how well it is used to increase the number, voice, and power of campaign volunteers. Campaigns need networks of people as much, if not more, than they need visibility in mass media networks. Turnout depends on the former. Democracies need maximum participation in campaigns to assure the legitimacy and vitality of the results. It is the online volunteer, clicking through to the campaign Web site and clicking its message forward to others, which carries the biggest promise of Net politics.

NOTES

1. Although Senator Dianne Feinstein of California posted a campaign Web site in 1994, online campaigning began in earnest in 1996.

2. The data in these two paragraphs are drawn from a November 2002 survey conducted by Princeton Survey Research Associates for the GWU Institute for Politics, Democracy, and the Internet, the Pew Internet & American Life Project, and the Pew Research Center for the People and the Press. For a full report, see www .ipdi.org.

3. Albert May, *The Virtual Trail: Political Journalism on the Internet*, August, 2002, GWU Institute for Politics, Democracy, and the Internet, www.ipdi.org.

4. "Ready on E-Day," Right Click Strategies, www.rightclicks.com/e-day.

5. Aaron Schatz, "The Lycos 50 Daily Report," November 13, 2002, http:// 50.lycos.com/111302.asp. In the week described in this report, "Election 2002" came from out of nowhere to be the fifth most requested search term, just behind the [video] game Grand Theft Auto, and just ahead of Harry Potter and Eminem.

6. As quoted in IssuesPA.org promotional material.

5

U. S. House Races

Republican Resurgence after Eight Lean Years

MAUREEN SCHWEERS
The House Race Hotline

"Since Republicans took the House in 1994, Democrats have not seen a national map so full of opportunity, as well as a national landscape and historical trends to turn those opportunities into control of the House."

The House Race Hotline made that evaluation in April 2002, and it's just as true after the dust settled on Election Day. Thanks to a redistricting year that generally favored incumbents, along with selective recruiting in an extremely small pool of truly competitive races, neither party had an upper hand as voters headed to the polls on Election Day. With a lagging economy as a backdrop for the 2002 elections, along with the historical trend of the president's party losing seats, it is *still* baffling how Democrats managed to lose ground in the House. While Democrats had significant success in holding back a predicted Republican edge after redistricting, that success didn't ultimately translate to a Democratic majority. A combination of factors, including the party's failure to find a consistent message to compete with the bully pulpit of a popular, war-time president; simply being outspent and outstrategized in a number of key races; and a few late, bad breaks with recruits contributed to Democrats' failures on November 5.

Republicans made small gains in their House majority, picking up six seats on election night. Gaining six seats—just 1.4 percent of the U.S. House of Representatives—hardly constitutes significant ground, when it comes to pure number-crunching. However, in the big picture of the 2002 battle for the House, six seats is a *huge* deal. Had the tables been reversed and Democrats picked up just six seats, the Democrats would have gained a majority, with Dick Gephardt taking the helm as Speaker rather than resigning from his position as Minority Leader.

Throughout 2002, the Democrats' rallying cry was "six seats to a Democratic majority"—a goal that sounded easy enough. However, in the months leading up to the election, numerous political analysts (ourselves included) calculated that it seemed virtually mathematically impossible for Democrats to reach that magic number, given the small number of competitive races, along with the fact that a majority of these competitive races were played out in Republican-held districts. (For those counting, Republicans found themselves defending 19 open seats, compared to 11 for Democrats; as for vulnerable incumbents, according to our final House ratings, ten Republicans were in truly competitive races, compared to just five for Democrats). Even though the majority of the battle for the House was fought on Republican home turf, for Republicans to pull off a six-seat pickup is still remarkable, considering the historical trends working against them.

However, one bright spot in an otherwise difficult year for the Democratic Congressional Campaign Committee (DCCC) came just over a month after Election Day. While most of the national political attention was focused on the Louisiana Senate run-off, the bigger surprise on December 7 was in the 5th District, where Democratic state Representative Rodney Alexander pulled off a slim, 518-vote upset over Republican Lee Fletcher in a Republican-leaning district. The DCCC actively recruited Alexander, a conservative Democrat who had experience garnering crossover voters, and endorsed him in the primary and put significant resources behind his candidacy, touting that their spending in the 5th District—a less pricey media market compared to other competitive districts—was the largest amount of advertising they spent in the last week of a campaign in any non-incumbent race this cycle. While the DCCC deserves major kudos for the win, it was a tough reminder for Democrats that, if the DCCC had the financial resources to play as hard as Republicans in other tight races, election night may have turned out *very* differently.

Despite Democrats' best efforts to make the economy, Social Security privatization, prescription drug coverage or corporate accountability a winning issue, no national issue or trend emerged to define the 2002 battle for the House, which was fought district by district. However, there certainly were plenty of interesting sidebars, with the most important (and lasting) being redistricting.

REDISTRICTING: AN INCUMBENT'S BEST FRIEND

Every ten years, state legislatures are required to redraw their states' congressional boundaries, based on the latest population count by the U.S. Census Bureau. Past redistricting cycles have produced an unusual number of competitive races. However in 2002, political mapmakers, with few exceptions, went for maximum incumbent protection plans. Take Iowa, for example, where an independent redistricting commission drew the state's five districts county by county without taking politics into consideration. That process netted more competitive seats in Iowa than in California, Texas, and Illinois combined—which make up nearly one-fourth of the U.S. House of Representatives. Nationally, of the 383 incumbents seeking reelection in 2002 in traditional incumbent versus challenger races (this excludes the member versus member races), just 23 incumbents received 55 percent or under in the general election—traditionally a sign of potential vulnerability—compared to 40 in 2000. That's a whopping 6 percent of incumbents who enter the 2004 election with an automatic bull's-eye on their backs.

Technology is the most significant factor that has changed redistricting in the twenty-first century. Traditionally, redistricting is the epitome of political deals in a smoke-filled room, with outside parties having little input on the process simply due to a lack of information and resources. Now, U.S. Census Bureau statistics are available to download on the Internet, and anyone with the right software can draw a congressional map. Moving district lines no longer involves long number-crunching sessions; it is as easy as pointing, clicking, and dragging a mouse. As a result, a majority of state legislators who look in the mirror every morning and see a potential congressman or congresswoman had their own "perfect district" to shop around. The process was further complicated by the fact that 2001 marked the first time redistricting took place under mandatory legislative term limits in 18 states. Other difficulties abound. In Florida, a tax bill was held up as a bargaining tool as state Senate and state House members squabbled over which of their colleagues would see their dream districts become a reality. Additionally, intrastate political fights tended to be a factor. In Ohio, Republicans controlled the entire redistricting process, yet Republican Governor Bob Taft got in the way of a maximum-impact Republican plan by insisting that mapmakers draw a safe district for Democratic Representative Sherrod Brown, who threatened to challenge Taft in 2002 if he saw his chances of reelection in the House diminish as a result of redistricting. As a result, there were no vulnerable incumbents in Ohio in 2002. Furthermore, in West Virginia, the collegial nature of the legislature may have helped one potentially endangered incumbent. The Democratic-controlled state legislature should have given freshman Republican Congresswoman Shelley Moore Capito a tougher district, but her former colleagues in the state legislature instead opted to give her a pass.

While personal politics certainly played a major role in some states' redistricting process, it was more common for state delegations to work across party lines to create bipartisan, compromise maps to secure *everybody*—particularly as the cost of holding one's seat in a competitive district skyrockets. As state legislatures faced the unenviable task of having to draw their own legislative lines, many weary state redistricting committees were more than willing to sign off on a plan that both Republicans and Democrats could agree on. However, while an exception to the rule, there were a few states where partisan mapmakers went for maximum impact in redistricting.

In perhaps the boldest partisan mapmaking, Pennsylvania Republicans, who were forced to eliminate two districts due to slow population growth, not only eliminated two Democratic districts, but forced another Democrat into retirement, drew two Democratic incumbents into one district, and created two seats for Republicans, which they ultimately ended up winning. Republicans also went for a power play in Michigan, which lost one seat in reapportionment. Republicans forced two Democratic incumbents to run against each other in a primary, pushed another Democrat into retirement, and drew the seat being vacated by House Minority Whip David Bonior, a candidate for governor, to be much more favorable to them. Republicans won each of those new seats.

The Democrats made their strongest redistricting play in Georgia, where the state gained two seats due to population growth. In addition to creating those two seats to be Democratic-leaning, they forced two Republican incumbents to run against each other in a primary; created a Democratic-leaning seat in a district being vacated by now-Senator Saxby Chambliss; and drew the two new seats to be Democratic opportunities. While the elections in Georgia didn't go as Democrats planned (they won just two of the four new districts drawn for Democrats in large part due to poor recruiting, and came close to losing a third new seat), Democrats did find redistricting success in Maryland, where they picked up two seats. Maryland was one of the few maps nationally that created competitive districts in a state where substantial changes were not forced by the state gaining or losing seats.

When all the maps were in, only three of the new districts created by redistricting emerged as pure swing districts, where either party had an equal chance of winning—Arizona's 1st district, Colorado's 7th district, and Nevada's 3rd district. While all three districts had dramatically different storylines, it's worth noting that Republicans did carry all three in 2002.

It's safe to say that these districts will always be top targets, and will be considered bellwether races in future cycles—at least until the next round of redistricting rolls around, after the 2010 census.

Looking back to 1994, Republicans found some success by picking off a number of marginal Southern districts, which were a result of minority voters being packed into majority-minority districts, thus draining Democratic votes from surrounding districts. Such a dramatic turnaround as a result of redistricting is unlikely in 2004; if anything, the only major changes that would take place in 2004 or in future cycles as a result of redistricting would be yet another redrawing of districts (which is being seriously considered in Texas where Republicans just took complete control of the state legislature in 2002; it's possible other states may follow) or as a result of a court decision (the U.S. Supreme Court this year will hear a case challenging Mississippi's redistricting map). Stay tuned.

Now, with redistricting out of the way, we can finally get to the individual races.

YOU ONLY HURT THE ONES YOU LOVE

The primaries weren't kind to avid C-SPAN fans, as voters ended the careers of some of the more—how shall we say this—colorful members of Congress. Among the more notable primary defeats, voters rejected the scandal-plagued Gary Condit of California; convicted felon James Traficant of Ohio; Georgia's Cynthia McKinney, who made a number of controversial comments following September 11; and lead impeachment manager Bob Barr of Georgia. So, perhaps the tone *is* changing in Washington—but George W. Bush can't take all the credit for that.

In addition, redistricting created four extremely uncomfortable primary matchups, with two incumbents forced to run against each other. Indiana, Georgia, Michigan and Pennsylvania all hosted these rare fights, which were some of the nastiest, most hard-fought primaries of the cycle, despite the fact that they typically feature two members of Congress with near-identical congressional records. In fact, because their records were near-identical, personal attacks tended to play a more prominent role in these races, with the ABSCAM scandal and questions about the validity of an incumbent's Purple Heart even cropping up in one district. Despite the more personal tone of these races, interestingly, they all had one element in common: a more senior member of Congress faced off against a younger, and in three out of four cases, scrappier colleague. In all four matchups, the more senior member, who was viewed as delivering more for the district, won.

Between eliminating the more controversial members and selecting experience in the member versus member matchups, one may look at the candidates who emerged from the primary field and conclude that savvy primary voters are simply choosing better (albeit duller) candidates. However, that's not an easy argument to make to Democrats, who saw not one, but two top candidates get lost in a crowded, seven-candidate field in the new, open 1st District of Arizona. An untested candidate emerged from the pack, likely costing the Democrats that key seat.

ONCE IN A BLUE MOON

While competitive Senate races are largely controlled by national operatives and typically feature polished candidates with a tightly controlled message, smaller House districts generally turn more on local issues and personalities, with each race dramatically different from the other, from the style of campaigning to the candidates themselves. (The best example: for a moment in time, there was a community of voters bounded by district lines who believed Jim Traficant best represented their interests.) That's the beauty of the direct representation of the House. However, when it comes to finding overall trends in a year that did not feature seismic movement on the national scale, the unpredictability that political junkies relish in the House for its intriguing storylines throughout the year suddenly proves to be a major obstacle.

Enter the general election incumbent-versus-incumbent matchups. These four pairings were the marquee races of 2002, not only because they were rare, every-ten-years occurrences, but because all assumptions about incumbency advantage could be thrown out the window, as two battle-tested incumbents faced off—a political analyst's dream. And, because these races feature two incumbents with long voting records and experience in Washington, national issues tended to play more prominently in these districts, making them a microcosm of the national debate. All issues that Democrats tried to take to a national stage—the economy, Social Security privatization, prescription drug coverage, and corporate accountability—took center stage in these districts, simply because both the Republican and Democratic nominees were already debating or working on these issues in Washington.

On paper, Republicans held an edge in every one of these districts (see table 5.1). Connecticut's 5th District had a slight Democratic tilt, but Republican Congresswoman Nancy Johnson was a moderate with experience running in a tough district, had higher name identification, significantly outraised Democratic Representative Jim Maloney, and held Maloney's

Table 5.1   House Incumbents Defeated in General Election, 2002

State	Candidate	Percent vote	Vote total
Connecticut	Nancy Johnson (R)	54	114,253
5th District	Jim Maloney (D)	43	90,576
Mississippi	Chip Pickering (R)	64	137,718
3rd District	Ronnie Shows (D)	35	74,878
Pennsylvania	Tim Holden (D)	51	103,176
17th District	George Gekas (R)	49	97,570
Illinois	John Shimkus (R)	55	133,690
19th District	David Phelps (D)	45	109,796
Florida	Ginny Brown-Waite (R)	48	121,983
5th District	Karen Thurman (D)	47	117,748
Maryland	Chris Van Hollen (D)	52	106,575
8th District	Connie Morella (R)	47	97,847
Minnesota	John Kline (R)	53	152,533
2nd District	Bill Luther (D)	42	121,072
New York	Tim Bishop (D)	50	80,864
1st District	Felix Grucci (R)	49	78,415

term limit pledge against him in the seniority debate. In Illinois's 19th District, lackluster top-of-the ticket performance by Republicans and the region's economic downturn gave Democratic Congressman David Phelps a strong chance in this Republican-leaning district, but not enough to put him over the top. Meanwhile, Democrats faced perhaps their longest odds: Mississippi's 3rd District, where Republican Representative Chip Pickering defeated conservative Democratic Representative Ronnie Shows. Two national issues played big here—Pickering's father was one of Bush's judicial nominees rejected by the Senate, which turned into a fundraising boon for the younger Pickering, and the district was home to the collapsed World-Com, which made corporate accountability a particularly relevant issue.

Like the three brand new swing districts mentioned earlier, these races trended Republican, again, indicating that a national Democratic tidal wave just wasn't in the cards. Of the four member-versus-member races, Pennsylvania's 17th District was the only one Republicans failed to carry in the general election. The race was a testament to how a good candidate and a strong campaign organization can overcome a tough district. We'll look further into that later.

THE BUSH BOUNCE?

When it comes to competing for the White House's attention, the House campaign committees typically find themselves overshadowed by their senatorial and gubernatorial counterparts. However, the Bush White House never took their slim, six-seat majority in the House for granted, and took an enormous gamble, actively campaigning for House candidates when historical precedent, coupled with a lagging economy, forecasted potentially dramatic losses for the president's party.

For the majority of the cycle, Vice President Cheney was the lead cheerleader for the House, raising money and campaigning in 52 districts—not including a number of repeat visits in the most competitive districts. In the final weeks of the campaign, with his job approval ratings still sky-high over a year after September 11, 2001, Bush began to campaign for House Republicans, stumping for Republican candidates in 23 of the most competitive districts and appearing in television ads for numerous others (a still shot of the candidate and Bush on the White House portico was a fixture in positive Republican ads in the final weeks). Just two of the candidates Bush campaigned for in the district lost; both were incumbents hurt by redistricting.

While it is certainly tempting for Republicans to declare the House victories a Bush victory or a Bush mandate, that may be somewhat of an overstatement. While significant, a six-seat pickup is hardly a tidal wave of 1994 proportions. The small pool of competitive races were won and lost district by district, with no overall national issue sweeping Republicans into victory. The popular war-time president's greatest accomplishment on the House front was creating an environment where being associated with him was not detrimental to candidates, and using the fundraising prowess of the White House to ensure that no potential Republican vulnerability lacked resources or attention.

LOOKING TO 2004

While former Florida Secretary of State Katherine Harris will likely be the face of the 2002 freshman class simply because of her notoriety during the White House 2000 recount, this new class is particularly notable for the number of former national strategists who now call themselves congressmen. The class, which includes a former Clinton White House senior adviser (Rahm Emanuel), a former National Republican Senatorial Committee executive director (Jeb Hensarling) and a former National Congressional Campaign Committee executive director (Tom Cole), is a strong recruiting pool for future campaign committee chairs. And, those future political strategists will have some unique challenges to deal with in the coming years.

An interesting trend seems to have emerged over the last few cycles. Many of the incumbents who lost weren't necessarily on the radar screen for multiple cycles. Instead, they were relatively untested members of Congress, caught relaxing and enjoying the advantages of incumbency.

The member-versus-member race in Pennsylvania's 17th District best illustrates this. Republican Representative George Gekas and Democratic Representative Tim Holden faced off in a heavily competitive race. Gekas, a ten-term member, had every possible advantage: a district drawn more favorably for him, a steady stream of top Republican leaders visiting the district on his behalf, and an extensive media campaign paid for by the National Republican Congressional Campaign Committee. Republicans may have underestimated Holden, a five-term member from the Republican-leaning 6th District, who survived the 1994 Republican tidal wave and was used to running in competitive races. Holden, a seasoned campaigner, narrowly defeated Gekas, who either ran unopposed or broke the 70 percent mark in every election in his heavily Republican district since 1984.

It goes beyond that. Look at who else lost in 2002—members like Florida Democratic Representative Karen Thurman, who hadn't been targeted seriously in three cycles, and Maryland Republican Representative Connie Morella, who was not a national target for years. In 2000, then-Congressman David Minge of Minnesota and then-Congressman Sam Gejdenson of Connecticut were ousted in surprise victories, while other districts in their states—deemed more competitive, based on the demographics of the districts—had the attention of national operatives.

Essentially we wonder if, given the choice of targeting another Republican Congresswoman Anne Northup or Democratic Representative Dennis Moore for the fourth cycle in a row versus challenging a veteran Congressman who has never had a real race in a slightly marginal district, that maybe challenging the member from the latter district would be the better strategy.

Yes, numbers are numbers, and Democrats believe that in order to get the majority back, they have to win back the Republican-held districts that former Vice President Gore either carried or nearly carried in the White House 2000 election. However, we've joked with some Democrats that they've probably helped make Anne Northup a Senator some day, as the tough contests she's won have prepared her well for a statewide race. The same could be said for Moore, for Iowa Republican Representative Jim Nussle, for Pennsylvania Democratic Representative Joe Hoeffel, for Pennsylvania Republican Representative Pat Toomey, to name a few. If the trend continues, two rising sophomores, West Virginia Republican Representative Shelley Moore Capito and Utah Democratic Representative Jim Matheson could be added to that list; Matheson is already being asked about a possible 2004 gubernatorial bid, given his strong performance in the GOP-trending areas of his district.

Just about every cycle, at least one tier-two challenger bubbles up to the surface and pulls off a surprise win. It's a tough call for the campaign committees to make—where to put last-minute resources to put these under-the-radar candidates over the top; but what if the Democrats had stayed and played in Texas's 23rd District or Oklahoma's 1st District? What if Republicans had stayed and played in Mississippi's 2nd District? In all three of those races, the opposition party made little to no investment; even so, the incumbents—Republican Representative Henry Bonilla of Texas, Republican Representative John Sullivan of Oklahoma and Democratic Representative Bennie Thompson of Mississippi—pulled off victories by closer-than-expected margins.

Initial target lists are traditionally comprised of open seats races, freshmen, incumbents who received 55 percent or under in the last election, and incumbents who hold seats where the opposing party carried the district in recent presidential elections. However, don't add the Henry Bonillas and the John Sullivans and the Bennie Thompsons to this "watch" list just yet. Typically, lightning strikes just once for these kind of upsets; it's no doubt those who had an unexpected scare in 2002, but survived, will run much better campaigns, focus more on their districts, and/or raise money earlier the next time around. In 2000, no challenger won revenge in a general election rematch of a congressional race from the previous year; in 2002, just one, now-Minnesota Representative John Kline, won a rematch, thanks in part to redistricting. The same held true in the primary season; just one candidate, now-Alabama Representative Arthur Davis, defeated an incumbent.

However, even with the unpredictability, playing in these "tier two" races may be necessary in future cycles. As stated before, redistricting strengthened incumbents; the relatively low number of incumbents who failed to break the 55 percent mark was a good indicator. Further, of the 18 new seats created in redistricting, just 8 had the new representatives scoring 55 percent or less. That means that if the campaign committees want to pull off upsets, they may need to resort to more unconventional targeting.

This sort of targeting is a gamble, even by political standards. However, it may be an unintended consequence of the incumbent protection plans that dominated this round of redistricting. If either side is going to make more than single-digit gains in election years, *creating* competitive districts through recruiting and resource allocation will be necessary rather than relying on demographic targeting. Otherwise, we may be in for four more cycles of status-quo elections, with a laser-like focus on the same 30 to 40 competitive races.

6

Iowa Senate

Harkin's Best Yet

MIKE GLOVER
Associated Press

Democratic U.S. Senator Tom Harkin began laying plans to run for a fourth term in office well before the 2000 presidential election, assembling a small cadre of key aides to begin drafting plans for organization of his next campaign. In a state with roughly 50,000 more Republicans than Democrats, Harkin's victory margins had been shrinking over the years. In 1996, GOP challenger Jim Ross Lightfoot closed fast and came within a couple of percentage points of Harkin. In addition to its obvious potential impact on control of the Senate, Republicans have made ousting Harkin a top priority. He ran for the Democratic presidential nomination in 1992 as an old-line liberal, but has been unbeatable in Iowa since he first went to Congress in 1974. That has frustrated Republicans, who view him as their top target each time he's up for reelection.

Republicans decided to switch tactics for this election cycle. Instead of running a staunch conservative against Harkin as they had in the past, the party's establishment settled on an urban moderate in Representative Greg Ganske, a plastic surgeon from Des Moines. Ganske had ousted 38-year-old Democratic U.S. Representative Neal Smith in the 1994 Republican tide, and made a name for himself by backing a version of the patient's bill of rights and using his status as a physician to argue for health care reform. Republicans argued that Ganske could run from the middle, casting Harkin as a liberal out of touch with his rural roots.

Harkin, 62, had won election to the House in 1974, and moved up to the Senate in 1984, while Ganske, 53, was a newcomer to politics when he ran in 1994. Republicans hoped to cast Harkin as part of the liberal Washington establishment.

Ganske formally announced his candidacy March 3, 2001, flying to a series of stops around the state with former Republican Governors Bob Ray and Terry Branstad in tow and joined by top GOP legislative leaders along the way, leaving no doubt about the preferences of the Republican establishment. His announcement stressed his backing for education for the disabled and health care reform.

Harkin had no primary opposition, but Ganske wasn't so lucky. A young Nora Springs farmer named Bill Salier didn't buy into the GOP's tactic. He labeled Ganske "liberal lite," and said Republicans couldn't beat Harkin without energizing the party's conservative base. A former Marine, Salier had never run for office, was little known and had virtually no money, rattling around the state in a battered pickup truck.

Ganske opted to ignore Salier, focusing his attention on Harkin—aides said privately that Salier's presence on the ballot could help Ganske by making him appear more moderate by comparison. Ganske and Harkin began trading attack television commercials even before the June 6 primary. However, Salier surprised many in that primary when his renegade candidacy gained him 41 percent of the vote, despite the virtual unanimous backing of Ganske from Republican regulars. In a fiery primary-night speech, Salier vowed that "the cultural wars will be waged for 30 years." He would later endorse the statewide Republican ticket and make occasional appearances on its behalf, but his activity level would be low, with ominous consequences for Republicans.

Public polling taken shortly after the primary showed Harkin hovering just above 50 percent, with Ganske at around 40 percent. The trends showed Harkin expanding his lead slightly by September, but final pre-election polls showed him with a lead ranging from 9 percentage points to 22 percentage points.

Harkin made a decision early on that would have great consequences for the campaign. Democratic Governor Tom Vilsack also faced a tough re-election campaign, and Harkin prepared a plan where Harkin, Vilsack and the state's Democratic Party would run a coordinated campaign in the fullest sense of the word. All three campaigns worked from the same office, and shared the costs of a $3.5 million grassroots organizational effort taking advantage of the newest technology. More than 100 field staffers were hired in early summer and dispatched to knock doors throughout the state, each carrying a hand-held wireless computer. They would survey voters on issues of importance, take absentee ballot requests and eventually would knock on

250,000 doors identifying potential voters. Each night they would download their daily data into a centralized database. At the end of the day, Democrats built a huge database on what was driving voters, doubled the number of absentee ballots they cast—a total of 108,000—and identified roughly 50,000 "marginal" voters, those who cast ballots in presidential elections but usually stay home in midterm elections. "The story of this election may be how we identified those marginal voters," said Harkin, greeting workers at a shift change the day before the election. Both candidates at the top of the ticket concluded that their messages might differ, but a potential Democratic voter identified and motivated by one would likely also vote for the other. That database allowed field staffers to more tightly focus turnout activities in the closing days of the campaign, shrinking the universe that had to be tapped by phone or mail. A conscious decision was made to not target party activists, who are likely to vote whether they are contacted or not. Republicans also mounted a turnout effort, but it was a far more traditional effort to distribute absentee ballots and run phone banks in the week heading into the election.

Harkin also gained an issue opportunity when Democrats gained control of the Senate, and he assumed the chairmanship of the Senate Agriculture Committee just as it got serious about writing a new farm bill, a key issue throughout the Midwest. Harkin eventually negotiated a new farm bill that returned traditional crops subsidies to federal policy, effectively setting a safety net under farm income. President Bush signed the measure into law, traveling to Iowa to call it "good for America and good for America's farmers." The measure had been pushed by the traditionally Republican Iowa Farm Bureau Federation, and that group joined virtually every commodity group in endorsing Harkin's election effort, giving him a key inroad into the heavily GOP farm vote. Ganske voted against the farm bill, arguing it was too heavily weighted toward Southern interests. Harkin called it a defining difference between the two candidates.

That played directly into one of Harkin's key strategies, an argument that his seniority had given him clout in Congress and throughout Washington that was crucial for a small, rural state like Iowa. "Iowans have invested a lot in me," said Harkin, arguing for another term to make a payment on that investment. Ganske rejected that argument, arguing that having clout mattered less than what was done with that influence. "His positions at times are extreme for Iowa," said Ganske. "Mine are more in the mainstream."

Neither campaign was lacking for money. Harkin would raise $8.5 million for the race, and Ganske would eventually raise $5 million, including $400,000 of his own money injected in the last week. Both were the beneficiaries of big spending by national campaign committees. The money flowed into attack television that flooded the state throughout the campaign, and occasionally became a campaign issue. Ganske's commercials attacked Harkin for ignoring looming problems in Social Security and Medicare. Harkin confronted Ganske directly on his backing for President Bush's tax cutting efforts, saying that cut raided the Social Security trust fund for a tax cut "that benefited the richest 1 percent of Americans."

The television commercials themselves occasionally became a campaign issue. One commercial aired on Ganske's behalf featured an elderly woman with a script having her say "I've trusted Tom Harkin for nearly 30 years," but this year had been betrayed by his neglect of Social Security and other health issues. Harkin's campaign leaped on the issue, pointing out that the woman was an out-of-state actress, charging that the spot was deceiving voters. Ganske retorted that the commercial wasn't made by his campaign but was produced by the National Republican Senatorial Committee (NRSC). Harkin quickly produced a new campaign commercial ridiculing the Ganske spot. Though Ganske disavowed the NRSC commercial, he quickly produced a spot with three Iowa women making the same charges.

The race was jolted again in late September with what came to be known as "tape-gate," when it was disclosed that a Harkin backer had attended a Ganske strategy session, surreptitiously taped the meeting and delivered the tape to Harkin's campaign office. A transcript of the tape was later leaked to a reporter. Iowa Republican Chairman Chuck Larson Jr. and Ganske campaign manager Bill Armistead began holding daily press conferences to charge that Harkin's campaign was behind an effort to illegally bug a private Ganske campaign event. After a week of exchanges, Harkin said an internal review had shown that a junior staffer had recruited a backer to give $50 to Ganske to get on his mailing lists, and encouraged him to attend the strategy session and tape the meeting. Harkin fired the staffer involved, and he accepted the resignation of campaign manager Jeff Link for not more closely supervising eager young staffers. Denver political strategist John Frew, who ran Harkin's first Senate campaign in 1984, was brought in to take charge. Local prosecutors began looking into the episode, as did a U.S. attorney in Chicago. Local federal prosecutors begged off because of ties with Ganske. Both quickly announced that no laws had been broken and dropped the case. Harkin apologized, and said it was time to move on to other issues. Ganske said the issue was one more example of how a bare-knuckled politician like Harkin crossed the line into dirty politics, but the issue quickly faded from public discussion. The only concrete fallout was polls that had been showing Harkin widening his edge began to flatten and stabilized with about a 10-point lead. In a poll published the Sunday before the election, the *Des Moines Register* gave Harkin a 50–41 margin in a poll with a margin of error of 3.5 percentage points. That telephone sample was among 807 likely voters and was taken the week before the election. The *Cedar Rapids Gazette* published a poll the same day giving Harkin a 51–29 margin with a 3.3 percentage point margin of error. That telephone survey was taken of 1,082 people the week before the election.

Ganske's effort to keep focus on the episode also suffered a blow when it was disclosed that 750 people had been invited to the strategy session, including many Democratic activists, making it far from a gathering designed to share sensitive strategic information.

Both of the candidates suffered a problem with competition for voter attention, but as the challenger, Ganske suffered the most. The 2002 election featured a competitive governor's race where the two rivals spent a total of nearly $13 million, and four of the state's five congressional races featured expensive and competitive races. In major media markets like Des Moines and Cedar Rapids, those contenders flooded the airwaves with such a blizzard of television ads that it was difficult for a single candidate to punch a message through the clutter. In the end, all of the incumbents fared well.

Campaign debates did not prove to be crucial in the race. They held two traditional debates, but one of those was broadcast on radio only, and the other was televised relatively late on a Sunday evening. The two also made a joint appearance in an interview program broadcast on public television, and none of the events saw new charges or major campaign-altering gaffes.

As the campaign entered its final phase, Ganske's message shifted in subtle but significant ways, taking on a more conservative tenor. His television commercials and stump speeches accused Harkin of favoring human cloning, opposing the death sentence even for terrorists and favoring a specific late-term abortion procedure critics call "partial birth" abortions. He also accused Harkin of wanting to roll back Bush's tax cuts and endangering national security by blocking plans to create a new agency focused on homeland security. In addition, Ganske began attacking Harkin on gun rights, charging that Harkin favored extremely restrictive gun control. Harkin's response was to don a sporting cap and invite Ganske to join him pheasant hunting on the opening day of the season. He then brought in paralyzed actor Christopher Reeve and Michael J. Fox, an actor who suffers from Parkinson's Disease, to testify about Harkin's long backing for stem cell and other medical research. Harkin also touted his role as lead author of the Americans with Disabilities Act, landmark civil rights legislation for the disabled that was signed into law by the current president's father. In his stump speeches, Ganske also began talking of retiring Harkin to his home in the Bahamas. References to Harkin's ownership of a vacation home in the Bahamas have long been an applause line at Republican gatherings.

By the campaign's final couple of months, Ganske rarely if ever mentioned health care reform, the patient's bill of rights or other issues designed to depict him as a moderate.

Polling itself became an issue in the race. Virtually all of the public polling showed Harkin maintaining a steady lead throughout the race, a finding that Harkin aides said was matched by their internal sampling. Republicans insisted their internal sampling showed the top races much closer, in some cases virtually tied. The difference was in methodology. Republicans polled only those with a history of voting in midterm elections while the other polls were among those who described themselves as likely voters. The thrust of that difference was that the GOP sampling would be more reflective of a low-turnout election, while the other polling would be more reflective of a stronger turnout. On Election Day, roughly 1 million voters cast ballots—60 percent of the state's registered voters—which is higher than the 55 percent that turned out for the 1998 midterm election. That's a strong turnout, particularly in light of the relentlessly negative tenor of the campaign, which often serves to suppress voter turnout.

Both sides had plenty of outside help in the campaign. President Bush repeatedly stumped in the state, including appearing at a big voter-turnout rally in Cedar Rapids the morning before the election. That appearance was part of Bush's campaign-closing blitz, but earlier appearances in the state were part of a strategy he developed of concentrating on states where the 2000 election was close. Bush lost Iowa to Democrat Al Gore, but only by about 4,000 votes. Bush also has worked hard to cement ties with the state's GOP establishment to avoid a challenge in the state's leadoff precinct caucuses. Iowa's caucuses mark the first test of strength among presidential candidates and get heavy attention every four years. Vice President Dick Cheney held a voter-turnout rally in heavily Republican western Iowa and most of the cabinet found reason to appear on Ganske's behalf. Those caucuses also brought some help for Harkin in this year's election. North Carolina Senator John Edwards donated $160,000 in computer gear that fueled the high-tech voter turnout effort. Massachusetts Senator John Kerry and Vermont Governor Howard Dean joined Edwards at the state Democratic Party's big annual fundraising event, and stumped often for Harkin.

In the end, Harkin scored a relatively easy victory compared to razor-thin margins in other states. He defeated Ganske by a 54–44 margin, piling up 550,156 votes to 446,209 for Ganske. His victory was far broader than earlier wins. Harkin piled up huge margins in the state's six largest counties of Polk, Linn, Scott, Dubuque, Black Hawk, and Johnson, as expected. He took a 20,000-vote pad out of Polk, which includes Des Moines, and an 11,000-vote margin out of Linn, which includes Cedar Rapids. But Harkin also won overwhelmingly rural and GOP-dominated counties like Adair, Allamakee, Calhoun, and Sac, where many Democrats don't bother campaigning. That offered evidence that his effort to build backing in the farm community with his farm bill and casting Ganske as an urban doctor with little connection to farmers worked. In addition, Harkin carried counties like Dallas and Warren, affluent collar counties around Des Moines where suburban sprawl makes them the fastest-growing part of the state.

While the collapse of the exit polling system denied much insight into the thinking of Harkin voters, an analysis of the public polling offers insight into how Harkin assembled his winning coalition, suggesting he won the election by holding his base better than Ganske, and by scoring with independents that decide the outcome of every election. There are 582,303 registered Republicans in Iowa, compared to 529,605 registered Democrats. Both are outnumbered by the 696,031 who have registered without declaring a party preference. Polls showed Harkin getting about 58 percent of the independent vote. In addition, roughly 12 percent of Republicans were abandoning Ganske, double the level of Democrats who abandoned Harkin. One explanation for this would be that the conservative base of the Republican Party wasn't energized by the Ganske campaign. Coupled with a loss of a gubernatorial election the GOP had great hopes of winning, it likely means that the party is in for a protracted debate over which direction it should take in responding to the verdict by voters. For Democrats, victories at the top of the ticket proved to have little in the way of a coattail effect down the ballot. Republicans went into the election with a 4–1 lead in congressional seats, and despite some noisy and competitive elections the GOP retained that margin after the election. In addition, Republicans maintained firm control over both chambers of the legislature.

With Republicans gaining control of the Senate, Harkin lost his chairmanship but will remain the ranking Democrat on the Agriculture Committee in a strong position to oversee implementation of the farm bill he authored.

The successful voter turnout effort by the coordinated campaign is likely to be developed further. It was designed by Link, and though he was forced to resign before the election, Link remains very close to Harkin. The state's Democratic Party has given him the assignment of spending a few months drafting and refining an organizational effort targeting states where moving as few as 40,000 votes can make a difference in an election. That program would be of little use in giant states like California or Florida, but could be crucial in the next round of Senate elections. States like Nevada and North Dakota are home to potentially vulnerable Democrats who could use tools which could inflate turnout at that level. Harkin scored his impressive victory on a night when Republicans were making historic gains, and at least five of his Democratic colleagues phoned Harkin to talk about how he pulled off the victory. The new effort will be modeled on the coordinated campaign that Harkin, Vilsack, and the state's Democratic Party ran in the 2002 election.

The twin victory by Vilsack and Harkin will make both early and important players in the next presidential campaign, which is already under-way and certain to intensify quickly. The two built an impressive political machine that will be ardently courted by a large and active field of potential candidates for the Democratic presidential nomination. Vilsack has said he will maintain his traditional neutrality, assuring there's a level playing field for all who want to compete in the state's precinct caucuses. Harkin endorsed Gore in the last campaign during the primary season, but has been quiet about his intentions in this election cycle. The presence of both assures that the state is a friendlier place for Democrats to campaign.

With the death of Democratic Minnesota Senator Paul Wellstone dur-ing the campaign, there will be pressure on Harkin to fill his role as a leading advocate for liberal causes. Harkin spoke at Wellstone's memorial service and described him as his best friend in the Senate.

Harkin's victory, his biggest yet, will make it tougher for Republicans to recruit against him in the future. Harkin's health is good and he ran a spirited and active campaign, so there's no reason to believe he's contem-plating retirement.

7

Minnesota Senate

Tragedy and Triumph in a National Headline Contest

DANIEL J. B. HOFRENNING
St. Olaf College

Paul Wellstone, the incumbent in the Minnesota Senate race, was a two-term Democrat whose maverick style and liberal voting record made him a beloved figure. While many politicians fled from the liberal label, Wellstone wore it proudly and never feared the political ramifications. He even titled his 2001 autobiography, *The Conscience of a Liberal*.[1] In 1996, Paul Wellstone was the only Senator up for reelection to vote against a very popular welfare reform bill that passed by wide margins and enjoyed bipartisan support. The bill was designed to put a limit on the time in which people could receive welfare benefits. Wellstone felt it was too punitive toward the poor. In 2002, he risked his political future again when he voted against President Bush's resolution authorizing the use of force in Iraq. He cast those votes, realizing that he might alienate the moderate voters he needed to win. While such liberalism is often a political albatross, Wellstone projected a sense of conviction and authenticity, not to mention a sense of humor, that enabled him to forge a unique bond with his constituency. Even among voters who were more moderate, his personal style enabled him to develop a relationship of integrity and trust.[2]

Twelve days before the election, Paul Wellstone died in a plane crash.

With him on the tragic flight were Sheila, his wife of 38 years, his daughter Marcia, three campaign aides, and two pilots. The calamity triggered a maelstrom of grief, tactical surprises, and a pressure-packed campaign that was neck-in-neck until the finish line. The mixture of profound grief and an imminent election created an atmosphere that was surreal. Despite being overwhelmed with grief, the Democrats first had to attend to the practical matter of finding a new candidate. Barely two weeks before the election, they desperately needed a well-known political leader who could carry Wellstone's political legacy and lead Minnesotans in their grief. Wellstone's surviving sons directed all eyes to former Vice President Walter F. Mondale.

Mondale is a Minnesota political icon. A native of Minnesota, he served his state and the nation as attorney general, U.S. senator, vice president, and ambassador.[3] As the Democratic nominee for president in 1984, he lost by a wide margin and carried only Minnesota and the District of Columbia. Despite his landslide presidential loss, his stature in Minnesota was still strong. Poll data indicated that very few Minnesotans had a negative view of the former vice president. He had never lost an election in his home state. Though 74 years old, Mondale was not in the midst of a sedate retirement. He regularly gave lectures at the University of Minnesota, served on several corporate boards, and worked for a major Minneapolis law firm. After Mondale became the Democratic nominee, the early predictions saw little hope for his opponent, former St. Paul mayor Republican Norm Coleman.[4]

But Coleman was a formidable Senate opponent. In 2001, at the very beginning of this campaign, it looked as if another Minnesota Republican leader would contest him for the Republican nomination—until the White House intervened. Vice President Dick Cheney called the potential opponent, Republican House leader Tim Pawlenty, and asked him not to run against Coleman. Pawlenty deferred to White House pressure and ran for governor instead. The way was cleared for an uncontested nomination and a unified Republican party. The White House felt that Paul Wellstone was the most vulnerable Senate Democrat. Eager to pick up a seat for the closely divided Senate, they were to devote significant resources to the Minnesota contest. Finding a strong Republican candidate was paramount.[5]

Just six years before he was recruited by the popular Republican president, Norm Coleman was a Democrat who supported the 1996 reelection efforts of both President Clinton and his future Senate opponent, Paul Wellstone. Shortly after the 1996 election, he defected to the GOP. His party switch and his changing positions on a few key issues led many to brand him as an opportunist. Paul Wellstone's campaign even ran a television commercial that featured a clip of Coleman at a Democratic convention extolling the virtues of President Clinton and Senator Wellstone. Another commercial featured "Coleman debating Coleman" to highlight the Republican candidate's changing issues on Social Security privatization, drilling for oil in the Alaska wilderness, and increasing the use of motor boats in the Boundary Waters Canoe Area. While Coleman's record showed some inconsistencies, to his credit he had been a conservative Democrat. His pro-life position on abortion and close ties to the business community made him anathema in many quarters of the Democratic Party. His move to the Republican Party was not too surprising.[6]

Coleman's record as mayor of St. Paul was the central message of his campaign. Over and over again, Coleman touted his mayoral experience as indicative of his leadership. His campaign theme, "Bringing People Together to Get Things Done," highlighted his pragmatism. While promoting his record of economic growth, he frequently noted that he had never raised taxes. He also championed the successful return of professional hockey and led the effort to build a new hockey arena. Some citizens refer to the arena as "the house that Norm built." While some charged that the city gave up too much to the private owners of the franchise, Coleman and others were proud of the result. Beyond hockey, 8,000 new jobs were created in St. Paul, representing a 10 percent expansion.[7]

While Coleman emphasized his practicality, Wellstone championed people. His campaign theme was that he would fight for the people of Minnesota. This populist perspective featured campaign commercials that emphasized his work for people, for senior citizens, for families with school children, and for citizens concerned with corporate corruption. While his liberal voting record alienated most Republican voters, he developed a unique ability to reach independent voters, many of whom did not agree with his position on the issues. He did it in part by an infectious personal style—Wellstone loved to campaign, and at political rallies he had a singular capacity to motivate people. His exuberance reminded some older voters of Hubert Humphrey, a very popular Minnesota politician who used to practice what was termed "the politics of joy." Wellstone also gained people's respect because of the clarity and force of his convictions. In the days following Wellstone's death, pundits, fellow political leaders, and ordinary citizens commented repeatedly on Wellstone's passion and authenticity.

THE ISSUES

Featuring these two highly skilled politicians, this campaign centered on issues including U.S. policy toward Iraq, Social Security, prescription drugs, and corporate accountability. On foreign policy toward Iraq, Norm Coleman expressed strong support for Bush's position. Criticizing Wellstone for being soft on defense, campaign commercials contrasted his opposition to defense spending with his support of "trivial" programs such as community theater. In truth, Wellstone was more a dove than a hawk. He began his Senate career by expressing strong opposition to the first Gulf War. At the Vietnam Veterans Memorial, he held a widely publicized and strongly criticized rally against the war. Veterans groups decried his use of the memorial.

But once in office, Wellstone's position on military issues evolved. He advocated veterans' issues, gaining the support of many veterans groups.[8] While opposing some defense appropriations, he supported the use of force in the former Yugoslavia and the missile attacks against Iraq ordered by President Clinton. After the terrorist attacks of September 11, Wellstone voted for all defense appropriations and supported the military campaign in Afghanistan. But he was one of twenty-three Senators who voted against the resolution giving President Bush the authority to use pre-emptive force against Iraq. Many constituents and observers respected his willingness to cast such a risky vote, comparing it to his 1996 vote against welfare reform. While his 1996 vote may have hurt his standing in the polls, his vote on the Iraq resolution surprisingly seemed to help him. His polling numbers went up after taking a stand on that issue.

On Social Security, the Democrats expressed their strong support of this so-called third rail of American politics. They urged protection of Social Security and lobbied for its preservation in its current form. In contrast, Norm Coleman wanted to allow younger workers to divert part of their Social Security contributions to personal investment accounts. Wellstone attacked Coleman for supporting privatization. On the defensive, Coleman accused Wellstone of scaring seniors; never, he intoned, would he support privatization. Coleman, and Republicans across the country, contended that they supported personal accounts—not privatization. While younger citizens could elect to put some of their Social Security money in the stock market, the account would be managed by government—not private investment managers. Hence, Republicans asserted that the program maintained its public nature and could not be termed "privatization." Coleman also pledged not to support any plan that could result in cutting benefits.[9]

On prescription drugs, Coleman criticized Wellstone and the Democratic Senate for not getting a bill signed into law. Coleman presented himself as the results-oriented pragmatist while his opponent was the strident ideologue. He averred that Wellstone had had twelve years to pass a bill and Minnesota's seniors were still waiting. In turn, Wellstone decried Coleman's fealty to the pharmaceutical industry. Drug companies were among Norm Coleman's largest donors of campaign funds and the St. Paul mayor could be expected to produce a bill that the industry favored. Wellstone argued that Republicans had failed to enact bills sponsored by Democrats because of opposition from the pharmaceutical industry. Coleman did support the more modest benefit that could be administered through the private sector. Wellstone, and later Mondale, wanted a more generous provision of benefits that was administered through the Medicare system.

Corporate accountability was another important issue in the race. In the wake of the Enron scandal, Wellstone disparaged Coleman for his reliance on campaign contributions from big business. In advertisements, Wellstone commended his own proposal to prevent corporate corruption, including offshore tax evasion by American businesses. Coleman maintained his respect for the law and cited his experience as a prosecutor for the Minnesota attorney general. In one debate, he referred to his experience prosecuting criminals, "whether they wore masks over their heads or business suits."

FUNDRAISING

This campaign was well funded and was one of the most expensive in Minnesota history. For Wellstone, this was a marked shift from his initial 1990 campaign in which his opponent, incumbent Senator Rudy Boschwitz, outspent him by a 6:1 ratio.[10] In the 2002 campaign, Coleman raised about $10 million and Wellstone matched it. A significant portion of Coleman's funds came from PACs, something Wellstone was quick to point out. Though he accepted some PAC money, Wellstone relied more on a broader base of small donors, averaging $51 per donor. Beyond the candidates, it is estimated that both parties poured in another $20 million of soft money for issue ads and other party-centered activities. Other independent groups such as the Americans for Job Security added a few million and funded some of the more negative ads of the campaign.[11]

These large sums funded a barrage of ads and a grassroots operation for both campaigns. Having cut his teeth on the protest lines of the 1970s and '80s, Wellstone took great pride in his grassroots operation, which he continued to grow from his three previous state-wide campaigns. The populism of his grassroots campaign was symbolized by a tattered green school bus that Wellstone used in all his Senate races. The bus was frequently seen at campaign events. In comparison, Coleman's grassroots operation seemed less extensive; however, the campaign's final days revealed an extensive get-out-the-vote operation and a series of exuberant rallies for the Republican candidate.

This was always a close race. Because of Wellstone's liberal voting record, Republicans perceived him as vulnerable and recruited a strong candidate. Unlike other incumbents who developed safe seats, Wellstone's races were always close.[12] For more than a year prior to the election, all the state-wide polls showed this race to be a statistical dead heat. More often than not, Wellstone had a slight lead, but it was never beyond the statistical margin of error. In the days prior to Wellstone's death, he seemed to be maintaining or increasing his lead in some polls. But it was always close.

Prior to the tragic plane crash, both candidates were locked in a ferocious face-off. Coleman questioned Wellstone's trustworthiness because he reneged on a pledge not to run for a third term. Wellstone countered that Coleman's record revealed "naked opportunism." Coleman questioned Wellstone's support of the military and even the war on terrorism. Wellstone charged that Coleman switched his issue positions often. In the heat of this political battle, Wellstone's death was a seismic event. The political combat was silenced. In this race and every other race across the state, candidates pulled their ubiquitous ads and ceased their public appearances. Televisions and newspaper reports were filled with moving testimonials to Paul Wellstone. Supporters draped black cloth on their green Wellstone lawn signs. Many politicians, such as Iowa's Senator Tom Harkin, wept openly. Several Republicans openly expressed their respect. Minnesota's Republican Representative Jim Ramstad, himself a recovering alcoholic, emotionally recalled working with Wellstone to increase insurance coverage for treating chemical dependency. Senator Pete Domenici (R-NM) broke down on CNN when he talked of Wellstone's commitment to helping the mentally ill.[13] Minnesota Governor Jesse Ventura (I) ordered the flags to be flown at half-mast. The depth and breadth of the response made clear that Minnesota had lost a beloved leader.[14]

But intense public grief did not deter strategists on both sides from working behind the scenes to recast the campaign.[15] On the day of Wellstone's death, his campaign manager, Jeff Blodgett, asked for a meeting with Minnesota's elder statesman. The next morning Blodgett, David Wellstone, and Mondale's advisor David Lillehaug met with Mondale at Mondale's downtown Minneapolis law firm. Wellstone's son asked, and Mondale agreed to consider it, but refused to talk publicly about it further so soon after the Senator's death. One of the five at the meeting leaked the meeting to the *Minneapolis Star Tribune* which featured it on the front page.[16] That report squelched speculation about any other potential candidate. The conventional wisdom was that Coleman was finished and that Mondale could ride a wave of sympathy to a fairly easy win. Mondale was a popular political figure even though nearly two decades had passed since his last election. It was as if the wise elder statesman came down the mountain for one last battle.[17]

The Coleman campaign was scrambling. Vin Weber, a former Minnesota Congressman and a national Republican leader, assisted the campaign by phoning Republican friends in Missouri to learn how they had handled Republican John Ashcroft's campaign after the tragic death of his opponent, Governor Mel Carnahan. In that year, Missourians elected the late Carnahan and the new governor appointed his widow to assume the seat. Missouri Republicans told Weber that after Carnahan's death, Ashcroft had completely disappeared from public view. In retrospect, they felt that public invisibility was a mistake.[18]

The Coleman campaign decided that their candidate should remain visible; he would maintain a low and respectful profile. On the afternoon of Wellstone's death, a somber Coleman summoned reporters to his St. Paul home. With his wife at his side, Coleman professed his deep respect for Wellstone. He recalled that although he disagreed with Wellstone on most issues, they had a struggle in which the competitors could hug each other after each round. When barraged with political questions, Coleman demurred and said that Minnesotans should think more about "being on bended knee" than on political calculations. Two days after Wellstone's death, Coleman held what he termed a "non-press press conference" and appeared on a Sunday morning national talk show. In each venue, he expressed his deep respect for the late Senator Paul Wellstone.

Meanwhile, former Republican leader Newt Gingrich assailed Mondale's record as vice president. He underscored the inflation and insecurity that marked the late seventies when Mondale and President Jimmy Carter occupied the White House. Minnesota Republican chair Ron Ebensteiner publicly issued a request for five debates with Mondale. Both men were roundly criticized for improper politics in this period of mourning. Because the Democrats had not yet selected him as their candidate, Mondale continued to refrain from any comments about a potential race. The first poll after Wellstone's death showed Mondale with a six-point lead, roughly the same lead that Wellstone possessed shortly before he died.[19] The period of mourning seemed to favor the Democrats. Some analysts suggested the wave of sympathy might help Democrats across the nation.[20]

On a Tuesday evening, four days after Wellstone's death, a three-hour memorial service was telecast across Minnesota and the nation. Twenty thousand people packed William's Arena. The crowd spilled over into another auditorium and people thronged to television monitors on the street surrounding the arena. Former President Clinton, former Vice President Gore, Minority Leader Trent Lott, and over half the Senate attended. The memorial was to honor not only Wellstone, but his wife, Shelia, his daughter Marcia, three campaign aides, Mary MacEvoy, Will McLaughlin, and Tom Lapic, and the two pilots who died. The event began with the poignant recollections of lost loved ones, but it ended as an unequivocal political disaster for the Democrats.[21]

Rick Kahn, Wellstone's campaign treasurer and close friend, gave a speech that transgressed the norms for memorial services. While eulogizing his friend, he repeatedly implored the crowd to "win this election." He went as far as to call on several Republicans by name, imploring them to work for a Democratic win as a tribute to Paul Wellstone. Wellstone's sons and Iowa Senator Tom Harkin, though not as shrill as Kahn, also roused the crowd to get back to the work of campaigning. Neither campaign organization immediately comprehended the significance of the event. The public expressed outrage at the memorial's improper partisan tone. Fundraising surged for the Republican Party during the memorial itself. Media outlets reported receiving hundreds of irate phone calls and e-mails. Post-election polls indicated that one in five Coleman voters were influenced by the service.[22] Some observers said that the event dragged down Democratic campaigns across the nation.[23] While many expected Mondale to benefit from an apolitical period of mourning and sympathy, the memorial service fueled the Republicans more than the Democrats. With six days to go before the election, the campaigns resumed with more intensity than ever before.

Walter Mondale received the nomination the day after the "memorial rally," as it was later referred to by some analysts. During his compressed campaign, he pledged to carry Wellstone's banner. Mondale was a liberal politician, but he was a bit more moderate than Wellstone. Unlike Wellstone, Mondale supported free trade and served on corporate boards. He never stressed that and instead pledged to carry the banner of Wellstone's campaign by fighting for all Minnesotans, especially working families and the poor. After receiving the nomination of his party, Walter Mondale had five days to campaign. During that time, he presented himself as the carrier of Wellstone's causes. He agreed to debate Norm Coleman and the two met for a one-hour faceoff on the day before the election.[24] Peggy Noonan, a noted speech writer for Presidents Reagan and Bush, termed it the best political debate of the season.[25] In it, Mondale aggressively attacked Coleman and defined the policy differences between them. Coleman for his part, stood his ground, and treated Mondale with deference, always referring to him as "Vice President Mondale." Most observers saw Coleman trying to establish his credentials as a respectful and conciliatory leader. On the issues, a group of debate coaches concluded that Mondale's positions were clearer and more specific.[26] On prescription drugs, for example, Coleman repeated his criticism of the current Senate's inaction and talked emphatically about getting a bill passed. Mondale retorted that Coleman's rhetorical emphasis on pragmatism masked his fealty to a right-wing agenda. Coleman responded by touting his St. Paul record and his commitment to changing the tone of Washington. Mondale defended his opposition to President Bush's Iraq resolution and Coleman attacked him for weakening the nation. Mondale said that his support of building a multilateral coalition led to true strength, while Bush's more unilateral approach actually led to weakness.

Deftly, Coleman repeatedly expressed his respect for the late Senator Wellstone. The attacker of Paul Wellstone became the more humane mourner of a great man's death. While negative ads were prevalent when he campaigned against Wellstone, he was able to end his campaign on a positive note. Most observers say that voters saw a transformed Coleman. His rallies in the final days pulsed with energy. Poll data showed that independents and younger voters came to vote Republican. On the final weekend, Vice President Cheney, First Lady Laura Bush, and President Bush all came to Minnesota.

The high-level visits, the aftermath of the memorial, and the nationwide Republican surge led to Coleman's victory. It was a cliffhanger, but Coleman won by 3 percentage points, and his victory became a key part of the Republican takeover of the Senate.

NOTES

1. Paul Wellstone, *The Conscience of a Liberal: Reclaiming the Compassionate Agenda* (New York: Random House, 2001).

2. For a discussion on the ways in which Senators and Representatives cultivate trust as they represent and relate to their constituents, see Richard Fenno, *Home Style* (New York: Longman, 2002) and *Senators on the Campaign Trail: The Politics of Representation* (Oklahoma City: University of Oklahoma Press, 1996).

3. For a fuller discussion of Mondale's career, see Steven M. Gillon, *The Democrat's Dilemma: Walter F. Mondale and the Liberal Legacy* (New York: Columbia University Press, 1992).

4. Tom Webb, "Tough to fight a legend," *St. Paul Pioneer Press*, November 2, 2002.

5. Tom Webb, "Bush Ups Ante in Minnesota's Senate Race, White House is Working Hard to Unseat Wellstone," *St. Paul Pioneer Press*, April 22, 2001.

6. Patricia Lopez, "Coleman's journey crosses political divide," *Star Tribune*, October 16, 2002.

7. Bill Salisbury, "Coleman Embraced a New Party and Adopted a New Goal," *St. Paul Pioneer Press*, July 28, 2002.

8. Mark Brunswick, "Veterans criticize Coleman ad that attacks," *Star Tribune*, October 1, 2002.

9. Eric Black, "Senate ads debate Social Security Plans," *Star Tribune*, October 6, 2002.

10. For an account of Wellstone's first race see Dennis McGrath and Dane Smith, *Professor Wellstone Goes to Washington: The Inside Story of a Grassroots U.S. Senate Campaign* (Minneapolis, Minn.: University of Minnesota Press, 1995).

11. Greg Gordon, "Senate race sets a $ record," *Star Tribune*, October 25, 2002.

12. For a fuller discussion of the vulnerabilities of incumbent Senators see Richard Fenno, *When Incumbency Fails* (Washington, D.C.: CQ Press, 1992).

13. David Westphal, "A Senator's Death: Tears and Tributes for a colleague and friend," *Star Tribune*, October 26, 2002.

14. "Paul Wellstone: An Idealistic Servant of Minnesota," *Star Tribune*, October 26, 2002.

15. Bill Salisbury and Tom Webb, "Despite quieted campaigns, parties are keeping busy," *St. Paul Pioneer Press*, 8A, October 29, 2002.

16. Eric Black, "Mondale close to yes," *Star Tribune*, October 27, 2002.

17. Bill Salisbury, "If Walter Mondale replaces Paul Wellstone as Norm Coleman's opponent for the U.S. Senate, a campaign entirely different from the last 18 months will ensue," *St. Paul Pioneer Press*, October 28, 2002; Brian Bonner, "Mondale has roots deep in Minnesota," *St. Paul Pioneer Press*, November 3, 2002; and Eric Black, "Mondale has a long history in Minnesota Politics," *Star Tribune*, October 27, 2002.

18. Eric Black, "13 Days: Behind the scenes of two campaigns in one extraordinary election," *Star Tribune*, November 10, 2002.

19. Eric Black, "Support shifts to Mondale, likely D-F-L replacement holds lead over Coleman," *Star Tribune*, October 30, 2002.

20. Lawrence M. O'Rourke, "Democrats talking up a 'Wellstone factor,'" *Star Tribune*, October 30, 2002.

21. Eric Black, "Analysis: Partisan Memorial aids Republicans," *Star Tribune*, October 31, 2002.

22. Rachel E. Stassen-Berger, "Poll shows independents tipped scales to GOP," *St. Paul Pioneer Press*, November 10, 2002.

23. Terry Collins, "Kahn's speech may have had national ripple effect, *Time* reports," *Star Tribune* November 14, 2002.

24. Bill Salisbury and Tom Webb, "Coleman, Mondale debate as Ventura picks his own," *St. Paul Pioneer Press*, November 5, 2002.

25. Peggy Noonan, "Lion vs. Tiger," *Wall Street Journal*, November 4, 2002.

26. Eric Black, "A vigorous debate, but did it sway voters?" *Star Tribune*, November 5, 2002.

8

Missouri Senate

Sympathy's Time Limit for Jean Carnahan

STEVE KRASKE
Kansas City Star

Jean Carnahan had the name, a presence that fired Democratic passions and a queen-sized advantage in fundraising. Republican Jim Talent had White House support. In 2002, that was enough to give Talent a slim one-point victory in Missouri's much-ballyhooed U.S. Senate race.

The contest will long be remembered as the campaign that Mel Carnahan's widow lost in her first bid for public office in 2000. Time may also show that Talent's victory was another sign that the GOP is ascendant in perhaps the nation's top bellwether state.

The story of Missouri's crucial 2002 Senate race began two years earlier when then-Governor Mel Carnahan died in a plane crash three weeks before Election Day. Up to that time, he had been locked in an often bitter Senate race against Republican John Ashcroft. Their clash had been billed as the battle of Missouri political titans.

Following his death, the late governor's name remained on the ballot, and he narrowly defeated Ashcroft. A new governor appointed Jean Carnahan to serve the first two years of the six-year term. During her brief Senate tenure, the low-key Carnahan rushed to establish a legislative record. Her inexperience showed at times—most glaringly in her first debate with Talent in which she stammered through several answers before gaining her footing. But she proved to be a resilient campaigner fortified by her belief that she was carrying out her husband's legacy.

Talent, a former four-term congressman with a disarmingly casual campaign style, referred to the tragedy as the "elephant in the room" because it could not be overlooked. But he insisted the race was about the future. It also came to be a race about the president's popularity. President Bush visited the state an unprecedented five times, including the day before the election as part of an 11th-hour, seven-state campaign blitz.

His father, former President Bush, visited Missouri twice, including a final-week stop in Springfield. Vice President Cheney flew to Cape Girardeau during the last week. Other administration visitors included Lynne Cheney, White House counselor Karen Hughes, Interior Secretary Gale Norton, Commerce Secretary Don Evans and adviser Mary Matalin.

This help buoyed Talent after Minnesota Senator Paul Wellstone died in a late-October plane crash stunningly reminiscent of Mel Carnahan's death two years earlier. Republicans feared another sympathetic wave for the Democrats.

But support from a Bush team gearing up for a possible war with Iraq kept coming.

"It's hard to run against a president," Carnahan said after the election. "He has a bigger canon than the rest of us."

And this White House had something else—boatloads of goodwill. On Election Day, 72 percent of Missouri voters said they approved of the president's performance.

NOMINATION CONTESTS

The primary race was a yawner and little more than a warm-up for the Carnahan-Talent clash that followed. Both leading candidates maintained a steadfast focus on November throughout. Talent urged his backers to "badger" other voters to get them interested in the midterm election, which typically draws fewer voters than in a presidential election year.

Carnahan told her supporters that she had taken a "giant leap of faith" in accepting the appointment. "You trusted me to do what was right for our state and nation, and I trusted God for the strength to do the job," she said.

Carnahan was pitted against Darrel Day, a long-jailed felon. Still, he got 17 percent of the vote. Talent, on the other hand, won 90 percent against four largely unknown opponents.

The GOP primary outcome in the state auditor's race contained a potential problem for Talent. In a surprise, Al Hanson defeated Jay Kanzler, the hand-picked choice of party leaders. Hanson had served nine months in a Minnesota prison almost a quarter century ago on felony theft and swindling convictions. GOP leaders disavowed him. Privately, they worried that Democrats would link Talent with Hanson. "Clearly, it's a problem," Talent said, though the Hanson issue never materialized.

Of the general-election campaign ahead, Talent mentioned a word that he would use often in the months ahead: experience. "It's a question of experience and issues for the voters to decide," he said of the matchup. Carnahan said she was proud of her record. "I'm sure Mel would be very pleased that we're carrying on," she told the Associated Press. "You don't give up on the things you believe in."

GENERAL ELECTION CAMPAIGN

Main Issues

Throughout the campaign, Carnahan and the Democrats strived to focus attention on domestic issues. Their top target was Social Security. Carnahan and the Democrats attempted to portray Talent as a threat to the system's long-term viability. Talent, they pointed out, had at one time favored "privatization" of the federal retirement system.

"An unstable economy. Falling financial markets. All that, and Jim Talent would invest Social Security money on Wall Street?" an ad by the Missouri Democratic Party stated.

In their own TV spot, Republicans responded: "Tell Jean Carnahan to stop scaring seniors."

At one point in September, three of Carnahan's Democratic colleagues, including then–Senate Majority Leader Tom Daschle, flew to Kansas City to train the media spotlight on what Carnahan called Talent's "risky" Social Security stance. They mentioned Talent's co-sponsorship of a bill in 1993 that would have required employees to set up individual retirement accounts.

Talent countered that he favored only "safe investments" with Social Security. Carnahan said she opposed any type of private accounts. Carnahan also emphasized a prescription-drug plan for seniors, saying the program should be run through Medicare with no deductibles. Talent said he wanted coverage through private insurers with a $250 deductible.

Carnahan also touted an education bill to reduce class sizes and hire more teachers. Talent emphasized his support for President Bush's homeland security bill. The Democratic Senate's refusal to pass a bill to the president's liking was one reason Talent labeled the chamber "dysfunctional."

"If you support the president, you have to give him the tools that he needs to do what he needs to do for us," Talent said.

On October 24 in their second and final debate in Columbia, Carnahan attempted to turn the issue to her advantage. Miffed that Talent again was emphasizing her opposition to Bush's plan, Carnahan walked toward Talent waving her finger.

"I resent being told I am unpatriotic by my opponent," Carnahan said in a scolding tone. "And I don't want you to do it again."

Talent said later he was merely questioning Carnahan's votes. He said the incident was a campaign tactic.

"It's easier to do that than to explain a vote," Talent said. The confrontation made headlines statewide and led television news broadcasts that night.

On the environment, Talent emphasized his support for oil drilling in Alaska to reduce dependence on Mideast oil; Carnahan was opposed.

Key Strategies

From the start, Talent's chief objective was to emphasize his tenure in Congress and the eight years he spent in the Missouri House of Representatives. Carnahan may be the incumbent, Talent said, but he was the one with the most experience.

"Experience counts," concluded one Talent television ad.

Carnahan appeared to recognize Talent's edge and worked feverishly to establish a record of her own to show Missourians she could do the job. Besides her education legislation, she sponsored bills to protect jobs in the wake of the Trans World Airlines bankruptcy, to extend health-care benefits to military personnel returning from Afghanistan, and to uncover insider stock trading.

"I had to prove myself in a year and a half . . . whereas the rest of them had six years," Carnahan told *The Kansas City Star* referring to her Senate colleagues. "I had to start from day one proving myself because I knew I was under a microscope."

But Carnahan's zeal to build a legislative résumé proved costly. In July, a Carnahan ad sponsored by the Missouri Democratic Party appeared to credit the freshman senator for being the prime mover behind efforts to merge bankrupt TWA with American Airlines, "saving 12,000 Missouri jobs."

But Republican Kit Bond, Missouri's other senator, played a key role in the merger. Within days, several former members of TWA's pilots' union asked Carnahan to withdraw the ad because they said it exaggerated her role. Talent's camp seized on the issue through television and radio spots. The ad, one political analyst said later, went a long way toward transforming Carnahan's image from grieving widow to everyday politician.

Talent received an unexpected boost in early July when national political analyst Charlie Cook wrote a column questioning Carnahan's abilities. Cook wrote that Carnahan appeared "lost in the Senate" and cited Democratic staffers and lobbyists—all unnamed—who had concluded that the junior senator was not on top of her duties. Cook also wrote that Daschle had "teed up issues for her to help her build a record of accomplishment."

A Republican ad seized on this column to make a harsh claim. "She lacks an understanding of the legislative process," the spot stated. Talent had never actually claimed that Carnahan lacked ability. But he referred to her publicly as "Mrs. Carnahan," not "Senator Carnahan." Leading Democratic women thought Talent's salutation was sexist, but the issue never attracted much attention.

Another Talent strategy was to close the gender gap. Carnahan's lead among women was in the high teens in some early polls. But by race's end, several surveys showed that advantage shrinking. A Fox News exit poll placed Carnahan's edge with women at seven points. Talent undercut Carnahan's female strength in part by bringing a parade of prominent women Republicans to Missouri on his behalf. The visitors included Hughes, Lynne Cheney, Norton and Matalin.

Republicans also worked to subtly remind Missourians of Carnahan's vote against John Ashcroft for attorney general. Ashcroft visited the state in mid-October and he was the subject of a spate of campaign advertising aired by the Missouri GOP designed to appeal to the party faithful.

"We have seen . . . our own John Ashcroft unfairly attacked because of his private religious beliefs," one radio ad that aired on Christian stations said. "On November 5th, let's make sure our voices are heard."

One of Carnahan's chief strategies was to portray herself as a centrist. She often talked about her vote for President Bush's tax cut and her support for his defense initiatives. Reviews of voting records showed Carnahan to be one of the more conservative Democratic senators.

Democrats also hoped to raise questions about Talent's ethics. They filed complaints in the first half of the year concerning Talent's use of two political committees that they contended illegally aided his Senate bid. In documents released about two weeks before the election, the Missouri Ethics Commission cleared Talent of the weightier of the two allegations, but said it was still pursuing a second case. That matter involved Talent's use of a debt committee in his 2000 run for governor. Republicans called the issue a "technical compliance" matter that would quickly be resolved. The issue soon faded from the headlines and with it, a potential silver bullet for the Democrats.

Taking the wind out of the pro-gun vote also became a Carnahan focus. On the last day of August, the picture in virtually every Missouri newspaper was of the 68-year-old Carnahan hoisting a 20-gauge Browning Citori shotgun as she prepared to blast clay pigeons out of the sky. The political implications were obvious. Carnahan's camp insisted the event had been arranged weeks before, but the shoot coincided with polls showing Carnahan's support among men weakening. Few voters needed reminding that the Carnahan name was strongly linked with gun control.

For both camps, get-out-the-vote efforts were key. Pro-Carnahan groups went door-to-door in the state's two big cities starting in early October. Unions boasted of unprecedented GOTV efforts aimed at their members. Pro-Carnahan radio ads featuring prominent African Americans aired on radio stations that attracted largely black audiences.

Talent's forces also said they focused more heavily on GOTV than Republicans had in past years. Their efforts included automated telephone calls from former First Lady Barbara Bush.

Polling Trends

The conventional wisdom early in 2002 was that this was Jean Carnahan's race to lose. An April poll by Zogby International showed Carnahan ahead 50–44 percent. But by late August, Zogby showed Talent ahead 47–46 percent. In early September, Research 2000 had it 46–45 for Carnahan, and the die was cast. The race was too close to call.

By late October, though, Talent appeared to be forging a small lead. A survey for *The Kansas City Star* two weeks before the election showed Talent up 46–41 percent. A Gallup Poll taken less than a week before the election showed him ahead 48–44 percent. One *Star* poll respondent, Ted Feldman, a retired salesman from St. Louis County, said he liked Talent "because he's more schooled. In the debates, he knew the answers right away."

Carnahan backer Rich Cohen of St. Louis County cited the senator's voting record. "I think she's much more progressive than he is," Cohen said.

The Advertising Push

If a trend emerged in Talent's advertising, it was his steady use of the word "experience."

"Jim Talent. Experience when it matters most." "Jim Talent has 16 years experience fighting for Missouri seniors." "Jim Talent has the experience to bring us jobs."

When Carnahan attempted to portray Talent as a soldier in the Gingrich revolution, Talent responded with a spot that began, "Jim Talent believes you can measure a society by how it treats its children."

Carnahan's advertising addressed a plethora of domestic issues. One theme: her work in the Senate was making a difference. Several of her ads attempted to duplicate the success of the single Jean Carnahan spot in the 2000 campaign in which a somber-looking Carnahan, just days removed from burying her husband, looked into the camera and told Missourians about the values she and her late husband championed together.

Her campaign's first 2002 ad featured her looking into the camera again.

"It's a matter of right and wrong," Carnahan said, referring to her legislation requiring corporate executives to disclose major stock sales. "We cannot let dishonest people in corporate board rooms get rich while the life savings of hard-working Americans dwindles away."

Several of Carnahan's ads attempted to portray her as having an impact. One ad highlighted her opposition to tax breaks for drug-industry advertising.

"Senator Jean Carnahan," the ad ended. "Standing up to the big pharmaceutical companies—to start bringing drug costs down."

Money

Talent went into the race with a reputation as a fundraising wizard. But on this front, Carnahan whipped him with an effort that began almost as soon as she was sworn into office. Using her head start to full advantage, she traveled the nation—from New York to Hollywood—in search of dollars. The net result: She outspent Talent $9.7 million to $6.0 million, or $5 to Talent's every $3. Democrats, though, insisted that pro-Talent independent groups more than made up the difference through soft-money advertising.

ELECTION RESULTS

Talent won 49.8–48.6 percent with two minor-party candidates claiming the remaining 1.6 percent. Talent received 934,204 votes to 911,558 for Carnahan.

Despite the defeat, the results suggest Democrats did well with their get-out-the-vote effort in their key target areas. Talent lost pivotal St. Louis County by 15,000 votes.

In the last mid-term election in 1998, Republican Senator Kit Bond won re-election in part by carrying St. Louis County by 10,000 votes. In St. Louis City, however, Bond lost by 26,000 votes. Talent lost by 54,000 city votes in 2002.

In Jackson County, home of Kansas City, Talent narrowly lost. In 1998, Bond carried the county.

But despite the financial edge and the solid voter-turnout effort, Carnahan still fell short.

"It's a very troubling sign for Democrats," said Missouri GOP executive director John Hancock.

Exit Polling

Talent won among men 53–44 percent, but lost among women 45–52 percent, according to Fox News exit polling. Asked which issue mattered most in deciding their votes, 21 percent, the highest total, said the economy. Of those, 56 percent voted for Carnahan, 43 percent for Talent.

One surprising result was that 17 percent, the second-highest total, cited abortion as the top concern, even though the issue received scant attention in the race. Of those, 80 percent sided with Talent, an abortion opponent, to 19 percent for Carnahan, who favors abortion rights.

If those numbers are accurate, Talent outpolled Carnahan by 190,000 votes based on the abortion issue—in a race decided by roughly 23,000 votes.

About a quarter of the voters, 27 percent, said they based their votes on "personal character or experience." Of those, 65 percent opted for Talent to 32 percent for Carnahan. Asked another question about experience, 42 percent said Carnahan lacked the proper background to be a senator. The remaining 58 percent said she did not.

Asked if Talent's positions on the issues were too liberal, too conservative or about right, 30 percent of voters said he was too conservative while 59 percent said he was about right. Carnahan was seen as too liberal by 39 percent and about right by 54 percent.

ANALYSIS

Even with a huge advantage in fundraising and a good performance in turning out the vote in the Democratic strongholds of St. Louis and Kansas City, Carnahan still fell short.

Bush's persistent support undoubtedly was crucial. It came as Missouri appears to be trending conservative. A Carnahan poll showed that a plurality of voters, 39 percent, identified themselves as conservative, compared with 36 percent who said they were moderate and 18 percent who said they were liberal.

Talent's anti-abortion stand also was critical. Even though abortion received little media attention, the issue appears to have influenced a substantial voting bloc.

CONCLUSION

The result of the 2002 Senate race may turn out to be another sign that Missouri, ranked as the best presidential bellwether state in the nation, is shifting Republican. George W. Bush defeated Democrat Al Gore in 2000 by 50–47 percent.

In 2002, the GOP captured the Missouri House of Representatives for the first time in half a century. That seismic change in state politics followed a year when the GOP took over the state Senate after a similar decades-long absence from power.

Although Democrats hold five of Missouri's six statewide offices, five of the state's nine members of the U.S. House are Republican. And save for Jean Carnahan's brief, two-year tenure in the Senate, Republicans have controlled both Senate seats since 1987.

Some analysts claim that Democrats are lucky to have controlled the governorship since 1993. Mel Carnahan won the preceding year largely due to legal problems that ensnarled Republican Bill Webster.

And the groundswell of pro-Democratic sentiment following the 2000 plane crash that killed Carnahan may well have elevated Democrat Bob Holden over Talent in that year's governor's race. Remove those improbabilities and Republicans could have controlled the state's chief executive's office since 1981.

Indeed, as 2002 came to a close, Missouri Democrats were searching for answers. Holden began 2003 with lousy job-approval ratings. And Democrats had no immediate first-tier contender to challenge Bond, who is expected to seek a fourth term in 2004.

9

New Jersey Senate

Back to the Future as Torricelli Yields to Lautenberg

BRUCE A. LARSON

Fairleigh Dickinson University

New Jersey has not been kind to Republicans of late. Democrats Bill Clinton and Al Gore carried the state in the 1992, 1996, and 2000 presidential elections. In 2001, following eight years of unified Republican control of the statehouse, Democrat Jim McGreevey resoundingly defeated GOP candidate Bret Schundler for governor by 14 points, bringing with him a Democratic majority to the state assembly and an even split in the state senate. But the New Jersey GOP has had a particularly long streak of bad luck in U.S. Senate contests, as 2002 Republican nominee Doug Forrester pointed out in one of his campaign's early direct mail pieces:

> 1972 sure seems like a long time ago. "Hawaii Five-0" was the hot TV show. Led Zeppelin had just released "Stairway to Heaven," and bell-bottom pants were the rage. 1972 was also the last time a Republican from New Jersey was elected to the United States Senate.

Yet Republicans had reason to be optimistic in the 2002 U.S. Senate race. Democratic incumbent Senator Robert Torricelli had been under federal investigation for accepting illegal gifts from a businessman seeking political favors, and a popular Republican president led a nation still reeling from the September 11, 2001, terrorist attacks. In the end, however, Republicans came up short again. The Democratic Party's ability to replace the ethically challenged Torricelli with former U.S. Senator Frank Lautenberg—and the failure of GOP candidate Doug Forrester to define himself as something other than the anti-Torricelli candidate—put the New Jersey seat squarely in the Democratic column on Election Day.

THE GOP NOMINATION CONTEST

Torricelli's troubles provide the backdrop for the 2002 Senate race. Elected to the Senate in 1996, Torricelli had been under federal investigation since 1997 for allegations that he accepted thousands of dollars in cash and several expensive gifts—among them a Rolex watch, several imported suits, and a large screen TV set—from businessman David Chang in exchange for assisting Chang in his business affairs with the North Korean government. Chang was sentenced to federal prison in May 2001 for laundering excessive contributions to Torricelli's 1996 campaign, but in January 2002, the U.S. Attorney's office in Manhattan dropped its case against Torricelli for lack of credible witnesses. (The primary witness was Chang himself.) Federal prosecutors turned their files over to the Senate Ethics Committee, which promised to review the case—and whose findings would haunt Torricelli later in the campaign. For the time being, though, Torricelli had ducked the issue, setting the stage for the 2002 primary contest.

The New Jersey Republican Party initially tried to lure into the race former two-term governor Thomas Kean (1981–1989), who, as New Jersey's elder statesman, remains immensely popular among the state's voters (including many Democrats). But after publicly flirting with a run—now a ritual for the former governor—Kean declined, saying he was happy at his current post as Drew University's president. With no other top-tier candidates emerging, the GOP was left with four relative unknowns: Essex county executive Jim Treffinger, former TV anchor and state senator Diane Allen, state senator John Matheussen, and businessman and former West Windsor mayor Doug Forrester. Treffinger, who had won his Essex County post partly on the basis of his clean reputation and was thought to be well positioned to run against Torricelli's ethically challenged record, was the favorite of New Jersey's GOP establishment. But on April 18, less than two months before the June 4 primary, the FBI raided Treffinger's office searching for evidence of illegal political favors.[1] The political fallout forced Treffinger, who was ultimately indicted on charges of extortion and obstruction of justice, to withdraw from the contest, leaving Allen, Matheussen, and

Forrester to battle it out for the GOP nomination. Even among the state's Republican voters, none of the three candidates was very well known, according to a Fairleigh Dickinson University poll released in late May.[2]

With Treffinger's withdrawal, Forrester—barely even on the radar screen of GOP leaders when he announced his candidacy—became the favorite of the GOP establishment. Forrester's position as a relative outsider, and a net worth estimated at $50 million, led some GOP leaders to believe they had found their own Jon Corzine. (Corzine, New Jersey's other U.S. Senator, spent more than $60 million of his own money on his 2000 victory.) By the end of April, Forrester had lent his campaign more than $3 million, and he said he would spend more if necessary. By contrast, Allen and, especially, Matheussen could marshal only fractions of that amount. Ideology also played a role in party leaders' preferences. Allen, a political moderate, had proven adept at attracting the support of women and independents in her legislative races, but she was disliked by the state party's conservative wing.

The primary campaign opened up with a three-way debate in which each candidate was perceived as having done well; the rest of the nomination campaign was relatively uneventful—especially compared to the events that would unfold in the general election campaign. Although several polls showed that Allen might have had a better chance against Torricelli,[3] Forrester ultimately won the June 4 contest, garnering 44 percent of the vote to Allen's 37 percent and Matheussen's 19 percent. Turnout was especially low, with only a small percentage of the state's Republican voters bothering to cast a vote.

Why didn't any prominent Republicans emerge to oppose Torricelli, given his liabilities? First, at the time would-be challengers had to make their decisions about running, no one anticipated just *how* vulnerable Torricelli would become. Second, Torricelli's reputation as a tireless fundraiser and a ruthless campaigner—his nickname is the "The Torch"—surely discouraged some top-tier opponents. Third, many of the state's top Republicans had fallen in recent elections: acting governor Don DiFrancesco was forced to withdraw from the 2001 gubernatorial contest because of allegations of financial improprieties, former House member Bob Franks had lost two statewide contests in two years (first to Jon Corzine in the 2000 U.S. Senate race, then to Bret Schundler in the 2001 GOP gubernatorial primary), and 2001 GOP gubernatorial candidate Bret Schundler was handily defeated by Democrat Jim McGreevey in the 2001 gubernatorial contest. Finally, the state's increasingly Democratic electorate made it appear unlikely that any GOP candidate could oust a Democratic incumbent—even one with Torricelli's liabilities.

ACT I—TORRICELLI V. FORRESTER

The general election campaign started off quietly, in spite of some signs that Torricelli would have a difficult race ahead of him. A Fairleigh Dickinson University poll in late May reported that 41 percent of New Jersey voters—including a large plurality (42 percent) of the state's critical bloc of independents—thought that Torricelli should be replaced with a new person, and only 35 percent believed he deserved reelection. The poll also showed that Torricelli's unfavorable ratings were creeping dangerously close to his favorable ratings.[4]

The Forrester campaign nevertheless kept a relatively low profile during the summer's early days, content to let the media do the dirty work against Torricelli with its persistent coverage of the Senator's alleged ethical lapses. Forrester's only message seemed to be that he wasn't Torricelli—and that in itself was sufficient reason for voters to choose him over the incumbent in November. "I'm the guy running against Torricelli," he would open his campaign speeches with.

Torricelli spent the early days of the summer trying to deflect attention from his alleged ethical lapses by portraying Forrester as a conservative extremist on gun control, abortion, the environment, Social Security, and health care—important issues to New Jersey's increasingly Democratic electorate. Torricelli also tried to depict Forrester as a heartless profiteer who made millions by overcharging seniors for prescription drugs. (Forrester's company, *BeneCard*, which he co-founded in 1989, sells prescription drug coverage plans to public and private sector clients.)

On July 30, the nature of the campaign changed abruptly. The Senate Ethics Committee released a letter severely admonishing Torricelli for violating the Senate's prohibition on accepting gifts valued at more than $50. Using information referred to it by the U.S. Attorney's office in Manhattan, the committee found that Torricelli improperly accepted a variety of expensive gifts from businessman David Chang at the same time he was assisting Chang in his business affairs with the North Korean government. Torricelli immediately went on the offensive. Within hours of the release of the Ethics Committee's letter, he delivered a speech on the Senate floor in which he appeared to simultaneously accept and reject the committee's findings:

> I want my colleagues in the Senate to know I agree with the committee's conclusions, fully accept their findings, and take full personal responsibility. It has always been my contention that I believe that at no time did I accept any gifts or violate any Senate rules.[5]

He also purchased more than $1 million in TV ads, in which he apologized to New Jersey voters for exercising poor judgment (while carefully noting that he broke no laws), asked for forgiveness, and touted his record of fighting for the state.[6]

The campaign took on an increasingly incendiary tenor after the Ethics Committee reprimand. In campaign ads, press releases, and two televised debates, Torricelli attempted to divert attention away from the ethics controversy by fiercely attacking Forrester as a conservative extremist and criticizing Forrester's company for driving up prescription drug costs.[7] Torricelli also reminded voters that the Democratic majority in the U.S. Senate was on the line, and that a vote for Forrester was a vote for conservative Trent Lott (R-MS) as Senate majority leader.[8] In turn, Forrester hammered away at Torricelli's ethical lapses, repeatedly calling on the Senator to resign. He also attacked the incumbent Senator's legislative record, arguing that Torricelli's efforts to clean up the state's Superfund sites had failed and criticizing (in light of the United States' new war on terrorism) a 1996 regulation spearheaded by Torricelli that curbed the CIA's ability to put certain informers on its payroll.[9] Although Forrester became briefly embroiled in a conflict with the media over comments he purportedly made about supporting an increase in the state's gas tax,[10] the main controversy in the campaign remained Torricelli's ethical transgressions.

After Labor Day weekend, the unofficial start of the campaign season in New Jersey, several polls revealed that the Senate Ethics Committee's reprimand had hurt Torricelli. A Fairleigh Dickinson University poll released on September 25 showed Forrester leading Torricelli, 42 percent to 38 percent, and indicated that Torricelli was having difficulty mobilizing his base. For Torricelli, the only bright spot in the FDU poll was that Forrester was still relatively unknown by many of the state's voters, indicating that many Forrester supporters were casting a vote *against* Torricelli rather than *for* Forrester.[11] But three days later, a *Star-Ledger*/Eagleton-Rutgers poll had worse news for Torricelli, showing him trailing Forrester by 13 percentage points as New Jersey's critical bloc of independent voters began moving toward Forrester. With the GOP seeing a chance to capture its first New Jersey Senate seat since 1972, President George W. Bush made a rare stop in the state to campaign on behalf of Forrester.[12]

The next two weeks would witness some of the most tumultuous politics in the Garden State's history.

On September 26, Torricelli was dealt a devastating setback when a federal court ordered the release of a sealed Justice Department memo outlining the evidence collected against him during the department's five-year probe. The nine-page memo appeared to provide corroborating evidence about additional gifts from David Chang—such as deliveries of cash to Torricelli by Chang and his bookkeeper, Audrey Yu.[13] With only five weeks left before the election, the memo dashed any hopes Torricelli had of refocusing the campaign on substantive issues. Meanwhile, Torricelli's Democratic colleagues in the Senate became increasingly concerned that the New Jersey race would cost the party its slim majority, and party leaders in Washington were frustrated at having to divert scarce resources to a race that should have been a shoo-in for the party.[14] New Jersey Democratic House candidates were also worried that Torricelli would hurt the ticket.

Trailing in the polls and unable to get his message out, Torricelli huddled with Governor McGreevey and Senator Corzine in the governor's mansion for a strategy session during the weekend of September 28. It's unclear whether Torricelli's fellow partisans pushed him out or encouraged him to fight on—the party line was the latter, though McGreevey surely had little love for Torricelli.[15] Either way, Torricelli emerged from the session concluding there was no way to move beyond the ethics controversy.[16] On Monday, September 30, Torricelli called a news conference and announced he was quitting the race for the good of the party. "I will not be responsible for the loss of the Democratic majority in the United States Senate," he said in his tearful, at times self-pitying withdrawal statement. "When did we become such an unforgiving people?" Torricelli asked—a brazen question coming from an incumbent so well steeped in the practice of scorched-earth politics. Torricelli's penchant for alienating even his fellow partisans prompted one commentator at the press conference to note that "there wasn't a wet eye in the house, except behind the microphone."[17] It was a remarkable turn of events for an incumbent who many assumed would fight to the bitter end to keep his political career alive.

INTERLUDE: THE BALLOT SUBSTITUTION

With Torricelli out of the race, New Jersey Democrats had to scramble— first to find a replacement candidate with enough statewide name recognition to win an abbreviated campaign and second to engineer a last-minute change in the general election ballot. Although former Senator Frank Lautenberg (1983–2001) ultimately received the nod, he was selected only after three other candidates declined the party's invitation to run.[18] Democrats' first choice was former Senator Bill Bradley, who represented New Jersey in the Senate from 1977 to 1997. Bradley had impeccable ethical credentials and high statewide name recognition, but he also had little interest in entering the race and immediately rejected Democrats' offer.[19] The party then turned to fifth-term Representative Robert Menendez, whose $2.4 million war chest and high profile made him an attractive candidate. But Menendez, a rising star whose position as vice chair of the House Democratic caucus made him Congress's highest ranking Hispanic, was content to stay put.

Democrats turned next to Frank Pallone, a seven-term House member from Monmouth County long known to have Senate ambitions. Pallone initially accepted the party's offer, but within an hour called Governor McGreevey and backed out—apparently at the insistence of his wife.[20] (Some also speculated that Senate Majority Leader Tom Daschle objected to Pallone.[21]) Rejected by three candidates, Democrats finally settled for 78-year-old former U.S. Senator Frank Lautenberg, whose earlier offer to take Torricelli's place was rebuffed by McGreevey. While Lautenberg had some liabilities (mainly his age) he also had the twin advantages of money: he is a multimillionaire who could bankroll his campaign and statewide name recognition, two critical ingredients in what would be a short campaign. Lautenberg's selection added insult to injury for Torricelli, who had feuded bitterly with Lautenberg when the two served together in the Senate—and who initially said he wouldn't withdraw from the contest if the party chose Lautenberg to replace him.[22]

Democrats then faced a substantial legal hurdle in getting Lautenberg's name on the general election ballot in place of Torricelli's. New Jersey election law states that a party may nominate a new candidate if a vacancy on the ballot occurs 51 days or more before an election. Torricelli, however, withdrew 36 days before the November 5 general election, and the law is silent on what options, if any, a party had under such circumstances.[23] On October 1, state Democratic Party lawyers petitioned the State Superior Court of Middlesex County to halt the printing of ballots in New Jersey's 21 counties and requested that the state supreme court hear the case on an emergency basis.[24] Both requests were granted.[25] The next day, lawyers from the Democratic and Republican Parties took their arguments before the state's high court. Republican lawyers contended that the law's language was clear and that a ballot switch so close to the election would deprive New Jersey military personnel stationed overseas, some of whom had already cast their absentee ballots, of their right to vote.[26] Democratic Party lawyers argued that broad principles of democracy, such as a voter's right to a meaningful choice in the general election, trumped the 51-day statutory deadline for replacing candidates on the ballot. Moreover, the 51-day deadline, Democrats argued, was meant only to ensure that ballots would be printed and distributed on time—a goal that Democratic lawyers insisted would not be endangered by a ballot switch. Democrats had support on this point from a representative of New Jersey's 21 county clerks, who told the court that new ballots—including overseas absentee ballots—could still be printed and distributed on time if the process began immediately.[27] On October 3, the Court, which includes four Democrats and three Republicans, ruled unanimously in favor of the Democratic Party, concluding that "the election statutes should be liberally construed to allow the greatest scope for public participation in the electoral process, to allow candidates to get on the ballot, to allow parties to put their candidates on the ballot, and most importantly, to allow the voters a choice on Election Day."[28] The Court also ordered the Democratic Party to pay the costs of all reprinted ballots, an amount estimated at $800,000. Republicans fiercely criticized the ruling, arguing that it would set a dangerous precedent of allowing parties to engineer last-minute ballot changes whenever their candidates appeared to be losing. With echoes of the tumultuous 2000 presidential contest, the GOP immediately announced it would appeal the decision to the U.S. Supreme Court. But the Court, perhaps wary of stepping into another electoral thicket so soon after *Bush v. Gore*, declined to hear the case without giving a reason.

The Democrats had their new candidate.

ACT II—LAUTENBERG V. FORRESTER

Until this point in the campaign, Forrester's strategy had been to make Torricelli the main campaign issue, and with only five weeks left to campaign, he had difficulty switching gears. He tried desperately to associate Lautenberg with Torricelli (despite the fact that the two Democrats were bitter enemies), referring implausibly to the "Lautenberg-Torricelli machine." The Forrester team also attempted to make an issue out of the ballot switch, running an ad on cable stations across the state that characterized the last-minute candidate substitution as unfair.[29] But it became clear that Forrester was mostly preaching to the choir. Polls showed that the ballot switch generally angered only Republicans and some independents. Democrats' maneuvering might help energize the GOP base, but that would not be enough to put the state in the GOP column on Election Day.[30] Meanwhile, Democratic leaders depicted Forrester's characterization of the ballot switch as disingenuous, since Forrester, they pointed out, had repeatedly called on Torricelli to resign. Now that Torricelli had in effect done so, Forrester was crying foul. Forrester, though, had good reason to feel threatened. Two polls released in the first week of October showed Lautenberg slightly ahead after only a week in the contest.[31]

With Torricelli no longer the main issue in the race and the election a month away, Forrester needed to quickly redefine himself while also attacking Lautenberg. He challenged Lautenberg to an extensive series of debates and criticized Lautenberg for not immediately accepting the challenge. The Forrester campaign also briefly tried to make Lautenberg's age a factor, issuing a news release that asked, "Is Frank Lautenberg running from his record or is he getting forgetful?" This was a risky strategy in a state with 1.1 million seniors, but Forrester pointed out that Lautenberg had made age an issue in his 1982 campaign against 72-year-old Representative Millicent Fenwick.[32] Either way, polls showed that most New Jersey voters were unconcerned with Lautenberg's age.[33] Recognizing that it would be difficult to prevail against a Democrat on domestic issues, Forrester attempted to shift the debate to defense and security issues, which typically play to the GOP's advantage—and which, the campaign hoped, might be particularly salient in a state that lost so many people in the September 11, 2001, terrorist attacks in New York City. Toward that end, he criticized Lautenberg's votes on military matters—highlighting the former Senator's repeated opposition to increased defense spending and his vote against the 1991 Persian Gulf resolution. (Lautenberg announced his support for the 2002 Iraq resolution, neutralizing it as a campaign issue.) Finally, Forrester called into question Lautenberg's effectiveness as an advocate for New Jersey's interests, pointing out that the state's share of federal dollars had decreased under Lautenberg's tenure as Senator.

Never known for his oratory and debating skills, Lautenberg needed only to avoid gaffes and act like an incumbent. His strategy was to minimize the number of debates, tout his record and experience as a senator, and focus on domestic issues that worked to the advantage of Democrats. On issues such as abortion, gun control, and environmental regulations, Lautenberg followed Torricelli's tack, depicting Forrester as a conservative extremist out of step with mainstream New Jersey voters.[34] He accused Forrester of supporting Social Security privatization, though Forrester denied ever backing such a plan, and he defended his positions on defense and security issues. To counter Forrester's attacks on his defense record, Lautenberg showcased his record of military service (he is a World War II veteran) and pointed out that Forrester had sat out the Vietnam War. To help hammer home the point, he enlisted decorated Vietnam War veteran and former Nebraska Democratic Senator Bob Kerrey, who came to New Jersey to campaign for Lautenberg. Lautenberg also made an issue of several columns Forrester wrote for a local newspaper between 1989 and 1993, which seemed to confirm Democrats' claim that Forrester was anything but a political moderate. In one column, Forrester lambasted the 1992 New Jersey assault weapons ban as political pandering; in another he criticized drunk driving checkpoints as "a gross violation of proper governmental boundaries." (In a column unlikely to garner Forrester much support in Atlantic City, he likened the city to "the unclean waters of a toddler's wading pool."[35]) Because Forrester had done so little to define himself earlier in the campaign, Lautenberg was able to claim that these columns represented the real Forrester.

After much quarrelling over a debate schedule, the candidates participated in two debates on the Wednesday and Saturday prior to Election Day. Both candidates held their own in the second debate, but Lautenberg's doddering performance in the first—he appeared unfocused and unprepared—made it clear why his campaign sought to minimize the number of debates. Fortunately for Lautenberg, few voters appeared to have tuned in.

Without exception, polls in the last few weeks of the campaign showed the Democrats' move had paid off. Forrester's problem was clear. Spending much of the campaign touting what he *wasn't* (Torricelli), Forrester never defined who he *was*. A Fairleigh Dickinson University poll released on November 3—two days before the election—reported that 24 percent of New Jersey's likely voters still didn't know enough about Forrester to form an opinion about him, and 9 percent had never even heard of him. Meanwhile, with 18 years in the Senate behind him, Lautenberg enjoyed de facto incumbent status. Some pundits speculated whether voters even knew that Lautenberg had left the Senate in 2000. As an indication of how completely Forrester's fortunes had reversed, President Bush declined to include New Jersey in his 11th-hour campaign barnstorm around the nation.

CAMPAIGN FINANCE

With all the controversy in the New Jersey contest, scant attention was paid to how the race was being financed. As with most New Jersey statewide contests, this race was expensive, owing in part to the state's unusual media setting. (Candidates must buy advertising time in the New York City and Philadelphia media markets—two of the most expensive in the nation.[36]) According to the Center for Responsive Politics, Torricelli, a prodigious fundraiser, raised $10.5 million, spent $5.6 million, and had $5.1 million on hand at the time he dropped out of the race on September 30. Seventy-five percent of Torricelli's total receipts came from individual contributors, 18 percent came from PACs (mostly business), and 7 percent came from other sources.[37] As of this writing, it was unclear whether Torricelli had given any of his campaign funds to Lautenberg or the Democratic Party.[38]

In contrast to Torricelli, Lautenberg and Forrester's campaign efforts were largely self-financed. As of October 16, 74 percent of the $1.3 million in Lautenberg's campaign account came from loans he made to his campaign. The balance of Lautenberg's receipts came from individual donors ($213,906) and PACs ($111,975). A similar story applies to Forrester, who loaned his campaign 80 percent of its total receipts ($8.7 million), collected $1.4 million from individual contributors, and raised $339,166 from PACs. GOP leaders initially backed Forrester in the primaries in part because of his ability to bankroll his campaign. But as the general election campaign unfolded, it became clear that Forrester, though wealthy, was no Jon Corzine. Much of Forrester's wealth, it turned out, was tied up in his business.[39]

Political parties also played a role in financing the New Jersey contest, though much of it was through undisclosed soft money expenditures. Other than the $16,500 contribution made to Torricelli by the Democratic Senatorial Campaign Committee (DSCC), Democratic Party organizations made no hard money expenditures in the race. (These figures reflect Federal Election Commission reports up to October 16, 2002, the last date for which data was available at the time this chapter was being written.) On the Republican side, the National Republican Senatorial Committee (NRSC) contributed $17,500 to Forrester, and the New Jersey State Republican Committee gave $10,000. In addition, the Republican National Committee (RNC) reported $634,000 in coordinated expenditures on behalf of Forrester. Both parties were reported to have spent significant sums of soft money on issue ads, direct mail, and get-out-the-vote efforts. (Federal law does not require political parties to itemize and report soft money expenditures, so these expenditures are based on estimates and the parties' own claims.) According to one account, the Democratic Senatorial Campaign Committee (DSCC) committed to spending $4.5 million in soft money on the New Jersey race, with an additional $3 million pledged by the state Democratic Party.[40] Republican Party committees were committed to spending similar amounts, according to the same account, though the GOP would surely become skittish about committing substantial resources to the race as Forrester fell behind in the polls. Several interest groups also made soft money expenditures on behalf of the candidates.

ELECTION RESULTS

On Election Day, Lautenberg defeated Forrester, 54 percent to 44 percent, with various minor party candidates garnering 2 percent of the vote. Voter News Service's (VNS) exit polling system crashed on Election Day and subsequently was unable to produce any data for the 2002 midterm elections. Nevertheless, we can briefly explore voters' decisions using an election-eve poll of 900 likely New Jersey voters conducted by Opinion Dynamics for Fox News. The numbers referred to in this section can be found in table 9.1.

For all the tumult of this campaign, the Lautenberg-Forrester race ended up closely resembling New Jersey's other recent statewide contests, with predictable groups making up each candidate's coalition of supporters. Partisan defections were relatively few in number, with 91 percent of self-described Democrats supporting Lautenberg and 89 percent of Republicans

Table 9.1   Election-Eve Poll of New Jersey Voters, 2002 (percentage voting for each candidate)

	Lautenberg	Forrester
Party		
Democrat	91	6
Republican	9	89
Independent	50	45
Other	53	26
Gender		
Female	60	37
Male	46	50
Race/ethnicity		
African American	93	4
Hispanic	69	26
Asian	53	40
White/Caucasian	48	49
Other	58	24
Age		
18–30	56	32
31–45	55	42
46–64	48	50
65 and over	59	38
Education		
Less than high school	68	24
Graduated high school	59	38
Some college/tech voc	52	45
Graduated college	45	51
Graduate/professional school	59	39
Income		
$0–7,999	81	10
$8–11,999	82	0
$12–14,999	48	36
$15–19,999	59	41
$20–24,999	65	35
$25–34,999	75	23
$35–49,999	59	35
$50–74,999	54	44
$75–99,999	53	42
$100,000 and above	43	55
Region		
Essex and Hudson Counties	81	16
Bergen and Passaic Counties	44	52
Central	55	42
South	51	44
Northwest	44	55

	Lautenberg	Forrester
Most Important Issue		
Social Security	69	29
Gun Control	68	30
Education	58	39
Environment	81	8
Economy	60	38
Iraq	37	57
War on Terrorism	22	72
Highest Priority for Nation		
Economy and Jobs	73	25
Terrorism and National Security	36	60
U.S. Invasion of Iraq		
Support	41	57
Oppose	82	14
Gun Owner in Household		
Yes, I own a gun	25	69
Someone else owns a gun	43	54
I and someone else own a gun	36	64
No, I don't own a gun	59	38
Opinion on Ballot Switch		
Fair	86	11
Unfair	21	75
Perceived Corruption in New Jersey		
More than in other states	39	58
Less than in other states	67	33
About the same	62	34
Importance of Senate Control		
Very important	55	43
Somewhat important	53	44
Not too important	52	43
Not important at all	48	42
Concern that Lautenberg is too old		
Very concerned	11	84
Somewhat concerned	34	63
Not very concerned	64	35
Not at all concerned	73	23

Note: The results are from a poll of 900 likely New Jersey voters conducted by Opinion Dynamics for Fox News. The margin of error is $+/-3.3$ percentage points. Sample subsets have a higher sampling error than the overall sample.

favoring Forrester. Since Democratic voters significantly outnumber Republican voters in New Jersey, however, Forrester would have needed to make up the difference by winning handily among the state's independents. But Lautenberg carried independents, and underwhelming as his margin was (50 percent to 45 percent), it sealed Forrester's fate.

Other groups also lined up predictably behind the candidates. Revealing a wide gender gap, Lautenberg fared substantially better among females than did Forrester (60 percent to 37 percent), whereas males favored Forrester over Lautenberg, though by a narrower margin (50 percent to 46 percent). Lautenberg ran ahead of Forrester among voters of nearly every age cohort, education level, and income level; he also captured an overwhelming majority of the state's minority and urban voters. Forrester outpaced Lautenberg only among college grads (though not those with post-graduate degrees), 46- to 64-year-olds, the wealthiest New Jerseyans, and suburbanites. He ran behind Lautenberg in every region of the state except Bergen and Passaic counties and the Republican-leaning northwest.

Consistent with each candidate's issue agenda in the campaign, voters concerned with domestic policy issues were more likely to support Lautenberg, while voters who named security and defense issues as priorities favored Forrester. Though Forrester and Lautenberg both announced support for the recently passed congressional resolution giving the President the authority to use force in Iraq, voters who opposed an invasion of Iraq nevertheless overwhelmingly supported Lautenberg (82 percent to 14 percent), while Forrester ran ahead of Lautenberg (57 percent to 41 percent) among voters favoring an invasion. Not surprisingly, gun owners (and voters who lived in households where someone owned a gun) were more likely to back Forrester, whereas Lautenberg ran ahead of Forrester among voters who didn't own guns.

Factors associated with the late-breaking tumult of this contest were also related to voters' choices. Not surprisingly, Forrester outpaced Lautenberg among voters who believed Democrats' 11th hour candidate substitution was unfair, while Lautenberg won by wide margins among voters who perceived the change as fair. Voter perceptions about political corruption in New Jersey also played a role in the outcome of the contest: Forrester ran ahead of Lautenberg (58 precent to 39 percent) among voters who believed New Jersey had more political corruption than other states, whereas voters who believed that the state had less or about the same amount of corruption as other states overwhelmingly favored Lautenberg. Concern over partisan control of the U.S. Senate seemed to play only a minor role in voters' decisions: those for whom control of the Senate was very important were slightly more likely to support Lautenberg than were voters for whom control of the Senate was not important at all. Finally, most voters said they were unconcerned about Lautenberg's age hindering his effectiveness. But voters who were concerned about Lautenberg's age were considerably more likely to favor Forrester over the former Senator.

CONCLUSION

The Democratic Party's ability to replace the ethically challenged Torricelli with former U.S. Senator Frank Lautenberg—and the failure of GOP candidate Doug Forrester to define himself as anything other than the anti-Torricelli candidate—put the New Jersey seat squarely in the Democratic column on Election Day. By failing to articulate adequately the moderate credentials he claimed, Forrester allowed Torricelli and Lautenberg to define him as a conservative extremist. In the end, voters opted for a known quantity in Lautenberg, who had served the state well during his 18 years in the Senate and whose ideological leanings were in tune with a majority of the state's electorate.

For all of the national focus on the New Jersey contest—many observers were rating it a toss-up by late September—the race had a decidedly anti-climatic outcome. The speculation that partisan control of the Senate might hinge on the outcome of the New Jersey contest turned out to be untrue, as Democrats' critical losses in Minnesota, Missouri, and Georgia would give the GOP control regardless of what happened in New Jersey. Still, by keeping the seat in the Democratic column, Lautenberg and the state Democratic Party prevented an even more disastrous midterm election outcome for national Democrats.

For those observing New Jersey politics from the inside, Lautenberg's victory provides further evidence that the Garden State is firmly in the Democratic camp. Absent an authentically moderate Republican who can get voters to move beyond their Democratic moorings, the GOP will have difficulty winning statewide contests in New Jersey for the foreseeable future. Conservative Republicans such as Bret Schundler—who lost the 2001 governor's race to Democrat Jim McGreevey by 14 points—only risk further sidelining the GOP, while candidates such as Forrester, who failed to stress his supposedly moderate credentials, will serve the party no better. What New Jersey Republicans need is precisely what they've been unable to come up with: an authentic moderate who can effectively communicate a centrist message. But even the best GOP candidates may have difficulty given state demographic trends that increasingly favor Democrats. As one Republican strategist recently put it, "We can either run moderates like Bob Franks and lose by 30,000 votes or run conservatives like Schundler and lose by 300,000 votes."[41]

If the 2002 contest raised questions about the GOP's viability in New Jersey, it also invited speculation about state Democrats. Lautenberg's age—he will be 84 at the end of his term—and Torricelli's spectacular political crash guarantee that neither will be part of state Democrats' long-term plans. This leaves Governor Jim McGreevey and U.S. Senator Jon Corzine as the most important players in the state Democratic Party, but it does nothing to answer the question of who will eventually succeed Lautenberg—a question that may need to be answered sooner rather than later, if, as some have speculated, Lautenberg chooses not to serve out his entire term. Only time will tell, of course, who steps up to take Lautenberg's place, but a Senate seat may begin to look more attractive to congressional Democrats if the Democratic Party in the U.S. House appears to be relegated to minority status for the foreseeable future.

Of course, any and all developments in New Jersey necessarily unfold in the context of the state's reputation for shady politics. If the past is any predictor of the future, voters here haven't seen the last of elected officials being brought down by allegations of political corruption.

NOTES

1. Mark J. Magyar, "Et Tu, Treffinger? The State GOP Reels Anew," *New Jersey Reporter* (April–May 2002): pp. 8, 12.

2. 49% of self-described Republicans had never heard of Diane Allen, 58% had never heard of Matheussen, and 44% had never heard of Forrester. See "Trouble for Torricelli," May 22, 2002, FDU PublicMind Poll, www.publicmind.edu.

3. A Quinnipiac University poll conducted in April showed Torricelli 12 points ahead of Allen, 15 points ahead of Matheussen, and 18 points ahead of Forrester. FDU's May poll also showed Allen running best against Torricelli.

4. According to the FDU poll, Torricelli's favorable ratings outnumbered his unfavorable ratings by only 8 percentage points. By contrast, Jon Corzine, New Jersey's other U.S. Senator, enjoyed a significantly larger favorable-to-unfavorable ratio in the poll than did Torricelli.

5. The transcript of Torricelli's floor statement was printed in the *New York Times*, July 31, 2002, p. B6.

6. Elizabeth Palmer and Jonathan Allen, "Torricelli's Ethics Admonishment Quickly Becomes a Campaign Issue," *Congressional Quarterly Weekly Report* (August 3, 2002), pp. 2104–2105. Laura Mansnerus, "In New Ad, Torricelli Apologizes for 'Poor Judgment,'" *New York Times* (August 2, 2002), p. B5.

7. David Kinney, "Hobbled Torricelli and Obscure Forrester Begin Race to November," *Star-Ledger* (September 2, 2002), pp. 1, 7.

8. Laura Mansnerus, "It's Either Me or the GOP, Torricelli Tells Democrats," *New York Times* (September 14, 2002), pp. B1, B5.

9. David Kocieniewski, "Torricelli-Forrester Fight Grows Fiercer by the Day,"

New York Times (September 7, 2002), pp. B1, B6. David Kocieniewski, "Challenger to Torricelli Attacks Curbs On the C.I.A.," *New York Times* (September 17, 2002), pp. B5, B6.

10. David Kocieniewski, "Forrester Denies Backing an Increase in the Gas Tax," *New York Times* (September 11, 2002), pp. B1, B5. David Kinney, "Hike Gas Tax? Not Me, says Forrester Now," *Star-Ledger* (September 11, 2002), pp. 15, 18.

11. A remarkable 47 percent of the state's likely voters reported never having heard of Forrester. See FDU PublicMind, "The Race for Senate: The Unpopular v. The Unknown" (September 25, 2002): www. Publicmind.edu.

12. David Kocieniewski, "Forrester Has 'Priorities Straight,' Bush Says at Stop in New Jersey," *New York Times* (September 24, 2002), pp. B1, B5.

13. Chris Mondics and Peter Nicholas, "Torricelli Accuser Bolstered in Memo," *Philadelphia Inquirer*, (September 27, 2002).

14. Hernandez, "Fellow Democrats Fret and Fume as Torricelli Campaign Struggles," *New York Times* (September 22, 2002), pp. 1, 44.

15. Torricelli alienated McGreevey in 2001 by unexpectedly announcing that he would challenge McGreevey for the 2001 Democratic gubernatorial nomination, putting state party leaders in the politically perilous position of having to choose between the two candidates. Torricelli withdrew two weeks after his announcement, after county party leaders lined up behind McGreevey. See David Kocieniewski, "Torricelli, Opposed Within Party, Drops New Jersey Governor's Bid," *New York Times* (August 1, 2000), pp. A1, B4.

16. David Kocieniewski, "Torricelli Quits Campaign, Citing Risk to His Own Party," *New York Times* (October 1, 2002), pp. A1, B4.

17. Paul Mulshine, "'Sopranos Fatigue Finally Caught Up With Torricelli," *Star-Ledger* (October 1, 2002), p. 27.

18. In addition to the candidates mentioned here, many others, including Rep. Robert Andrews, were also reportedly in the mix.

19. Raymond Hernandez and Alison Mitchell, "Democrats Scramble for a New Contender, But the GOP Vows to Fight To Keep the Old One," *New York Times* (October 1, 2002): p. B5.

20. Jonathan Allen and Jonathan Riehl, "Democrats Scramble to Recover From Sen. Torricelli's Downfall," *Congressional Quarterly Weekly Report* (October 5, 2002), pp. 2580–2584. David Kinney and Jeff Whelan, "Lautenberg's Return: Ex-Senator is Picked to Run In Torricelli's Place," *Star Ledger* (October 2, 2002), pp. 1, 8. Steve Kornacki, "After Two Long Days, Democrats Tap Lautenberg," Politics NJ.com (October 2, 2002).

21. Steve Kornacki, "After Two Long Days, Democrats Tap Lautenberg," Poli ticsNJ.com (October 2, 2002).

22. Raymond Hernandez and Alison Mitchell, "Democrats Scramble for a New Contender, But the GOP Vows to Fight To Keep the Old One," *New York Times* (October 1, 2002), p. B5. Jonathan Allen and Jonathan Riehl, "Democrats Scramble to Recover From Sen. Torricelli's Downfall," *Congressional Quarterly Weekly Report* (October 5, 2002), pp. 2580–2584. Raymond Hernandez, "Fate Linked Two Rivals; Bad Blood Keeps Them Apart," *New York Times* (October 3, 2002), p. B6.

23. According to New Jersey election law, the governor also has the power to postpone a U.S. Senate election if, within 30 days of the election, a ballot line becomes vacant. Democrats never publicly considered that course of action, however. Iver Peterson, "Election Statute Offers No Clear Answers," *New York Times* (October 1, 2002), p. B5.

24. Robert Schwaneberg, "Leading Issues in Contest Are Now The Legal Ones," *Star-Ledger* (October 1, 2002), pp. 1, 10.

25. Robert Rudolph and Lawrence Ragonese, "Judge Halts Printing of Ballots: Order Creates Trouble For Counties and Could Be Costly For Taxpayers," *Star Ledger* (October 2, 2002), p. 8.

26. Iver Peterson, "Both Sides Say Protecting Voting Rights Is the Issue," *New York Times* (October 2, 2002), p. B4. Robert Schwaneberg, "N.J.'s Highest Court To Decide Which Democrat Tops Ballot," *Star-Ledger* (October 2, 2002), p. 9.

27. David Kocieniewski, "New Jersey Court Lets Lautenberg Into Senate Race," *New York Times* (October 3, 2002), pp. A1, B6.

28. *The New Jersey Democratic Party v. Sampson*, Supreme Court of New Jersey, A-24, September Term 2002, 53,618, p. 5.

29. Richard Lezin Jones, "Ad By Republicans Continues to Stress the Democrats' Ballot Switch," *New York Times* (October 11, 2002), pp. B1, B5.

30. See, for example, the *Star-Ledger*/Eagleton-Rutgers Poll of October 8, 2002, "Lautenberg Substitution Revives Democrats' Chances Even While Energizing Republicans."

31. *Star-Ledger*/Eagleton-Rutgers Poll, "Lautenberg Substitution Revives Democrats' Chances Even While Energizing Republicans," October 8, 2002. Quinnipiac University Poll, "Lautenberg Inches Ahead In Jersey Senate Race," October 7, 2002.

32. David Kocieniewski, "After Torricelli, Race Now Suits The Democrats," *New York Times* (October 13, 2002), pp. 1, 38. David Kocieniewski, "Questioning Lautenberg's Age Could Backfire on Forrester," *New York Times*, New Jersey Section (October 27, 2002), p. 15.

33. For example, a poll by Fairleigh Dickinson University found that 71% of the state's likely voters thought that, at 78, Lautenberg "can still be effective."

34. Forrester supports abortion rights, opposes late-term abortions, opposes Medicaid funding for abortions, and supports parental notification laws for teenagers seeking abortions. On gun control, Forrester supports more adequately enforcing present laws rather than enacting new measures. On the environment, Forrester favors using government money to facilitate a more rapid cleanup of the state's Superfund sites, whereas Lautenberg supports tracking down polluters and making them pay for cleaning up the state's sites.

35. David Kocieniewski, "Forrester on the Defensive For Old Newspaper Columns," *New York Times* (October 15, 2002), p. 15.

36. Barbara G. Salmore and Stephen A. Salmore, *New Jersey Politics and Government: Suburban Politics Comes of Age*, 2nd ed. (Lincoln: University of Nebraska Press), p. 80.

37. In mid-September, Forrester criticized Torricelli for accepting campaign contributions from supporters of a group listed by the State Department as a terrorist

organization, The People's Mujahedeen of Iran. The group opposes Iran's present government. See David Kocieniewski, "Challenger Says Senator Took Donation from Supporters of a Terrorist Group," *New York Times* (September 14, 2002), p. B5.

38. As of October 16th—the last date for which Federal Election Commission data is available for this writing—there was no indication that Torricelli had given any money to Lautenberg or to the Democratic Party.

39. David Kocieniewski, "Forrester's Estimate of Wealth Seems to be Hurting, Not Helping," *New York Times* (October 24, 2002), pp. B1, B6. David Kocieniewski, "After Torricelli, Race Now Suits The Democrats," *New York Times* (October 13, 2002), pp. 1, 38.

40. Iver Peterson, "Senate Candidates Using Their Own Money, Disclosure Forms Show," *New York Times* (October 25, 2002), pp. B5.

41. The quote is by Roger Bodeman, who was Governor Kean's campaign manager. Cited in Iver Peterson, "The GOP Is All Dressed Up But It Has No Place to Go," *New York Times*, New Jersey Section (November 18, 2002), p. 2.

10

New Hampshire Senate

Down to the Wire in New Hampshire

LINDA L. FOWLER

Dartmouth College

When Kenneth Mehlman, deputy assistant to the president, briefed Republican strategists in June 2002, his confidential memo listed New Hampshire as one of two states where Democrats had a "strong chance" to pick up a seat. The state's senior senator, Republican Bob Smith, was in trouble with voters at home, and New Hampshire's popular Democratic governor, Jeanne Shaheen, was poised to take advantage of his vulnerability. Throughout the campaign season, analysts labeled it one of the few "toss-up" contests in an election year that proved overwhelmingly favorable to incumbents. In the end, three-term Congressman John Sununu saved the day for the Republicans, winning the race by 20,000 ballots with a close, but convincing 52 percent of the two-party vote.

By some measures, the New Hampshire seat should never have been in play to attract the attention of the White House and millions of dollars of outside party and interest group money. Heading into the election, only 27 percent of New Hampshire's registered voters were Democrats and its four-person congressional delegation was solidly Republican. The state's economy was still robust with an unemployment rate well below 5 percent, well under the national average. Yet Senator Smith's narrow reelection victory in 1996 and his quixotic three-month abandonment of the Republican Party to run for president in 1999 made him an inviting target.

Furthermore, two trends in the state created doubts that New Hampshire still deserved its reputation as a conservative Republican bastion. First, undeclared voters had become the single largest electoral group thanks to the in-migration of high tech workers and professionals. Outnumbering registered Republicans by a few percentage points, they were disinclined to embrace a conservative social agenda, although many agreed with tight-fisted fiscal policies. Shaheen's ability to win three consecutive two-year terms indicated that these independent-minded voters would support a Democrat. Second, the social and religious conservatives that constitute such a critical element of the Republican base in other states appeared unable to mobilize a significant number of activists in New Hampshire. Bush lost the 2000 presidential primary to John McCain by 18 percentage points and carried the state in the general election by only 7,000 votes. He probably would have lost the state—and the presidency—had Green Party candidate Ralph Nader not been on the ballot. In short, it was not clear that the president's 69 percent approval rating in the state would translate into grassroots activity.

If local personalities and political dynamics combined to make the Senate race competitive, they also determined its outcome. In anti-tax New Hampshire, the platform of the Democratic gubernatorial candidate to adopt an income tax in order to fund state aid for education brought a surge of new voters to the polls. Democrats at all levels felt their wrath, as the GOP swept the governor's race, gained overwhelming majorities in both chambers of the state legislature, held the two seemingly marginal congressional seats by comfortable margins, and retained the prized U.S. Senate seat. President Bush had put his political prestige on the line in New Hampshire, first recruiting a challenger to depose Smith and then making two visits to the state, including one on the weekend before the election. Despite his significant influence, the election was not a referendum on Bush's leadership but a repudiation of progressive efforts to make state revenues and expenditures more equitable. Ironically, Shaheen, who had opposed a state income tax, succumbed to the "ticket of taxers" label that brought down the entire party.[1]

THE NOMINATION CONTEST

The Democratic nominee for the U.S. Senate race, three-term governor Jeanne Shaheen, age 55, had defied political odds in 1996 by becoming New Hampshire's first female governor and first Democrat to hold the state house since 1982. Shaheen was a moderate in the Clinton-Gore mold and had been on Gore's short list as a possible vice presidential nominee in 2000. She had a reputation as a formidable grass roots organizer, and she had developed useful contacts outside the state among the many politicians who take an interest in New Hampshire's first-in-the-nation presidential primary. Her name recognition, fundraising potential and gubernatorial experience all combined to make her the strongest senatorial contender the Democrats had fielded in many years.

Shaheen adopted a pragmatic progressivism while in office, focusing on education, electric utility deregulation, export industry development, land conservation, and lower prescription drug prices. During her tenure, the GOP controlled at least one chamber and some times both houses in the state legislature, so Shaheen faced significant constraints in tackling the major issue of her governorship—a state supreme court decision requiring equity in public school funding. Shaheen had helped secure her election by "taking the pledge" against an income tax, a demand imposed on several generations of New Hampshire politicians by the ultra-conservative *Manchester Union Leader*. After the judges struck down her initial plan to address the disparity in school revenues between wealthy and poor communities, she resisted pressure from the liberal wing of her party and threatened to veto an income tax. Instead, she negotiated a statewide property tax and an assortment of business taxes with Republicans in the legislature. These proved highly unpopular with wealthy donor towns, imposed hardship on low income residents in affluent communities—particularly seniors—and failed to satisfy the original litigants. The unresolved issues surrounding school funding became a major liability for Shaheen during the general election campaign.

In contrast to Shaheen's uncontested nomination, 38-year-old Republican John Sununu faced a bruising battle against two-term incumbent Bob Smith. The Bush White House quietly encouraged the three-term House member to challenge Smith in the belief that Sununu had a better chance against Shaheen. With the balance of power teetering in the Senate, national Republicans took the unprecedented step of opposing an incumbent reelection bid in order to keep the seat in the GOP column. Opinion polls throughout 2001 and early 2002 consistently showed Sununu doing better against the governor. In addition, there was residual resentment among Granite State Republicans about Smith's mercurial presidential bid as an independent. Smith described his decision as a matter of principle, chastising his party that its commitment to gun owners and the unborn "was a fraud and everyone knows it."[2] His return to the party fold in order to take up a newly vacant chairmanship of the Senate's Committee on Environment and Public Works struck his disgruntled fellow partisans as opportunistic.

Sununu was the son of a former three-term governor of the state who had served as the first President Bush's chief of staff. Although the younger Sununu had no prior political experiencein politics, his family's name recognition in the state had proved invaluable in winning the 1996 GOP nomination in an open seat long held by Republicans. Ironically, the current President Bush had been the one to discharge Sununu's father after misuse of White House perks had become embarrassing to the previous Bush administration. Nevertheless, the younger Sununu had profited from his Washington connections, receiving choice committee assignments on the Appropriations and Budget Committees and becoming vice chairman of the Budget Committee in 2000 at the urging of House Speaker Dennis Hastert. Sununu's voting record in Congress was strongly conservative, but he was not a zealot. Nor was he closely identified with the religious right, although he did oppose abortion except in cases of rape, incest or endangerment of the pregnant woman's life. Sununu had a surprisingly weak showing in his 2000 reelection bid, however, and he failed to keep pace with either Smith or Shaheen in early fundraising. Nevertheless, with half the state in his constituency, including the state's largest city of Manchester, Sununu's name recognition, low-key persona and outside contacts made him an extremely competitive challenger to Smith and a formidable opponent for Shaheen.

Incumbent senators rarely lose a primary challenge,[3] however, and Senator Smith promised a tough fight. Although he had won his previous election with a narrow margin, Smith's outspoken conservatism and passionate opposition to abortion gained him a dedicated following among some Republican activists. He was a determined advocate for veterans and was known for quirky causes, such as trying to prevent the return of a young Cuban refugee, Elian Gonzalez, to Cuba. He used his new chairmanship to cultivate environmentalists, championing restoration of the Florida Everglades and protection of the Arctic National Wildlife Refuge from drilling. Among Republican primary voters, then, Smith appealed to an unusual mix of social conservatives, conservationists, and rural inhabitants, while Sununu attracted members of the business community and suburban professionals concentrated along the southern border.

By late summer, Smith had raised $2.9 million in campaign contributions to Sununu's $1.4 million[4] and had secured the endorsements of such prominent Republicans as Senate Minority Leader Trent Lott. His deficit in the polls had already closed in June to within eight points.[5] Yet Smith had lost the backing of the *Manchester Union Leader*, which turned its scathing editorial gaze on his efforts to claim credit for porkbarrel projects. He did pick up the support of the more moderate *Concord Monitor*, which charged that Sununu lacked "fire in the belly" to be a credible campaigner.[6] The two men had very few differences in their voting records as indicated by various interest group scores;[7] and in debate they revealed few differences on the issues.[8] Thus, their rivalry boiled down to the question of who could best represent the GOP in November.

On September 10, the Republican primary produced a surprisingly easy victory for Sununu with 54 percent of the vote. Sununu's claim that he "had never done anything that was not in the interest of the Republican Party" was convincing to the party faithful, yet it was a quote that came back to haunt him in Shaheen's campaign ads.

GENERAL ELECTION CAMPAIGN

Sununu and Shaheen were well-matched in their brief, but intense, campaign. Both candidates had widespread name recognition, extensive public records and ample resources to get their message across to voters. Although neither candidate scored high in terms of personal charisma, each came across as thoughtful and well-informed on the issues. No obvious personal deficiencies, no taint of scandal nor embarrassing connections hindered either candidate. In short, this campaign would be about pure politics: who could devise the most compelling message and who could get their supporters to the polls most effectively.

New Hampshire has consistently high turnout by national standards in both presidential and off-year elections. In recent years, voters had been setting records each time they went to the polls, demonstrating that they were susceptible to mobilization. At the same time, both parties had already tapped into the easiest targets so that the effort necessary to turn out additional voters at the margins was increasing.

Shaheen had the more difficult task for several reasons. As the minority party candidate, she started as the underdog, and had to make up the deficit with undeclared voters. Such voters are less likely to turn out in off-year elections, so Shaheen was relying on women's groups, teachers, environmentalists and senior citizens to help augment her coalition. In some close off-year election contests, formidable grassroots activity organized by the AFL-CIO had made the difference,[9] but unions were not particularly strong in New Hampshire—although they had helped Al Gore win the 2000 Democratic presidential primary.

Historically, Republicans have an advantage in off-year elections because their more educated and affluent identifiers are likely to vote without the stimulus of a presidential campaign. Yet Sununu's partisan advantage in turnout and registration was not necessarily secure, because of the divisive Republican primary. Some political observers thought that the momentum of victory in the primary would help Sununu in the general election, but others thought it would eat into his Republican base. Although Senator Smith had endorsed Sununu after the primary election, he kept his distance and did not campaign for him. Vocal Smith supporters vowed to write in his name on the November ballot and some claimed that they would vote for Shaheen. Smith did not publicly encourage such declarations, but he did not silence them either. Thus, Sununu, too, needed a significant percentage of undeclared voters.

Shaheen's strategy mirrored the approach of Democrats around the country. She emphasized domestic issues that advantaged her party and declared her support for the president's foreign policy, including the resolution to authorize the use of force in Iraq. She had established a record on improving primary education, had developed a plan to lower prescription drug prices, had led the state in deregulating electric utilities and had strengthened conservation programs. She identified herself as being "on the side of New Hampshire families," while she labeled Sununu a friend of corporate interests. Her mailings and advertisements charged that Sununu was in the pocket of the oil companies and the pharmaceutical industry and attacked his votes against special education, college scholarships and toxic waste cleanup. Most damning, perhaps, were her claims that Sununu favored privatizing Social Security and had supported a special loophole in the tax code that enabled companies to move their headquarters off shore to avoid paying taxes. The indictment of Tyco International Ltd.'s founder for defrauding investors of $600 million gave the issue of corporate malfeasance particular salience, because the company originated in New Hampshire and recently had moved its offices to Bermuda. In addition, Shaheen stressed the importance of maintaining a pro-choice majority on the Supreme Court and stressed Sununu's opposition to environmental regulation. She ridiculed his comment in a public debate that polar bears "enjoy walking on the pipeline" because they gain a better vantage point as predators. The issue that worked best, however, was Sununu's loyalty to the GOP leadership in Washington and his comment noted above about supporting the party's interests.

Sununu's voting record provided ammunition for his opponent, but he had neatly finessed the most dangerous fallout of a primary campaign by avoiding a pull farther to the right. Because his battle with Smith hinged on whom could best represent the GOP rather than issue differences, he did not have a lot of ideological baggage to shed during the general election. He stood firmly with the president on making the 2001 tax cuts permanent and found good cover in the party's alternative prescription drug plan. He somewhat disingenuously denied having supported partial privatization of Social Security and claimed to judge each vote on its merits, citing several instances when he had gone against the party's position. Sununu's most effective weapon against Shaheen, however, was New Hampshire's school funding crisis. The national Republicans had run ads against Shaheen all summer decrying her lack of leadership in solving the problem, and Sununu picked up the theme in September. He accused her of "failed leadership" and of shifting positions like a "weathervane" with respect to school finance. Most telling of all, Sununu linked her to gubernatorial candidate Mark Fernald's proposal to replace the hated statewide property tax with an even more hateful income tax. Almost overnight, the moderate Shaheen was transformed into another "tax and spend liberal" and the co-author of the "Shaheen-Fernald income tax plan."

Driving home the messages on both sides were the state and national party organizations, as well as advocacy groups that ran independent ads on the state's major television station, WMUR, and on the Boston radio and television networks. By November 1, the national parties had transferred significant funds to the state parties, thus enabling the New Hampshire State Democratic Committee to spend over $800,000 and the New Hampshire State Republican Committee to pour $1.1 million into ads just for New Hampshire's WMUR-TV.[10] Then, on the weekend before the election, the Republican Party pumped an additional half million dollars into advertising at WMUR, plus the Boston and Portland, Maine, stations.

Issue advocacy groups that ran ads included the usual suspects as well as some of mysterious origin.[11] Those backing Shaheen included the Sierra Club, National League of Conservation Voters, the National Abortion Rights Action League (NARAL), People for the American Way and the Voter Reform Project (a campaign finance reform group), which spent at least $600,000 between September 11 and November 4. Those supporting Sununu included the U.S. Chamber of Commerce, the National Rifle Association, Americans for Job Security, Club for Growth, United Seniors Association (a group funded by the pharmaceutical industry), and National Right to Life organization, which spent a combined total of at least $400,000.

The candidates also raised and spent plenty of money on their own from individuals and political action committees.[12] Shaheen's major donors included organized labor, Emily's List and such corporate PACs as AT&T Wireless and Oracle. Sununu's most generous contributors were energy and oil companies, the pharmaceutical industry, and banking and accounting firms. As with the primary, Sununu lagged his opponent raising $2.45 million to Shaheen's $3.71 million.[13] Given the edge he enjoyed in party support, however, the difference was not significant.

New Hampshire is used to political heavyweights in the state during the presidential primary season, but in 2002 major figures from both parties made frequent visits. In addition to prominent party leaders, committee chairs and senators, President Bush made two stops in the state. The second one occurred on the weekend before the election and seemed to have had two effects. First, it brought some disgruntled Smith supporters back into the party fold, and second, it energized the Republican get-out-the-vote effort. The result was an insignificant write-in for Smith and a record turnout on Election Day.

ELECTION RESULTS

The 20,000-vote margin for Sununu on November 5 came as a surprise to political observers in New Hampshire and around the country and helped the Republicans secure a slim 51–49 majority in the Senate. The race had appeared so close that the threatened write-in by Smith supporters or the few thousand votes on the Libertarian line could have been decisive. Last minute polls showed the race too close to call, but they are notoriously unreliable in New Hampshire because of the state's same-day registration laws, which enable last-minute voters to participate. Throughout the precampaign and campaign season, Shaheen had trailed Sununu in the polls. In October 2001, she was down 38 percent to 50 percent, and in June 2002 she was still behind 42 percent to 51 percent.[14] When the general election campaign began in earnest, Shaheen steadily gained ground, closing to 44 percent to 47 percent in early October and pulling ahead 46 percent to 42 percent at the end of October. A final poll in the field from October 30 to November 2, had the candidates in a dead heat with 45 percent for Shaheen and 46 percent for Sununu. The difference for Shaheen appears to be the headway that she made among undeclared voters, where she led her opponent in an internal campaign poll by 15 percentage points.

In the absence of exit surveys,[15] it is difficult to tell why the race was not quite as close as the polls predicted. The race generated record turnout with fully 65 percent of registered voters casting ballots. The write-in for Smith generated only 2,396 votes, and the Libertarian candidate received an additional 9,835. Sununu could do without those supporters, however, given the surge in same-day registration. In 1998, roughly 16,000 new voters had registered on Election Day, but in 2002, the figure was 32,602—8 percent.[16] The new registrants boosted the GOP's share to 36.7 percent, just one percent shy of the total number of undeclared voters and over 10 percent more than the new low of 25.6 percent for registered Democrats. They provided the margin Sununu needed to offset the write-in and Libertarian vote. Nationally, the Republican Party had copied a strategy from the Democrats to increase turnout in key races, and in New Hampshire they had the powerful pull of local anti-tax sentiment to complement their efforts. A Zogby International poll conducted shortly after the election indicated that taxes were the number one issue on New Hampshire voters' minds.[17]

CONCLUSION

The 2002 election set the Democratic Party back a decade in the Granite State and had significant consequences for the distribution of political power in the U.S. Senate. The battle over local income taxes that decimated Democratic candidates at all levels of office already has forced the party to begin reexamining its future strategy. After such a debacle at the polls, there are no obvious political figures to lead the rebuilding effort. Governor Shaheen's reputation seems relatively intact, because political observers credit her with having run an effective campaign that very nearly succeeded against tough political odds. Neither Shaheen nor any other Democrat, however, will have as promising an opportunity to pick up a Senate seat as the one they just lost. New Hampshire's junior Senator Judd Gregg, also heir to another political dynasty, has built a strong reputation as a pragmatic conservative with a willingness to use his seat on the Senate Appropriations Committee to benefit the state.

Indeed, Gregg's Senate position poses some difficulties for the newly elected Sununu who had begun to carve out a niche for himself in the House as a fiscal expert. New Hampshire will not get two seats on appropriations, and competition is fierce for the Finance and Budget Committees. Sununu presumably extracted some promises from the party when he agreed to give up his House seat to challenge Smith, but as of mid-December, it was not clear what opportunities he would have. Whatever the outcome of the committee assignment process, Sununu's elevation to the Senate has several implications for policy making in Washington.

First, he reflects the steady transformation of the Republican Party from a strident conservatism to a soft-spoken conservatism. When Republican governors engineered the selection of George Bush as the party standard bearer, they endeavored to shift emphasis away from the "movement" conservatives who saw politics as a crusade against moral decline. Senator Smith was a vocal advocate of causes dear to the Christian right, and his successor brings none of that passion to the floor of the Senate. Sununu is as conservative as their champion Smith on most issues, but he appears to care more about rewriting the tax code than about the culture wars. Although colleagues may welcome the respite from Smith's graphic depictions of aborted fetuses, social conservatives—already restive at the perceived lack of attention from the Bush Administration to their issues—may become more alienated from their loss of voice in the Senate.

Second, his election helped to stall the realignment under way in New England away from the Republican Party. The prominence in the party of Southern conservatives has become increasingly problematic for socially progressive Republicans from the Northeast, a fact that Vermont's formerly

Republican Senator Jim Jeffords lamented when he left the GOP with such momentous consequences in 2001. A Democratic victory would have given the jittery moderate Republicans in neighboring Maine and Rhode Island powerful incentives to buck the party leadership on key votes, such as the environment, women's issues and social welfare concerns. These lawmakers still hold a pivotal position in the narrowly divided 51–49 Senate, but they have used their power only sparingly. With Sununu rather than Shaheen in the Senate, they may have even less leverage among their more conservative colleagues.

Finally, Sununu's election proved disappointing to activists pushing for an increase in the representation of women in the Senate. With the defeat of Missouri Democrat Jean Carnahan and the election of North Carolinian Republican Elizabeth Dole, the Senate tally for female members remains at thirteen. Given the lack of progress in the House and net gain of only two pickups for female governors, Shaheen's loss was particularly disappointing to women's groups.

Voters in New Hampshire were among the lucky few in the nation that had competitive campaigns for all of the state's major offices—governor, both House seats, as well as U.S. Senate. Some complained about the negative tone of these races, but for the most part, the ads, while aggressive, focused on the candidates' records and public statements rather than personal attacks. The record turnout suggests that voters will go to the polls when political parties make the effort to mobilize them and candidates deliver clear, hard-hitting messages. Although the outcome of the Senate election was critical to the balance of power in the Senate, perhaps its greater significance is in demonstrating that genuine competition still exists in the United States, if only in a tiny corner of New England.

NOTES

1. Lisa Wangsness, "Income tax, turnout hurt Democrats," *Concord Monitor*, November 7, 2002, p. 1.

2. Michael J. Barone et al., *Almanac of American Politics: 2002*. Washington, D.C.: National Journal, 2001, p. 961.

3. In the previous decade, the only elected incumbent senator to lose a primary was Illinois Democrat Alan Dixon.

4. www.FEC.gov.

5. Granite State Poll, University of New Hampshire Survey Center, www.unh.edu/survey-center.

6. *Concord Monitor*, "Editorial: Bloodless Coup?" August 13, 2002, http://www.cmonitor.com/stories/senaterace/2002/edit081302%5F2002.shtml.

7. Barone et al., pp. 966–969.

8. Jerry Miller, "First Smith-Sununu debate finds few differences," *Manchester Union Leader*, August 14, 2002, http://www.the unionleader.com/Articles_show .html?article = 13280&archive = 1.

9. David B. Magleby, ed., *Outside Money: Soft Money and Issue Advocacy in the 1998 Congressional Elections*. Lanham, Md.: Rowman & Littlefield, 2000.

10. *Valley News*, November 1, 2002, p. A7.

11. Estimates of the expenditures by independent groups are unavoidably imprecise because groups do not have to file with the Federal Election Commission. The Shaheen campaign tracked ad buys in New Hampshire, Boston, and Portland, Maine, and made its lists available to the author. The data provide a rough approximation of which groups were involved and how much they spent.

12. *Valley News*, November 1, 2002, p. A7.

13. http://www.opensecrets.org/states/summary.assp?State = NH&cycle = 2002.

14. Polls conducted by the University of New Hampshire Survey Center for the Granite State Poll, WMUR-UNH Poll and *USA Today*/CNN NH Election Poll.

15. Technical difficulties at the Voter News Service prevented the timely release of exit poll data.

16. http://www.state.nh.us/sos/general2002/namessum.htm

17. Morton M. Kondrake, "Democrats Lost Economy Issue on Election Day," *Roll Call*, November 18, 2002, p.5.

11

North Carolina Senate

Dole Finally Beats Clinton (Sort Of)

RYAN THORNBURG

washingtonpost.com

AN OPEN AND SHUT CASE

The Senate seat of Republican Jesse Helms has been one of the most sought after—and most elusive—prizes of North Carolina Democrats for 30 years. Helms was first elected in 1972, the first Republican to win the office since Reconstruction. With his revolutionary and legendary direct mail fundraising efforts, he held on to the seat through some of the nastiest and most expensive Senate races—always with less than 55 percent of the vote. His failing health and an evenly divided Senate made his seat a Democratic target from the first hours of the 2002 election cycle.

In August 2001, Helms confirmed rumors that he would not seek reelection. For the first time since Sam Ervin retired in 1974, North Carolina would have a Senate race with no incumbent. Although Republicans were winning at other levels in the state, Democrats were fresh off two encouraging victories. In 2000, they kept the governor's office in Democratic hands after four-term governor James B. Hunt retired. Two years before that, political novice John Edwards had unseated Republican Senator Lauch Faircloth. Without the advantage of incumbency, the Helms Senate seat appeared within reach for Democrats.

For the fifth straight time, however, Republicans ended up dashing

Democratic hopes, and kept the Helms seat on their side of the aisle. As part of a White House–led national effort to retake control of the Senate, Republicans recruited Elizabeth Dole to run in her native state. Democrats, too, fielded a candidate with Tar Heel roots and Washington experience— Erskine Bowles, a former chief of staff in the Clinton White House. Although Bowles received more votes in his losing effort than Edwards did in his 1998 win, Dole's popularity, Republican discipline, and an unusually long, contested Democratic primary propelled her to victory in the state's most lopsided Senate race in nearly a quarter century.

THE PRIMARIES: THE ROCK STAR
AND THE RICH KID

The 2002 Senate race began early and ended late. Helms' age and declining health prompted candidates on both sides to begin planning their campaigns in December 2000. Court battles over the state's legislative redistricting plans forced the scheduled May 2002 primary to be delayed until September. Although Bowles and Dole appeared to be the odds-on favorites to win their parties' nominations, the primary landscape was so unusual and so uncertain that there were plenty of opportunities for both of them to lose their footing along the way.

Helms' retirement announcement came on August 22 and was celebrated in grand style. He was given live television time on Raleigh's CBS affiliate, WRAL, where Helms got his political start as a conservative commentator. Following the 6 p.m. statement was an hour-long special on Helms' career and interviews with some of his potential successors. Dole made no comment, but the next day she notified the state of Kansas that she would be switching her voter registration to her childhood home of Salisbury, North Carolina. The kickoff to Dole's campaign was scheduled for her hometown on September 11, 2001.

The Dole candidacy and the terrorist attacks quickly sucked all the air out of the race. With the help of circumstance and party leaders, Dole began to clear a path to the nomination. She was the party's "rock star" candidate, as she was often described by newspaper reporters covering her campaign stops. At almost every appearance, Dole's celebrity status brought out crowds of supporters and local reporters to describe her charm and the positive reception. On November 6, two-time gubernatorial candidate Richard Vinroot was the last of Dole's substantial primary opposition to step aside. Four weeks later, the Republican National Committee sent Vinroot a check for $200,000 to help retire his earlier campaign debts.

Dole started the race with 93 percent name recognition and a trove of acknowledgments as one of the most popular and admired women in America. She was the endorsed candidate of Helms and President George W. Bush. Perhaps as daunting as Dole's popularity was her experience. She had been president of the American Red Cross, secretary of the U.S. Departments of Labor and Transportation, and had three advanced degrees from Harvard.

But Dole had also run a presidential campaign in 2000 that was often described as overly scripted and that failed to meet many people's expectations. She also couldn't avoid the obvious comparisons to Hillary Clinton as a political wife who was talented in her own right and ran for the Senate in a state where she didn't live. Dole's opposition to abortion was too soft for some of the state's Christian conservatives. Her support of a ban on assault weapons and mandatory child trigger locks during the 2000 presidential campaign had alienated her from the National Rifle Association.

With Dole's path clear of substantial challengers, she spent the first five months of her campaign making stops in each of the state's 100 counties. But her enthusiastic receptions were only half of the story during the Republican primary. The other, which was more prominent in the larger media markets, was that Dole was running a cautious campaign. Reporters complained that Dole was inaccessible. She rarely granted one-on-one interviews and made no scheduled campaign appearances with the few minor Republican challengers who continued to dog her from the right.

While Dole was able to run as the de facto incumbent through most of the summer, Democrats struggled to find a nominee to challenge her. Before Helms announced his retirement, several top-tier Democratic candidates had publicly declared their intentions not to run. Even Bowles initially demurred from the campaign, after showing initial interest. (He eventually joined the race in October 2001, citing a post–September 11 call to civic duty.) In March 2002, the State Board of Election postponed indefinitely the May 7 primary. For Bowles, the early frontrunner, a delayed primary meant that he would have even less time to chip away at Dole's popularity.

It also meant he would have to endure more than nine months of criticism from his two most prominent Democratic opponents—state representative Dan Blue and Secretary of State Elaine Marshall. In 1991, Blue had become the South's first African American leader of a state legislative chamber since Reconstruction. But following the GOP takeover of the state House, he had angered the party's white leadership and continued to be a thorn in their side. Marshall had defeated NASCAR legend Richard Petty in 1996 to ascend to her office from a short career in the legislature.

The son of 1972 Democratic gubernatorial candidate Harlan "Skipper" Bowles, Erskine was well connected to all elements of the state's leadership. Bowles, however, was no rock star. His name recognition was less than

50 percent, and much of his fame was owed to his dubious association with Clinton—not a popular figure in North Carolina.

Like Dole, Bowles had roots in North Carolina but had made his career outside the state. He was an investment banker who worked in Charlotte and New York, the former head of the Small Business Administration and chief of staff to President Clinton. He owned part of the NFL's Carolina Panthers and had sat on the boards of Merck and First Union, among other companies. His wife, Crandall Bowles, is the CEO of her family's Spring Industries textile company. According to his disclosure statement, he and Crandall have assets worth between $26 million and $67 million. Writing about Bowles shortly after he reentered the campaign in October 2001, *The News & Observer* of Raleigh described him as "the new rich kid in the neighborhood."

In a campaign year during which Democrats pinned their early hopes on their ability to draw connections between Republican policies and corrupt big business, Bowles was perhaps more connected to Wall Street than any other Democratic Senate candidate in the nation. In an effort to illustrate his ability to work across party lines, Bowles featured in his first television ad a picture of himself with Senate Republican leader Trent Lott—and not President Clinton.

Bowles was criticized from the left during the primary. Blue railed against Bowles at every turn—for being too closely tied to the pharmaceutical industry, for aligning himself with a national group that supported school vouchers, for his former memberships in exclusive dining and sporting clubs, and for his support of NAFTA that had cost North Carolina jobs. Bowles did earn the AFL-CIO's endorsement in the primary, dealing a blow to Blue and Marshall's attempts to paint him as a foe of North Carolina workers. But the state teachers' union endorsed Blue in the primary and refused to back Bowles in the general election.

It wasn't until late July that the eventual September 10 primary date was set. This schedule didn't allow enough time for the state's customary primary runoff to be held between September 10 and the general election, so it was cancelled. The primary runoff is a relic of the state's racist past, created as extra insurance that African Americans wouldn't unite behind a single candidate and defeat a slate of white candidates who would split the white vote. A primary runoff must be held if no candidate receives at least 40 percent of the ballots. With African Americans comprising between 22 and 30 percent of the Democratic primary vote, it appeared as if Blue's chances improved with the decision to forego the runoff.

As it turned out, Bowles received 43 percent of the primary vote and would have won the nomination outright in any circumstance. Blue won 28 percent of the vote, and Marshall received 15 percent.

Dole walked to victory in the Republican primary with 80 percent of the vote. She entered the general election campaign with nearly a million dollars more than Bowles had in the bank and with a 49 percent to 35 percent lead in a Mason-Dixon poll of likely voters.

THE GENERAL ELECTION: DON'T BRING ME DOWN

The general election hinged on whether Democrats would be able to thread the needle of negativity. They needed to attack Dole enough that she would appear to be just another politician rather than the third most admired woman in the world, as a 1998 Gallup poll had dubbed her. At the same time, Dole was so popular that Democrats feared a backlash of sympathy if they attacked her too much.

Democrats began their attack on Dole in January, with an ad tying her to the Enron accounting scandal. Republicans responded with an ad that said Democrats were trying to divide the nation at a time when it needed to be united. An Elon University poll in early February showed that 52 percent of adults had seen the Democrats' ad, but only 13 percent had a more negative view of Dole as a result. A further indication that it wasn't successful: it was the only television ad criticizing Dole that Democrats aired until September.

North Carolina media outlets hired the Mason-Dixon polling firm to test public opinion throughout the general election. In its first poll after the primary, conducted September 12 to September 14, Dole enjoyed a 56 percent favorable rating and a 12 percent unfavorable rating. Thirty-nine percent of North Carolinians viewed Bowles favorably, while 19 percent viewed him unfavorably. His name recognition had risen to 87 percent, but it still trailed Dole's 99 percent recognition rate. She led the horserace poll, 49 percent to 35 percent.

The North Carolina Democratic Party began its post-primary criticism of Dole by following the national Democratic strategy of attacking Republicans on Social Security. While the Democratic Party was forced to change the content of the ad—twice—Dole spent the first days after the primary promoting her "Dole Plan" for North Carolina. She also proposed that both sides pool their money to air a series of televised debates, rather than spend their money on television ads. With this two-headed strategy she deftly answered criticism that her popularity was based on personality more than concrete ideas. The debate proposal was one to which Bowles could have had no winning answer. If he declined, he would have been criticized as a candidate who would rather run attack ads than debate the issues. If he accepted he would have removed from his arsenal the best tool he had for increasing negative opinion of Dole.

Bowles and Dole eventually agreed to two debates. The first was taped in secret at Meredith College in Raleigh, and later released to the state's television stations. The second debate was aired live in front of an audience from East Carolina University, and was a bit livelier. Dole and Bowles walked out from behind their podiums to echo the criticisms that were being aired in television ads.

The second debate aired on October 19, just as the tone of the television ads were getting more negative. The National Republican Senatorial Committee was running an ad criticizing Bowles for being named as a defendant in a Connecticut lawsuit against investment firm Forstmann Little. The company had lost $100 million of a state pension fund while Bowles was a general partner. In ads, Bowles criticized Dole for being part of the Reagan administration and "the largest tax increase in history." If Democrats appeared to raise Dole's ire the most with their Social Security criticisms, then Dole appeared equally able to get under Bowles's skin with an ad criticizing his wife's company for sending North Carolina jobs to Mexico.

Polls throughout the campaign indicated that a substantial majority believed the political ads in the state were mostly negative. However, by North Carolina standards these ads were pretty tame.

Even though the race was the most expensive in the country, it was also cheap by North Carolina standards. When adjusted for inflation, the $20.6 million spent by the Bowles and Dole campaigns through mid-October was only the fifth highest tab for a U.S. Senate race in North Carolina. Dole, who raised more money than any other Senate candidate in the country in 2002, spent far less than Helms did in any of his reelection efforts.

Including the more than $4 million dollars that Bowles contributed to his own campaign, he raised more money than all but three U.S. Senate candidates in 2002. He also raised more money than all but two other Democratic Senate candidates had ever raised in North Carolina.

According to the Center for Responsive Politics, 45 percent of Dole's regulated contributions of more than $200 came from outside North Carolina. Bowles raised 33 percent of his money from outside the state. Through mid-October, Dole had raised nearly $12 million, while Bowles had raised $5.8 million in addition to the money he kicked in.

In late October, polls showed the race tightening. The percentage of North Carolinians who had an unfavorable impression of Dole had risen, but so had the percentage of people who had a negative impression of Bowles.

With the race tightening as both sides had expected, Dole aired a positive ad featuring an image of President Bush. Bush arrived to stump with her in Charlotte three days later on October 24. It was the sixth and final campaign stop that Bush made in North Carolina in 2002. On October 29, Vice President Cheney made his second stop in the state for Dole. President Clinton made no similar appearances for Bowles.

The final Mason-Dixon poll, conducted on October 28 and October 29, showed Dole leading a six-point race, with 10 percent undecided. The percentage of North Carolinians who saw Dole in an unfavorable light had nearly doubled since the primary. But more people had a negative impression of Bowles, and his favorability rating hadn't budged.

Although polls showed the election closing to within striking distance for Bowles, a surge in turnout carried Dole to the widest winning margin of any Senate candidate from North Carolina since 1978. About 320,000 more voters cast ballots in the 2002 Senate race than in the 1998 Edwards-Faircloth race. Bowles received nearly 20,000 more votes than Edwards received in his 1998 victory. The percentage of registered voters who cast ballots increased in almost every county, regardless of the county's partisan or racial composition. However, some of this increase may be attributed to a decrease in registration following a cleaning of the voter rolls in 2001.

Dole won across most geographic and demographic lines. Although Democratic support of Bowles increased at the end of the campaign, it was much weaker than Democratic support for Edwards in 1998. Over the course of the campaign, he was able to win back much of the female vote that started in the Dole column, but he also lost support among independents at the end of the campaign. Bowles was able to more than double Dole's unfavorability rating, from 12 percent to 28 percent, but he suffered from lower name recognition, much lower favorables and slightly higher unfavorables than Dole.

CONCLUSION

Despite the initial misgivings of some Republicans to have Dole carry the mantle for North Carolina Republicans, the party united behind her as the candidate most likely to keep Jesse Helms's seat in the Republican column. Dole was the de facto incumbent for the state's first open Senate seat in 30 years—more like Frank Lautenberg in 2002 than Hillary Clinton in 2000.

Dole helped the party by raising money for legislative candidates and by boosting Republican-tilting turnout. Despite the Democratic advantage in voter registration, North Carolina Republicans were able to pass the torch from a candidate who had his roots in the state's conservative Democratic, rural politics of the 1950s to a candidate whose story has its roots in a struggle for gender equality, who was educated at Harvard, and who—like many of North Carolina's people—did not live in the state ten years ago. Assuming that President Bush and Senator Dole remain popular figures in North Carolina, their presence at the top of the ticket could energize Republican voters in 2004.

The next election cycle will also be the first indication of whether Dole's victory can be attributed to her unique personal popularity, to the disciplined strategy of the Republican Party or to a true shift in partisan preferences among new North Carolina voters who may be more comfortable with a Dole Republican than a Helms Republican.

12

South Dakota Senate

George Bush vs. Tom Daschle, Once Removed

DAVID KRANZ
Sioux Falls Argus Leader

THE HARDER ROAD

In the last quarter century South Dakota started getting used to national political attention. A combination of Senator George McGovern's opposition to the Vietnam War, his quest for the presidency, and Senator Tom Daschle's assent to Senate Majority Leader raised the notoriety to a level far greater than most small states are accustomed to.

Then came the 2002 elections. Democratic Senator Tim Johnson and Republican Representative John Thune would wage a battle key to control of the U.S. Senate.

But this race would not just be viewed for its role in determining balance of power. The national news media billed it early as a surrogate race between President George W. Bush and Daschle—the nation's most powerful elected Republican and Democrat officials.

Johnson and Thune didn't like the implication much. Both were quick to remind people that they welcomed help from the powerful leaders of their party, but they wanted to win the race on their own.

Late in the campaign Daschle weighed in on the characterization of his role in the race. "I think it demeans both candidacies, minimizes the candidates on both sides, and that is unfortunate," Daschle said. "People know

Tim Johnson. They know John Thune. And they are going to vote for them for their abilities, for their records."

A Johnson-Thune match-up was anticipated two years before the election, but it took awhile to unfold. At one point early in 2001 the anticipated match-up began to unravel. Some of Thune's closest allies wanted him to run for governor and eventually the pressure went well beyond his friends.

When it comes to the governorship, Republicans own South Dakota. Only five men in the state's 113-year history were not Republican. Four Democrats and one Populist held that job.

Holding that job is the ultimate power position here where the state is defined, jobs are handed out, and money can be raised for the party.

Key Republicans thought a Thune-for-governor campaign was the silver bullet needed to keep the domination. Thune downplayed on his Senate aspirations and agreed to form an exploratory committee for governor. Within a few weeks $500,000 was raised for the cause and the gubernatorial campaign seemed closer to a reality. Most who knew Thune well did not think he really wanted to be governor, but this was a way to keep Republican powerbrokers content until the inevitable happened.

And it did.

A call came from the White House. The president invited Thune and his wife, Kimberley, to the White House on April 9, 2001, to dine with him, his wife Laura and his mother-in-law.

At the end of the evening no deals were made.

"It doesn't change where I am at other than to make me more keenly aware of how badly I want to see this president succeed," Thune said after the meeting. "He knew I have a strong interest in running for governor, and we talked a lot about being governor. But he also made it clear what he wanted me to do, run for Senate."

Thune's options were limited since he already term-limited himself in the House before he got there, making a primary campaign promise of six years and out. The guessing games strung out, but it gradually became clear that he would abandon the exploratory committee and accept Bush's request.

Johnson's campaign could read the writing on the wall and quickly responded to the hint. Steve Hildebrand, who managed Vice President Al Gore's Iowa caucus victory in 2000, had been tapped to run the Johnson operation.

He told a Minnehaha County Democratic Forum in Sioux Falls the following Friday that Thune looked like he was planning to "do what was best for Washington, not what was best for South Dakota."

Thune still lingered publicly with his decision, waiting until mid-September before telling it to a flag-waving crowd in Jones County gym where he starred as a basketball player. Responding to anticipated criticism that he was passing up a sure-bet governor's race, he said, "This is not the time to shrink from our duties or to choose the easy path. I have chosen the harder road."

And he told the crowd about the strength he would bring to the state.

"These times are without precedent in our nation's history. Consider this: Tom Daschle leading the Democrats in the Senate and John Thune working with him and with the Republican leadership in Congress and with President Bush. South Dakota would be better positioned than ever before at the federal level."

That became his argument for the rest of the campaign even as Democrats and some Republicans cautioned about the dangers of taking away from South Dakota the position of power that Daschle held. Thune also tried to shift thoughts away from the idea that the president was his only influence in the decision.

"A lot has been made of the president's influence, but I did not make my decision on his influence alone," Thune said.

THE PRELIMINARY CAMPAIGN

Johnson's entry was a matter of saying out loud what everyone already knew. He would run for a second term. The delayed official announcement caused some Thune campaign staffers to fire up the rumor mill, suggesting that Johnson was contemplating a bid for governor.

The much-heralded race finally became a reality in February when Johnson returned with his family to their Vermillion home and announced for a second term. The lawyer and former state senator had already served five terms in the U.S. House and was completing his first term in the Senate. He won that seat in 1996, the only Democrat that year to defeat an incumbent Republican, three-term Senator Larry Pressler. Johnson has never been a flashy campaigner, but he prided himself in hard work and an understanding of the issues.

Stressing his value and work as a member of the Appropriations Committee was essential in his dialogue. And he included his standard line: What a great team he and Daschle as majority leader will continue to make for the state. Early on he painted Thune as the one who was at fault for negative television commercials, an issue that grew in significance as the campaign progressed.

"I'm not going to get down in the gutter with John in these ads. I'm disappointed by that, but all I can do is control what I can control," Johnson said.

He framed his issues: Social Security, lower cost of prescription drugs for seniors, veterans' benefits, agriculture. As most politicians do, Johnson read polls. South Dakotans would respond to those surveys saying they weren't quite sure what Johnson's successes were on the Appropriations Committee.

Johnson wasn't one for ranting and raving about political successes, but he knew he had to face voter perception. So he began a statewide tour in the spring of 2002 with Daschle at his side. It would be one of only a few joint appearances in this "do it by myself" campaign. They made the most of their time together, hitting communities where Johnson scored successes.

Daschle brought the humor with the team to the campus of South Dakota State University. "How many people heard them say, 'Join our party' and came here thinking it would be a kegger?" Daschle asked.

Johnson trumpeted his education success, telling students about a bill he authored to ease the burden of student loans. The punch line: President Bush had just signed it into law. The trip was designed to talk about the nursing reinvestment act, getting computers for school systems, helping the Milbank community save their hospital.

"South Dakota senators have never been in a better position to deliver on South Dakota priorities, South Dakota values," Johnson would say.

Personal contact is still the way South Dakotans like to hear from their politicians, but this campaign would be fought on television and in the mailboxes. Even though Thune often said he was running this race based on his skills, not the president's, Bush figured prominently in the campaign. The follow-up to one of his visits brought a well-done Thune-for-Senate television spot showcasing him with the president. An impressive newspaper also arrived. Johnson's campaign quickly gathered a focus group of undecided voters to view one of the coattail ads.

To their satisfaction they found that the vast majority of the participants saw the Bush-Thune TV ad suggesting that the congressman depended on the president and possibly he would be only a rubber stamp for Bush's policies.

Some 21,000 ads were run, driving up the cost of a campaign in a usually cheap state. It also helped make this the most expensive in the state's history.

An estimated $6 million to $7 million will have been spent by each candidate when the numbers are added and third-party advertisers will have spent about $7 million on each candidate. Previously, the 1996 race between Johnson and Senator Larry Pressler topped all races with $4.5 million spent by Pressler and $3.2 million by Johnson.

The television ads were oftentimes the subject of voter wrath. Early on the League of Conservation Voters upset Thune by suggesting in a television ad campaign that Thune opposed measures that would reduce the level of arsenic in water. That made Thune mad and he often began speeches by holding up a glass of water to jokingly check it for arsenic.

The ad that infuriated Johnson was one paid for by the Thune campaign shortly after the first anniversary of the September 11, 2001, terrorist attacks. It only ran in the western part of the state. It showed a picture of Saddam Hussein and talked about military preparedness. Several Johnson votes against a missile defense system were cited.

THE STAGE IS SET

Johnson argued that Thune was questioning his patriotism. He also became part of a surrogate blitz by former President Bush and Mary Matalin, a current White House aide, questioning Johnson's judgment about opposition to the 1991 Gulf War and his alignment with 58 other U.S. House members to file suit against former President Bush to determine if he could declare war without consent of Congress.

Thune said in an ad: "It is not a South Dakota value to sue the President of the United States."

Johnson saw this as an orchestrated effort to question his patriotism. So once again he reminded voters through a television ad that his son, Brooks, was a member of the 101st Airborne. He reiterated how he voted for this president's resolution of force against Iraq knowing his son may be put in harms way.

Support came from Mark Shields, a national columnist and member of CNN's "Capital Gang," who told readers and listeners on several occasions that Johnson was the only senator with a son in the military and eligible to fight in any conflict.

GUN CONTROL

The gun issue also had some explosive moments in the campaign. National Rifle Association (NRA) officials came to Sioux Falls to proclaim Thune as their candidate. A visit in mid-October from Charlton Heston, president of the National Rifle Association, rallied support for Thune. The suggestion was that Johnson was anti-gun and they were giving him a "C" for his voting.

Johnson's campaign countered with television ads and press conferences by Tony Dean, a respected outdoorsman who said the NRA had the wrong idea about Johnson.

Dean's television ads were forceful, saying gun ownership is important, but so is conservation. He also took to the Internet with his newsletter, criticizing the NRA's position on Johnson.

"I didn't understand the vehemence that those influenced by the NRA and their view on gun rights would carry into this race. I assumed that most gun owners are also sportsmen and that habitat and conservation issues would also matter to them. I was wrong about that group. I've concluded that for them, guns are the only things that matter," Dean wrote.

PRESIDENTIAL SUPPORT

When Bush promised support for Thune's candidacy he meant business. During the campaign cycle he made five trips to South Dakota, setting an all-time record for presidential visits to the state. Some were billed as policy, others were purely political, but all showcased Thune.

The first was in March 2001 before Thune's announcement, but considered a mission of encouragement as well as a successful effort encouraging Johnson to back his tax cut. He returned the next year with rallies in April, August, October and November.

A final analysis of Thune's defeat caused some supporters and critics to revisit the August 15 speech designed to highlight Homeland Security at Mount Rushmore. State ranchers and farmers were struggling with the drought and this would certainly be an opportunity for Bush to give Thune the boost he needed, going outside of the new farm bill to provide much-needed aid.

That didn't happen. Bush said the assistance would have to come from within the farm bill. It sent the Thune campaign rushing on two fronts: find a way to show the people the president did care about them and convince them that he does have influence with the president.

On that last trip on November 3, while critics were suggesting too many presidential visits were taking away from time needed for the workers to prepare a successful get-out-the-vote campaign, Thune gave a poignant thank you speech to the president for keeping a promise and standing with him until the end.

But it wasn't just the president. Several cabinet members, including Secretary of Agriculture Ann Veneman, Secretary of Interior Gale Norton, and Secretary of Education Rod Paige, visited the state on "official" visits.

Karl Rove, the president's top adviser, showed up for a fundraiser. Vice President Dick Cheney arrived during the home stretch for a Rapid City rally. His wife Lynne came to Sioux Falls. Laura Bush made a three-city tour in November. Congressman J. C. Watts (R-OK) and former New York Mayor Rudy Giuliani came to drum up Thune support.

It caused one member of the national media to wonder of Thune as he watched him on stage with the president: "Doesn't he ever campaign alone?"

While stars were shining on Thune, his opponent was doing just the opposite, keeping his distance from big-name Democrats like former President Bill Clinton, Senator Hillary Clinton (NY), Senator Ted Kennedy (MA), all names that would tie Johnson to a liberal label.

It wasn't anything new for Johnson. He didn't ask President Clinton to campaign in the state in 1996 during his close race with Pressler. But the president came in anyway on his own behalf, making South Dakota his last stop on election eve, the last of his political career. Instead Johnson banked on a low-key visit by Senator Daniel Inouye (HI) and a key visit to charge up veterans by former Senator Bob Kerrey (NE). Massachusetts Senator John Kerry and New Jersey Senator Jon Corzine showed up for an early fundraising visit and former Clinton operative James Carville hosted Johnson at a Washington, D.C. event.

Senator James Jeffords (VT), whose change from Republican to Independent shifted the balance of the Senate, was considered a safe invite, but his trip was grounded by airline problems. He never rescheduled.

While Bush was drawing packed houses down the stretch, Johnson preferred campaigning with Daschle. Even with the senior senator at his side, the events were low-key, usually a pep rally for workers or a parking lot speech before they went door-to-door looking to influence undecided voters.

ADVERTISING

Television ads still played a key role as the race neared an end. Politicians try to balance their message in accordance to what is publicly acceptable. That became an increasingly sensitive issue in the last week of the campaign. Johnson knew studies showed negative advertising worked, so he offered an olive branch to Thune during a television debate. Stop all unflattering advertising from here on.

Thune balked and continued running what he called "information" spots critical of Johnson. This came at a time when news of possible voter fraud was filtering through voters' minds.

Allegations surfaced that the state Democratic Party was involved in an effort to pay contract employees to secure registrations and absentee ballot applications on the reservations. Republican officials investigating the case pointed to one woman from Flandreau and one man from Rapid City. The woman was working as a contract employee with Democrats at the time, but the state attorney general, a Republican, would not concur with other party leaders that this was a "massive problem."

Thune took the opportunity during the debate to tell Johnson he would agree to go completely positive in the ad campaign if Johnson would "come clean" about his role in the vote fraud. Johnson reiterated again that he had no part in it. So the Thune ads continued, including one running exclusively in the western part of the state.

In part it said: "Tim Johnson sided with the environmentalists who threaten lawsuits to stop any timber clearing. John Thune's been a leader for West River, working to remove dead timber from the Hills. When we needed help, John Thune stood with us in West River." It was Thune's closing argument to the voters, summarizing his case against Johnson throughout the campaign.

Both finished with direct mail blitzes. Johnson reminded voters of the areas where polls showed he was strong. Thune got support from the state Republican Party and the state Right to Life Party, contrasting in at least 15 separate mailings the positions on abortion and cloning.

ELECTION DAY

As most national politicos predicted, the Johnson-Thune race would be the closest in the nation. It was even tighter than polls predicted. Most of those independent readings kept the margin in the range between a dead heat and three points for the duration.

The apparent winner wasn't determined until 5 a.m. the next day after Clark, Davison, Hamlin, and Shannon counties reported in.

Johnson was ahead by 528 votes, but Thune did not concede, waiting for a canvass of votes the following Friday. That showed Johnson winning by a 524-vote margin. The close vote produced allegations about the lateness of Shannon County on the reservation, reigniting the possibility that voter fraud had something to do with the results.

When Thune conceded, he hinted again that there may have been some irregularities in the count; yet he decided not to seek a recount or contest the election, concluding, "It's not helpful."

Yet Barnett continued to stand by his position. Three weeks after the vote he stood by his statement that no tainted votes were known to be cast. In the end, only the South Dakota race was a genuine match-up where the stakes involved Bush and Daschle.

Daschle won.

Johnson is now preparing to serve in the 108th Congress, still on the Appropriations Committee, but also as a member of the minority party. An irony in the results is that a large number of Republicans voted with Johnson, more than enough to reelect him. Many were supportive of the idea that a vote for Johnson meant a vote to keep Daschle as majority leader. Others were not happy with Thune's work on drought relief and position on veterans issues.

With the 2002 South Dakota Senate race decided, voters now have had a good night's sleep and are ready to debate Daschle's future in 2004.

13

Tennessee Senate

The Resurrection of Lamar Alexander

JAMES W. BROSNAN
The Memphis Commercial Appeal

When Senator Bill Frist, chairman of the National Republican Senatorial Committee, surveyed his home state of Tennessee in the summer of 2001 he was like a college basketball coach uncertain whether his star center would return for the next season or go pro.

Senator Fred Thompson, the hulking movie actor and lawyer of Watergate committee fame, was the most popular politician in the state despite occasional grumbles from conservatives about his tendency to go off the reservation on issues like campaign finance reform.

In 1994 he swept aside a rising Democratic star, Congressman Jim Cooper, by a 60–40 margin to win the last two years of the term of Vice President Al Gore. He duplicated the margin in 1996 against Houston Gordon for a full term. The speculation on the Democratic side was who would be the sacrificial lamb to take Thompson on in 2002.

But Thompson was indicating to Frist that he might not run. Even though he would only turn 59 that summer, an age at which some begin their Senate careers, Thompson was restless.

As a character actor, Thompson had found he could make lots of money for little work and still leave time for lobbying and an active social life as a much-in-demand bachelor. He came to the Senate as a reformer, determined to push issues like term limits, two-year budgets and reforms of government procurement and personnel rules.

But his colleagues' appetite for reform did not match Thompson's zeal and the Senate's willingness to spend endless days and long nights on mundane matters did not match his mood or lifestyle.

His campaign finance investigation was short-circuited by partisanship and time limits. As a member of the Intelligence Committee he was increasingly drawn to foreign policy and defense issues like nuclear weapons proliferation.

He wondered whether he could not contribute on a part-time basis on the outside while still maximizing his income as an actor and speechmaker. He chafed at having to turn down the role of a commander of a Navy diving school in "Men of Honor." (Hal Holbrook got the part.)

Politically Thompson had decided against running for president in 2000 and wasn't close enough to the Bush family to be in the running for vice president. Many Republicans back home wanted Thompson to run for governor—but the state's finances were in a mess and the incumbent, Republican Don Sundquist, was becoming an outcast in his own party for pushing an income tax. With Thompson uncertain, Frist quietly began recruiting a replacement.

There was plenty of interest. Three of Tennessee's five Republican congressmen had displayed statewide ambition—Ed Bryant, Van Hilleary and Zach Wamp. But when Republicans commissioned pollster Whit Ayres to survey Tennesseans that June the name that jumped to the top was that of former Governor Lamar Alexander.

Alexander had not held elected office since his last days as governor in January 1987. He had not been in public office since a two-year stint as education secretary to President George H. Bush ended with Bush's defeat by Bill Clinton in 1992.

Alexander had twice run for president and failed. He was lampooned by the press in 1995–96 for wearing his trademark red-plaid shirt at his announcement, but Alexander had nearly beat out Bob Dole for second place behind Pat Buchanan in the New Hampshire primary.

His run for the 2000 nomination went badly, however. Tennesseans who had contributed $5.6 million to launch his 1996 campaign had coughed up only $1.6 million by the summer of 1999. Texas Governor George W. Bush had captured Alexander's moderate support, including some inside the state, with his call for "compassionate conservatism," which Alexander called "weasel words" in a vain attempt to outflank Bush to the right.

When Alexander finished an embarrassing sixth in an Iowa straw poll on August 14, 1999, he pulled out of the race two days later, declaring, "This has been my last campaign for public office."[1]

Since then Alexander had concentrated on numerous business interests and teaching government courses at Harvard. As governor, he had refused entreaties to run against Gore for the Senate in 1984 and repeatedly offered the view that his executive temperament was not suited to the Senate, even though he had started his political career there as an aide to Howard Baker.

But Alexander was intrigued by the Ayres poll. It showed that Alexander was known by 93 percent of Tennessee voters, was viewed favorably by 66 percent and was viewed unfavorably by 16 percent. The ratings were only a few points below the ratings for Thompson and Frist.[2]

No matter how Alexander was viewed nationally at home he was still the man who walked across the state and was sworn in early to oust "Pardon Me" Ray Blanton before he could commute the sentences of any more murderers in the clemency-for-cash scandal. (Blanton would later serve federal prison time for scheming to award state liquor store licenses to cronies.)

Alexander had recruited two auto plants—Nissan and Saturn—to Tennessee and led the state and the National Governors Association in pursuing education reforms.

But September 11, 2001, seemed to make the poll moot.

Thirteen days later Thompson announced he would seek reelection after all.

"I simply don't think I would have been very happy off somewhere enjoying life, picking up the paper and seeing these things, what other people were doing, the changes in our country, the dangers, and knowing that I walked away from an opportunity to have an impact," said Thompson.[3]

But a personal tragedy would cause Thompson to change his mind again. On January 30, 2002, his 38-year-old daughter, Elizabeth Panici, died of what a medical examiner later declared was an accidental overdose of the painkiller hydrocodone. On March 8, Thompson told President Bush and colleagues he would not run after all.

"You know life takes us on twists and turns and for me it has resulted in me just not having the heart to run another campaign and serve another six years in Washington," said Thompson.[4]

Thompson's decision transformed Tennessee from a political backwater in the contest for control of the Senate to a battleground state. And it would be a sprint. The August 1 primary was four months away, and early voting began July 12. But Frist's recruiting efforts in 2001 had paid off.

Alexander said September 11 had changed his mind about not running for office again. Alexander said he faced a choice between teaching about government at Harvard or being involved in the process.

"I thought this was time when if you have an opportunity to serve you should. My experience gives me the best chance of any Republican to hold the seat," said Alexander.[5]

But Alexander was not the first Republican in the race. One day after

Thompson's announcement, Bryant said he would oppose Alexander. Bryant, 54, was only eight years younger than Alexander, 62, but he represented a different strain of Tennessee Republicans.

Alexander was born in Maryville, the heart of East Tennessee, a section of the state that had been loyal to Republicans ever since it sided with the Union in the Civil War. The son of a school principal and a teacher, Alexander's Republicanism was as much a part of his upbringing as the Presbyterian Church.

Bryant was born and raised in Jackson, the center of agrarian West Tennessee. Historically, West Tennessee elected Democrats, but it was the first section of the state to go right when Democrats went left, to Alabama Governor George Wallace first and then Republican presidential candidates.

But in the Bryant household there wasn't much talk of politics. His father was an electrician; his mother a nurse. He was inspired to be a lawyer by watching "Perry Mason" and "The Defenders." After six years as an army lawyer, he moved back to Jackson and joined a law firm that he found out later had strong ties to the Republican Party.

He also joined a church affiliated with the conservative Presbyterian Church in America, which split from other Presbyterians over issues like the inerrancy of Biblical Scripture and ordination of women. Bryant and his wife led a Bible study in their homes for married couples.

After several stints as a Republican campaign worker, Bryant lost a race against Representative John Tanner (D-TN) in 1988. The next year President Bush named him U. S. Attorney for West Tennessee, replacing Hickman Ewing, later a deputy in Ken Starr's Whitewater investigation team.

Bryant inherited the prosecution of Congressman Harold Ford Sr. on bank fraud charges. After the first trial ended in a hung jury in Memphis, prosecutors arranged to have the jury for the second trial picked from a pool in West Tennessee, but in 1993 the Justice Department, under pressure from the Congressional Black Caucus, ordered Bryant to ask for a Memphis jury. He refused and resigned. (The judge also wouldn't go along, but the West Tennessee jury found Ford not guilty anyway.)

The publicity helped Bryant win the congressional seat vacated by Sundquist. In eight years in the House his only national attention came as a member of the Clinton impeachment team. He deposed Monica Lewinsky, with little success at getting her to attack Clinton.

In 2001, Bryant had stockpiled more than $500,000 in his House campaign fund anticipating a Thompson retirement and he wasn't about to let Alexander or Frist or White House pressure keep him out of the race.

While the Republican field was set in three days, a slightly longer drama played out on the Democratic side. The four Democratic congressmen—Tanner, Bart Gordon, Bob Clement and Harold Ford Jr.—all said they would consider the race, but it was the youngest who talked loudest at first. Ford, 32, was a rising national star, boosted by his keynote speech at the Democratic National Convention. He hungered to find out if an African American could cut across the racial divide to be elected senator in Tennessee and had toyed with running against Frist two years before.

But African Americans made up only 14 percent of Tennessee's electorate and the Ford name was controversial not only because of the congressman's father, but his uncle, sharp-tongued state senator John Ford, who was embroiled in controversies ranging from speeding tickets to lobbying to ease regulations on cronies in the daycare business.

One day after Alexander announced, the three other Democrats met privately in Washington, and armed with some polling from the Democratic Senatorial Campaign Committee, persuaded Ford to give way to Clement.

Clement, 59, also was the son of a famous Tennessee politician, Governor Frank Clement, and like Ford, got an early start in politics with election to the Tennessee Public Service Commission at age 29. But his record afterwards was mixed.

He lost a primary race for governor to Jake Butcher in 1978 and four years later lost a general election battle to Sundquist for a congressional seat that ran from the Nashville to Memphis suburbs. He settled in Nashville and won a safe Democratic seat in 1988. He kept eyeing races for governor, but in May 2001 concluded he couldn't match the wallet of Nashville businessman and former mayor Phil Bredesen, the 1998 nominee.

But while the congressmen were settling on Clement, a new name came in from left field—Tipper Gore, the wife of the former vice president.

Although the idea began with a former staffer, and was not taken seriously by Gore at first, she began getting calls from senators and other Washington insiders urging her to run. As a name, money would not be a problem. Her husband even shaved his beard as a sign of support. But it would complicate another Gore run for the White House. Tipper Gore cherished her private time and had never been a policy person except on a handful of issues, like mental health and the family.

When Clement announced on March 18, Tipper Gore was on the stage. Clement had persuaded every other potential big name opponent to stay out of the race and he promptly disappeared from the news.

It wasn't just the Bryant-Alexander contest that was grabbing the headlines. The legislature was grappling with Tennessee's fiscal crisis, putting even more attention on the race for governor, where the two front-runners, Bredesen and Rep. Van Hilleary (R-TN), each faced some opposition.

The governor's race and the late start also complicated fundraising. Alexander fell $200,000 short of his goal of raising $2 million by Memorial

Day. Neither Bryant nor Clement was able to raise $1 million from individuals by June 30, but they were able to transfer large amounts from their House campaign funds, $375,000 for Bryant and $407,000 for Clement.

Plus, Tennessee candidates face an expensive task in reaching the state's 3 million registered voters. There are five multimedia markets—Memphis, Nashville, Chattanooga, Knoxville and the Tri-Cities area of Upper East Tennessee, plus smaller print markets like Jackson, Clarksville and Oak Ridge with their own unique interests. Candidates often tailor ads to specific regions or skip some markets altogether, particularly in primaries.

Alexander was the first Senate candidate to air commercials, using $100,000 he loaned the campaign to run radio ads on conservative talk radio shows that stressed his conservative credentials and praised President Bush. The ads were meant to protect Alexander against what would be the theme of Bryant's campaign—that he, not Alexander, was the real conservative and the real loyalist in the race.

Bryant had neither the time nor money to introduce himself in East Tennessee, which historically produces more than half the GOP primary votes. So he went on the attack.

In his first dash across the state, Bryant said Alexander was to his left on abortion, gun control, crime and taxes. Hitting the state's hottest issue, Bryant said Alexander advocated a state income tax in 1985; Alexander said he considered, but rejected the income tax.

"Tennessee is a conservative state. It needs conservative representation . . . that is proven and consistent," Bryant said.[6]

In late June, Bryant opened up his television ad campaign—only in East Tennessee markets—with a 30-second spot mocking Alexander's plaid shirt as representing less than pure conservative credentials.

"Don't be plaid, be solid for Bryant," said the ad's refrain.[7]

Alexander promptly responded with an ad accusing Bryant of wasting taxpayer money by leasing a car with his office allowance, even though such expenditures are allowed by House ethics rules. Some of Alexander's advisers thought the Bryant ad was not worth going on the attack. But Alexander had always thought he lost the New Hampshire primary because he didn't counterattack Bob Dole when Dole went after his tax record in Tennessee. He was signaling that mud would be met with mud.

The temperature of the race bothered Frist. He urged Alexander and Bryant to "tone down the rhetoric." Frist was ignored. After all, in his own primary in 1994, his campaign manager called an opponent "pond scum."[8]

Bryant was hoping to stir the kind of outpouring from the Christian right that had propelled the Republican sweep of the three statewide offices in 1994 and President Bush's victory over Gore in 2000. But even if Alexander wasn't exactly their kind of Republican, he had a winning message—he was the best candidate to hold the seat for the Republicans, to keep Clement from moving Thompson's seat to the Democratic side of the Senate.

In the primary, Bryant won his own district, a few other West Tennessee counties, the Memphis suburbs and the Republican stronghold of Williamson County south of Nashville, but not a single East Tennessee County. He won the hard right, holding Alexander to a 54–42 margin, but Alexander had shown the Howard Baker wing of the party could still win.

Bryant also had forced Alexander to spend money, while Clement began the general election with more than $1 million in the bank. Nonetheless, it was Alexander who again took the initiative. In mid-August, Alexander launched an ad in which Thompson reminded voters that he had been asked by Alexander to help "clean up the corruption" in the governor's office.[9]

After his Watergate heyday, Thompson had returned to Nashville to practice law. One of his clients was Marie Ragghianti, who was appealing her firing by Blanton as chairman of the Board of Pardons and Paroles. The case would lead to the Sissy Spacek movie *Marie,* and Thompson's first acting job, playing himself. But the day after Alexander was sworn in, he called Thompson to the Capitol and somewhat to the lawyer's surprise announced that Thompson would be reviewing pending clemency orders.

On the stump, Alexander was attacking Clement as too liberal for Tennessee. Clement had voted both for the Bush tax cut and the recent resolution authorizing the use of force against Iraq. He had voted with Bush 52 percent of the time according to *Congressional Quarterly,* one of the highest ratios for any Democrat in the House; but according to Alexander this wasn't good enough.

Still, Alexander was determined not to nationalize the elections. He talked about helping cities create jobs as if he was still recruiting auto plants. In Memphis he promised to support the fledgling biotech industry. In East Tennessee he focused on the Oak Ridge-Knoxville technology corridor. He turned down interviews with out-of-state reporters.

In the governor's race, Hilleary and the state GOP apparatus were mocking Bredesen's refusal to campaign with Gore. Yet even though Gore had appeared with Clement, Alexander would not make him an issue. Although the two disagreed on most issues, they held a mutual respect. Gore had called Alexander to offer consolation after his early exit from the 2000 race. More importantly, Alexander wanted Gore's supporters to vote for him.

There was little coordination between the Alexander and Hilleary campaigns anyway. Many of Alexander's supporters had backed Jim Henry, a former House Republican leader when Alexander was governor, in the primary. Some of Alexander's biggest business supporters, like Frederick W. Smith, chairman and CEO of Memphis-based FedEx, were backing Bredesen. One Alexander ad even featured a testimonial from a former business associate who was on Bredesen's finance committee.

Clement was on the stump too but he did not air any commercials in August. Bill Fletcher, his Nashville-based media consultant, argued that voters weren't paying any attention. For similar reasons they delayed until after the September 11 anniversary. Fletcher would later admit, however, that money was a factor in the late ad start.

The first Clement commercial in mid-September emphasized his experience across the state. The East Tennessee version said he graduated from the University of Tennessee, where Clement attended for his undergraduate degree. The West Tennessee version said Clement graduated from the University of Memphis, where he got his M.B.A.

Clement also emphasized standard Democratic themes. He promised a prescription drug plan as a standard benefit under Medicare, protection for Social Security and an increase in the minimum wage, which Alexander opposed.

But when the campaign began in earnest it was clear that as in the primary the principle issue was going to be Alexander himself. This time it was not his conservative credentials, but his knack for making money through the friends he gained as a politician.

It started in 1981 when the publisher of the now-defunct *Knoxville Journal* gave Baker, Alexander and three of their associate's options to buy the paper for $1 a piece in hopes they would find a buyer to keep its Republican orientation alive. They couldn't, and sold the paper to the Gannett chain, getting Gannett stock in return. No one in Washington seemed to mind that the Senate majority leader was getting such a boon, but Alexander put the stock in a trust until he was no longer governor. That proved to be a wise financial move when years later he sold the stock for $620,000.

The Senate's confirmation of Alexander to be secretary of education was temporarily delayed in 1991 because of disclosures that as president of the University of Tennessee, Alexander had directed fourteen university functions to be held at an inn where his wife Honey held a one-third interest.

In his 1996 race, Alexander was dogged about $236,000 he received as a settlement of his compensation as a board member of Martin Marietta when it merged with Lockheed Martin. Democrats criticized the payment because thousands of Martin Marietta employees were laid off.

By the time of the Senate campaign, Alexander was earning more than $1 million a year from investments and salaries and was a board member or adviser to thirty-two companies or nonprofit groups, all of which he would have to resign from if elected. One corporate board especially caught Fletcher's eye.

Education Networks of America (ENA) held the state contract to manage the computer network for Tennessee schools. A competing company had charged favoritism when ENA was awarded the first contract for $74 million in 1998 because the company's president, Al Ganier, chaired Sundquist's inauguration committee in 1995. The independent state comptroller's office and the FCC denied the protest.

Alexander joined the ENA board in 2000, receiving $5,000 a month. He said he avoided any contact with Tennessee officials when the contract was renewed for five years at a cost of $102.5 million.[10]

Clement saw a way to tie Alexander to the unpopular Sundquist and corporate scandals. Alexander had said in July that the marketplace and existing laws would punish most corporate wrongdoers, but then endorsed the tougher penalties passed by Congress.

On a Nashville radio forum on September 23 Clement suggested that Alexander's role with ENA was a potential conflict of interest.[11]

A week later, at their first debate in Chattanooga, Clement called on Alexander to resign from the ENA board. But Alexander was ready with a countercharge—that Clement in the early 1970s had served on the board of Jake and C. H. Butcher's City and County Bank of Knox County, part of the banking empire whose collapse in the early 1980s cost thousands of Tennesseans some of their savings.

"If you want to talk about Enron capitalism, let's talk about the Butcher banks," said Alexander.[12]

Clement could have easily deflected the charge. After all, Clement had lost the Democratic primary race to Jake Butcher for governor in 1978 and Alexander as governor had intervened with regulators to try to save the banks. Instead, Clement denied that he served on the Butcher bank board, surprising Alexander for the first and only time in the campaign, said Alexander's campaign manager, David Kustoff.[13]

After the debate the Alexander campaign gave reporters copies of a photo showing Clement in a group photo of the board. Clement said it was a community advisory board and didn't vote on policy.

At their second debate October 6 in Jackson, Clement regained his footing, handing Alexander a dollar bill and asking him to "turn it into $620,000 for Tennessee's children," a reference to the Knoxville *Journal* deal. [14]

Few sparks flew the next day at their third debate in Knoxville, but in their final debate in Memphis on October 20, Alexander sought to undermine Clement with black voters.

As a student editor at Vanderbilt University, Alexander argued (unsuccessfully at the time) to integrate the campus. As a candidate—like Baker before him—he courted the black vote. He was the first Southern Republican governor to urge President Reagan to back a federal holiday to honor Dr. Martin Luther King.

Earlier in the campaign Alexander had appeared in Memphis with several young black supporters, including Rodney Herenton, the son of Mayor Willie Herenton. Officially the city's first African-American mayor was neutral in the race, but his preference was obvious.

Now Alexander asked Clement why he hadn't supported his appointment of George H. Brown Jr. in 1980 as the first black justice on the Tennessee Supreme Court. (Brown was defeated by a white Democrat later.) Again, Clement was blind-sided. After the cameras were off he recalled that at the time he was serving on the board of the Tennessee Valley Authority, a federal position that barred him from political involvement.

To win Clement had to count on undercutting Alexander in East Tennessee and get a huge vote from African Americans in Shelby County (Memphis), which Gore carried by 48,000 votes in 2000 even though he lost the state.

A poll by Ethridge & Associates for *The Commercial Appeal* of 819 Tennessee voters between October 18 and 21 showed that Clement had not accomplished either task. It showed Alexander ahead by 13 percentage points in East Tennessee and with 19 percent of the black vote. Clement led with 43 percent of black voters, but one-third claimed they were undecided. Alexander's overall lead was nine percentage points.[15]

Perhaps more significantly, Clement was not damaging Alexander's image despite a barrage of negative ads, including one that charged that Alexander "takes care of number one" through questionable financial deals. It depicted a check signed by Sundquist to Alexander for $102 million, implying that Alexander personally received money from the ENA contract. Alexander responded with an ad in which Thompson called the charges "misleading."

The Commercial Appeal poll found that Alexander was the only one of the four statewide candidates viewed favorably by more than half the voters—54 percent.

"He did a good job for Tennessee when he was governor," Yvonne Curtis, 68, a high school worker in Millington told *The Commercial Appeal*. "I just feel that he'll do a good job again. He brought some jobs to Tennessee."[16]

Clement was viewed favorably by 46 percent of the voters, but one-fifth had no opinion. Ayres had asked voters in August whether they thought Alexander made his money through honest hard work or sweetheart deals. Only 18 percent chose sweetheart deals. By mid-September that number had gone up by one, said Ayres.

"Bob Clement was not going to be able to make the voters of Tennessee think Lamar Alexander was a corporate crook. It was very clear in August they were going to try and in fact we rejoiced that they did," said Ayres.[17]

Alexander shifted his ads in the last stretches of the campaign to education and a proposal to restore the teaching of civics. Money woes forced the Clement campaign to "go dark" two weeks before the election, Fletcher admitted after the election. The Democratic Senatorial Campaign Committee filled in with a "soft money" funded ad attacking Alexander's "sweetheart deals." Frist responded in kind with an ad attacking Clement for not voting to use his office mail accounts to finance free mail for U. S. troops during the Gulf War.

The Saturday before the election, Bush came into Blount County, but it was clearly a rally intended to try to boost Hilleary in a close race. Alexander's only public event the next day was at a ceremony in Knoxville to honor the state historian. Monday he and Thompson flew around the state together.

Clement spent the last two days of the campaign in Memphis, starting with visits to black churches Sunday. Ford Sr. escorted Clement while the newly elected African-American mayor of Shelby County, A. C. Wharton, escorted Bredesen. Congressman Ford was visiting black churches in Chattanooga for Bredesen.

On November 5 Alexander won the election 54 percent to 44 percent, with a smattering of votes going to seven independent candidates. He carried 27 of the 30 largest counties, including Shelby County by 285 votes. Herenton introduced Alexander at the victory rally. A Shelby co-chairman, District Attorney Bill Gibbons estimated Alexander got as much as 10 to 12 percent of the vote in some middle-class black neighborhoods. Congressman Ford doubted Alexander got more than 5 to 7 percent of the black vote.

"Lamar ran an effective campaign. He is a moderate candidate who was a popular governor," said Ford.[18]

Bredesen eked out a 51–47 win to capture the governor's mansion.

Ayres said that if the money and candidate are equal, a Republican should win Tennessee. Gore started giving interviews after the election. On Tennessee, he said, "I've got a lot of work to do."

As for Frist, he said he felt Tennessee was secured the day he recruited Alexander.[19]

NOTES

1. R. Locker, "Alexander Pulls Plug on 6-Year Quest for Presidency, Bush Blitz Dried up Fund-Raising," *The Commercial Appeal*, A1, Aug. 17, 1999.

2. J. W. Brosnan, "Lipman Has Advice on Airport Security," (column), *The Commercial Appeal*, B5, Oct. 1, 2001.

3. J. W. Brosnan, "Attacks Gave Thompson a Reason to Stay Put," *The Commercial Appeal*, A7, Sept. 25, 2001.

4. J. W. Brosnan, B. Dries, "No Heart to Run Says Thompson, Rethought Re-election After Daughter's Death," *The Commercial Appeal*, A1, March 9, 2002.

5. Interview with J. W. Brosnan, March 27, 2002.

6. T. Humphrey, "Bryant Takes Stinging Jabs at Alexander Campaign, Gets in Gear," *The Commercial Appeal*, B1, April 2, 2002.

7. J. W. Brosnan, "Don't Get Plaid, Bryant Says in E. Tennessee," *The Commercial Appeal*, B2, June 22, 2002.

8. J. W. Brosnan, "Frist Urges Alexander, Bryant Rein in Rhetoric," *The Commercial Appeal*, A16, June 27, 2002.

9. J. W. Brosnan, "Alexander Launches TV Campaign, Ads Feature Thompson Endorsement," *The Commercial Appeal*, B2, Aug. 20, 2002.

10. J. W. Brosnan, "Education Expertise Has Paid Off for Citizen Alexander," *The Commercial Appeal*, B1, April 16, 2002.

11. R. Locker, "Clement Says Alexander's Business Role Risks Conflict," *The Commercial Appeal*, B2, Sept. 24, 2002.

12. R. Locker, "Alexander, Clement Clash on Board Roles," *The Commercial Appeal*, B1, Oct. 1, 2002.

13. R. Locker, J. W. Brosnan, "Alexander Tops Clement for Senate," *The Commercial Appeal*, A1, Nov. 6, 2002.

14. R. Locker, "Senate Duo Exchange Salvos of Innuendo," *The Commercial Appeal*, B1, Oct. 7, 2002.

15. J. W. Brosnan, "Alexander Holds Edge for Senate—Poll: Clement Falling Short Among Women, Minorities," *The Commercial Appeal*, A1, Oct. 28, 2002.

16. Ibid.

17. J. W. Brosnan, interview with Ayres.

18. J. W. Brosnan, "Urban Appeal Paid Off for Big Winners," *The Commercial Appeal*, A8, Nov. 7, 2002.

19. J. W. Brosnan, interview with Frist.

14

Texas Senate

A Race about Race

JAY ROOT
Fort Worth Star-Telegram

The day after former Dallas Mayor Ron Kirk won the hard-fought Democratic nomination for U.S. Senate, the Republican in the race—already anointed by his own primary voters and the Bush White House—unveiled what would become the central theme of his campaign.

"Our team will be the team of President George W. Bush," said John Cornyn, state attorney general, former state Supreme Court judge and political acolyte of White House adviser Karl Rove. "The other team will be headed by (Senator) Tom Daschle, who wakes up every morning trying to figure out new ways how to frustrate President Bush's agenda for the American people."[1]

Over the next seven months, many other issues would emerge in the 2002 open Senate race—military spending, the candidates' ties to failed Houston energy giant Enron and even rap music, to name a few.

But Cornyn again and again would return to his verifiably strong ties to Bush. And in Texas, where the native son president enjoyed approval ratings around 70 percent, who could blame him?

Certainly not Kirk, who called Bush "well-loved" and who praised many of his policies, including his stance on Iraq, the war on terrorism and even the 2001 tax cuts. Indeed, barely a month before Cornyn trounced him 55–43, Kirk, who portrayed himself as a bipartisan consensus-builder, suggested he might vote for Bush when the president makes his expected re-election bid in 2004.[2]

In the end, it's unclear if any changes in strategy could have netted more votes for Kirk, the black component of a racially diverse Democratic "Dream Team" that also included a deep-pocketed Hispanic running for governor and a popular Anglo running for lieutenant governor.

Perhaps Kirk could have rallied more traditional Democrats to the polls by stressing his differences with the Republicans instead offering a qualified "me, too" message on tax cuts and foreign policy.

Kirk could have made fewer mistakes, too. One that haunted him with conservative and independent voters—thanks in part to Cornyn's incessant reminders—was Kirk's complaint that the troops who might fight in Iraq would come disproportionately from the ranks of minorities and the poor. Kirk apologized for the way he said it, but it probably cost him some swing voters in places like Dallas–Fort Worth, where the former mayor is still popular.

Thus, in hindsight, it seems possible that Kirk could have garnered more than the 1.9 million votes he got on Election Day—maybe even tens of thousands more. Victory, however, was probably beyond his grasp. Nationwide, Republicans used Bush's popularity and jet-setting activism to defy history by picking up seats in both houses of Congress for the first time since 1934.

In George W. Bush's Texas, that national tide was more like a tidal wave: Not only did Republicans pull off a fourth consecutive sweep of all statewide offices, they made gains in the already solidly Republican state senate and gained a majority in the state house for the first time since 1871. The Dream Team turned out to be a nightmare for Democrats.

"If you didn't have an 'R' next to your name, you were dead," said Kirk campaign manager Carol Butler.[3]

Had they seen it coming, Democrats obviously would not have picked 2002 as the year to stage an expensive and flashy comeback effort. Alas, it had seemed for a while that the once-dominant Democrats—eyeing a faltering economy, Republican ties to Enron and their own potential to score big with minority voters—were poised for at least a few upsets.

And they were delirious at the prospect of humiliating Bush in his own backyard.

GRAMM EXITS

The first sign of a rare Senate job opening came in the summer of 2001. Rumors began circulating that arch-conservative Republican Senator Phil

Gramm, first elected in 1984, would step down from the seat once held by Lyndon Johnson.

The colorful Gramm denied it for weeks, but the rumors kept coming.

"What else do I have to do?" the senator asked reporters in June. Less than three months later, on September 4, he answered that question by announcing his retirement from elective politics.

"Remarkably, the things I came to Washington to do are done," he told a packed news conference on Capitol Hill. "I felt it was time to quit."[4]

While several Republican names immediately surfaced, none were as sure a bet to run as Cornyn, 50, a former judge whose white hair and formal, stately manner already gave him the uncanny look and feel of a United States senator.

More importantly, Cornyn wanted the job and he was part of the Bush White House's inner circle. Aides say he began sewing up financial commitments with 72 hours of Gramm's withdrawal and then scheduled a formal announcement on September 12—barely a week after Gramm made it official. Cornyn postponed the announcement, but not his decision to run, due to the September 11, 2001, terrorist attacks.

At least one big hurdle remained: There was rampant speculation that Gramm would resign and let Republican Governor Rick Perry appoint a replacement. Many Republicans favored the selection of a Hispanic who could further the party's Latino outreach goals and give the GOP candidate an incumbent edge against whomever the Democrats nominated.

But there was a hitch: Republican sources say Perry favored Tony Garza, a close Bush confidant and rising GOP star, while Gramm wanted U.S. Representative Henry Bonilla, a Republican from San Antonio. (Garza has since been named U.S. ambassador to Mexico.)

It was an awkward moment for Republicans when word of a possible deal began leaking out. The *Houston Chronicle* reported on September 6 that Bush had met with Perry at the White House to discuss "possible inducements" to get Gramm to depart early. In return, Gramm reportedly wanted a good replacement job and a say in who succeeded him.

Asked about it publicly, Perry said the senator was "still going through a thought process of whether or not he would resign early."[5]

That prompted a heated denial from Gramm's camp, and the specter of insider political trading played right into Cornyn's hands, Republican sources say.

"Once it got out, then it looked like they were working a backroom deal," said a GOP operative with close ties to Cornyn. "If they had been willing to work out that deal, you would have had a Hispanic, I suspect, and Cornyn would not have been able to run. History was altered by premature leakage of a news story."

Publicly, Cornyn allowed for an appropriate post–September 11 pause, though he had quietly set up a federal fundraising account on September 14. By the time he made his public entry into the race on September 21, he had all but locked up the nomination. Bonilla and another Texas congressman, conservative Joe Barton from the Dallas suburbs, were still theoretically interested but they got no encouragement from the White House or from key party financial backers, who were lining up behind Cornyn. He had the momentum and the golden perception that he was Bush's choice.

In Texas, little else was needed.

"Every day that went by was a day Cornyn made progress. They were all considering the race. We were in the race," said Ted Delisi, Cornyn's top consultant and a Rove protégé himself.

Not two weeks later, Bonilla and Barton dropped out. So, with more than a year to go before the election, Cornyn had unofficially secured the nomination without a drop of blood spilled, and he had taken a giant step toward becoming the next U.S. senator from Texas.

He won his March primary with 77 percent of the vote against four fringe candidates.

DEMOCRATS PREDICT COMEBACK

On the Democratic side, the jockeying began even before Gramm got out, in part because Democrats felt sure this was their time to stage a comeback after years of defeat and humiliation.

Democrats hadn't been competitive in major open races since 1990, when Ann Richards was elected governor and her party won all but one of the top-ballot races. Just eight years later, Bush—who had beaten Richards in 1994—presided over a GOP sweep of every statewide office in Texas.

This year was supposed to be different. The favorite son was gone now, the Democrats happily crowed, making 2002 the first year without a George Bush on the ballot in more than a decade. Moreover, a wealthy Latino named Tony Sanchez was promising to spend millions of his own money pursuing the office of governor, so the increasingly important Hispanic voters were expected to turn out like never before. It was against this hopeful backdrop that a crowded Democratic primary—with three viable candidates—began to take shape.

Schoolteacher Victor Morales, the 1996 novice candidate who waged a populist campaign against Gramm from the front seat of his white Nissan pickup truck, couldn't resist another bite at the apple. He had gotten a respectable 44 percent of the vote after spending less than $1 million on a

1996 campaign that Gramm—who had run for president and lost the same year—spent $14 million to wage.

Also tossing his hat in the race was U.S. Representative Ken Bentsen, the nephew of former Senator Lloyd Bentsen. The elder Bentsen had been the last Democrat to win an open Senate seat in Texas. (It was 1970, and the loser was George H. W. Bush, the current president's father.)

Of all the candidates, though, it was popular Dallas Mayor Ron Kirk who generated the most excitement in the Democratic establishment—what was left of it, anyway. By late September, his list of supporters began to look like a who's who of Democratic heavyweights, including Beaumont trial lawyer Walter Umphrey, state house speaker Pete Laney and former Governor Richards.

It was clear there would be a runoff, but any combination of the three candidates seemed possible. On Election Day, Kirk won by running up the scoreboard in Dallas–Fort Worth, and he cut deeply into Bentsen's Houston base. Morales ran predictably well in South Texas, where he undercut Bentsen's strong family ties. Thus, Bentsen was the odd man out with 27 percent of the vote, while less than 1,000 votes separated Kirk and Morales, who each got 33 percent.

While the Bentsen-Kirk fight sparked split allegiances in the party's upper reaches, there was no such dynamic in the Kirk-Morales April runoff. Morales was a populist insurgent with no official party backing, and that's exactly how he ran.

Kirk had already hard-wired the party hierarchy to his candidacy. Many Democratic leaders, such as former Housing Secretary Henry Cisneros, were already beginning to tout the "dream team" concept, whereby blacks drawn to Kirk and Latinos flocking to Sanchez in the governor's race would spark Democratic victories up and down the ballot. With Kirk's easy 60–40 win over Morales, the dream team was finally on the field. And it would not take Texans long to notice.

CORNYN STUMBLES

Three days after the Democratic primary ended, Cornyn convened a press conference that might best be described as the beginning of a brief period in which Democrats seemed to have a plausible chance of staging a dramatic upset in Texas.

What appeared that day under the klieg lights was a nervous, unsure Republican candidate—a stark contrast to the confident attorney general still known to many as "Judge Cornyn." He had called reporters to his campaign headquarters to rebuke a top aide, his spokesman Dave Beckwith.

At issue: a story carried by the Associated Press the day after the primary runoff, in which Beckwith had criticized the diverse Democratic slate as a sort of racial engineering.

"This dream ticket is cynical," Beckwith said. "It is based on a racial quota system. In the end, it will not work, because most people vote on issues and philosophy, not on race."

Cornyn called the comments "shocking" and vowed that race would not "play any part in this campaign." Cornyn might have sincerely hoped that would be true, but race would prove to be a central feature in the Senate contest.

For one thing, Kirk's ethnicity made the election interesting. Only two blacks from the South had previously served in the U.S. Senate, and both were sent by legislatures before the direct election of senators.

That an African American from a former Confederate state—Bush's Texas, no less—could actually win was news in and of itself.

Texans who knew him were not surprised that Kirk, 48, might be the one to pull it off. He seemed to have defied political gravity by easily winning two terms as mayor in fractious and racially divisive Dallas, where support from the mostly white Republican power grid is indispensable.

If ever there were an African American "good 'ol boy," it is Kirk, a wily lawyer who can work a black church and a corporate boardroom in a single afternoon. What's more, he was a moderate, pro-business candidate who could appeal to independent swing voters.

The national press gushed. An August *New Yorker* piece entitled "Why George Bush is scared of Ron Kirk" spoke of the Democrats' "giddy optimism" that Kirk might embarrass the president at home and cement the party's grasp on the U.S. Senate.[6] Similarly, *Time* magazine said Kirk was giving the White House "jitters on Bush's home turf."[7]

The Kirk momentum seemed to surge in the summer. Kirk, who in 1995 became the first African American elected to a major Texas city, had just run in a highly publicized primary and was better known than Cornyn.

Kirk also benefited from the perception that the Cornyn campaign had stumbled over the "racial quota" remark and was tarred by Enron. In the spring, the attorney general belatedly decided to give his $200,000 in Enron-related donations to charity—after he said he would not give up the contributions.

A statewide poll conducted in July by the University of Houston also fueled Democratic hopes. It put Kirk eight points ahead of Cornyn, leading some Texas Republicans to hit the panic button.

"I more or less knew what to expect," Cornyn recalled in a September interview, as the polls started turning decisively his way. "Some of the folks who maybe hadn't been through those statewide campaigns before kind of got worried that six months out, we're neck and neck."

KIRK'S MISSTEPS

The Kirk boomlet turned out to be short-lived. For starters, the highly disciplined Cornyn campaign repeatedly pounded Kirk for his out-of-state fundraising tours and appearances, including one that featured Hillary Clinton, and used those associations to portray the Democrat as liberal and out of step with mainstream Texas.

In one September news release, the Cornyn camp found particular delight in noting Kirk's appearance at a California fundraiser featuring liberal Representative Barbara Lee (the only House member to oppose the war in Afghanistan), Congresswoman Nancy Pelosi and Senators Dianne Feinstein and Barbara Boxer—all of California.

"I don't understand how my opponent can talk strong on national defense," Cornyn seethed, "and then cavort happily in San Francisco with the very people who are trying to subvert his agenda."

Even more damaging than Cornyn's predictable tarring of his opponent with the dreaded "L" word were Kirk's own missteps and gaffes, which prompted embarrassing apologies and revealed weaknesses in the Kirk campaign organization.

The first shoe dropped in late August, when Kirk apologized to a law enforcement organization for overly politicizing his criticism of Cornyn on capital punishment. A few days later, Kirk stumbled again. His staffers had botched an attack on Cornyn's role in a state flap over racist testimony that had been used by prosecutors in several death penalty cases.

Kirk's campaign erroneously asserted that Cornyn had played a role in the use of that testimony. In fact, Cornyn had won praise from Democrats after going to the U.S. Supreme Court to have the testimony thrown out and new trials ordered. That prompted another costly admission of error from the Democrats.

Finally, on September 13, Kirk stepped on a racial landmine. He was trying to explain why some in his party were hesitant to give Bush carte blanche in a war against Iraq, but it came off sounding more like class and race warfare.

In an emotional speech before a group of veterans in San Antonio, Kirk complained that wars were fought disproportionately by low-income minorities, saying "people who look like us" are over-represented in the graves of the war dead but underrepresented on Wall Street and in corporate scandals.

"Those who question our patriotic duty to make sure we have a chance to win, I wonder how excited they'd be if I get to the United States Senate and I put forth a resolution that says the next time we go to war, the first kids have to come from families who earn $1 million or more," Kirk said before a group of veterans in San Antonio.[8]

Cornyn aides smelled blood. Believing Kirk had undermined his moderate appeal with an Al Sharpton-esque speech, they began calling all the senior political reporters to make the candidate available for interviews, which ran in stories across the state.

Again, Kirk issued a statement saying he regretted the way he had said something. And Cornyn, who called the statement "divisive" and "puzzling," would repeatedly exploit the fallout in subsequent news releases and campaign appearances.

It was one in a long string of instances in which ethnicity had bubbled to the surface, and which Cornyn seized upon and used to his advantage. In the final days of the campaign, Kirk's appearance with a hip-hop musician who had written lyrics disparaging police officers also provided fodder for Cornyn's attacks, prompting Kirk to charge the attorney general was trying to "frighten" white voters.

Whether or not that's what Cornyn intended—he says it's not—pre-election polls showed that Democrats were losing big in large part because so few Anglos, about a third or less, were supporting them.

And Kirk's missteps did nothing to close that divide.

By September 21, Cornyn saw that victory was within his grasp. Returning home in his campaign plane from an East Texas fundraiser with the legendary actor and gun enthusiast Charlton Heston, the Republican cited Kirk's "gaffes" as the turning point in the race.

"They've made kind of outrageous statements and have had to apologize, and I think at some point people wonder does this guy have the temperament to serve in the United States Senate," Cornyn said.[9]

DREAM TEAM FAILS TO DELIVER

Like the governor's race in Florida, which featured the president's brother, the Senate campaign in his home state was personal, and Bush left nothing to chance.

By the time voters went to the polls, Bush had visited the state three times on Cornyn's behalf; he twice sent Vice President Dick Cheney, and dispatched his wife Laura and über-adviser Karen Hughes to hold fundraisers or make campaign appearances with him.

Likewise, the national Democrats, hoping to deal Bush a setback at home, pumped millions into issue advertising in the state, and made sure he had the resources to be competitive.

Records compiled by the non-partisan Center for Responsive Politics through October 16 show Kirk raised $7.7 million compared to Cornyn's $9 million. If the trends hold once all the reports are in, Texas will have drawn more money than all but two Senate races, with some $16.6 million in contributions.

While the money contest was close, the election results were not, despite polls showing a tight contest even in the final days. Cornyn trounced Kirk 55–43, winning all but a handful of counties—such as liberal Travis (Austin) and union heavy Jefferson (Beaumont)—outside of heavily Democratic South Texas. Kirk barely won his own Dallas County.

In the context of the larger Democratic strategy to capture power back in Texas, Kirk was no more of a failure than his cohorts on the statewide ballot. Once again, Republicans had swept every office and increased their legislative gains.

And with the exception of a couple of counties in South Texas, projections of a huge Hispanic turnout failed to materialize. An analysis by the *Fort Worth Star-Telegram* found that turnout in counties that were 75 percent or more Hispanic saw turnout increase only four percent over 1998—which had set a modern record for low voter participation.

Given the unexpectedly large Republican gains nationwide, it is reasonable to conclude—as Kirk did after the election—that running as a Democrat in post-September 11 America, against the president's candidate in his home state, did not present ideal circumstances.

While a few Texas voters might have been turned off by "all this diversity manifesting itself at one time" on his party's ticket, Kirk noted accurately that the electorate didn't seem to like Democrats of any color.

It only took him about eighteen months to figure that out.

"If I knew then what I know now," Kirk said, "I just would have stayed out of the water."[10]

NOTES

1. *Fort Worth Star-Telegram*, April 11, 2002.

2. *New York Times*, "Tough Senate Race in Texas Gets Bush in Gear," April 6, 2002.

3. *San Antonio Express-News*, "Ever-Present Talker for GOP Unbeaten," November 17, 2002.

4. *Fort Worth Star-Telegram*, "Gramm Bowing Out," September 5, 2001.

5. *Fort Worth Star-Telegram*, "Perry: Gramm May Exit Early," September 8, 2001.

6. *The New Yorker*, August 12, 2002.

7. *Time*, "Can He Rope Texas," August 11, 2002.

8. *San Antonio Express-News*, "Kirk: Race, Class Affect War Views," September 14, 2002.

9. Interview with author, September 21, 2002.

10. Interview with author, November 18, 2002.

15

It's a Sonny Day in Georgia

CHARLES S. BULLOCK III
University of Georgia

Independent analyst Rhodes Cook's newsletter published just before the 2002 election lists records for continuous electoral success. The longest was Democratic control of Georgia's governorship for fifty consecutive elections, a record that began even before federal troops left and Reconstruction ended. Democratic success in gubernatorial elections was largely replicated in lower offices. No Republicans won congressional office in the 20th century until Goldwater's coattails brought a House victory. Statewide success first came when Mack Mattingly defeated Senator Herman Talmadge in 1980. Not until the 1990s did Republicans become a significant force winning their first constitutional statewide offices in 1994, the same year they took control of the state's congressional delegation.

During the 1990s, Republicans saw their ranks in the state legislature double to more than 40 percent. Since 1996, Republicans have received the bulk of the votes cast in state legislative elections, although this never translated into a majority of the seats. An audacious Democratic gerrymander sought to translate minorities in the state electorate into a majority in the state legislature and to transform the 8–3 Republican majority in the congressional delegation to a 7–6 Democratic majority.[1] Going into the 2002 election Democrats appeared likely to extend their record of gubernatorial and legislative success. Governor Roy Barnes, whose activist first term won plaudits from business leaders and appeared to cut into the natural Republican constituency, led a ticket of Democrats seeking reelection.

The best laid plans of the Democratic Party fell apart on election night.

In a stunning upset, Sonny Perdue, the former Democratic president pro temp of the state Senate before converting to the GOP, upended Barnes by garnering 51 percent of the vote. Less surprisingly, Representative Saxby Chambliss ousted Max Cleland to become Georgia's third Republican senator in modern times. Republicans won the open post of state school superintendent and defeated two members of the Public Service Commission giving the GOP eight of fifteen positions elected statewide.

Republicans derailed the Democratic gerrymander express winning 2 open congressional seats to retain an 8–5 advantage. Down ticket, Tom Murphy who had served as speaker of the House for 27 years, lost. In the state Senate, Majority Leader Charles Walker was beaten along with 5 other Democratic incumbents. The redistricting plan designed to net Democrats 5 additional seats in the Senate, instead yielded a gain of 3 seats to Republicans pulling them to a 26–30 share of the seats. Within a week after the election, four Democrats changed parties to give Republicans a Senate majority for the first time in more than 125 years.

GENERAL TRENDS IN THE ELECTORATE

Neither Barnes' tracking polls nor surveys conducted by the media hinted at the incumbent's vulnerability. Late polling showed Barnes gradually pulling ahead, edging above 50 percent. With hindsight's perfect acuity we can suggest causes of the dramatic upsets. In navigating the post-election sea of data without the pole star of exit returns, several things can be deduced. First, Republicans who won statewide offices must have largely bridged the gender gap. It is relatively easy for southern Republicans to attract 60 percent or more of the votes from white males. Since however, a Republican statewide victory in Georgia requires approximately 60 percent of the white vote, attracting a narrow majority among white females usually is insufficient. This was not a problem for Perdue, who beat Barnes in 95 of 96 counties where blacks constituted less than 35 percent of the population. Bill Shipp, the dean of Georgia political journalists, sees in the 2002 results the demise of the Democratic coalition as white rural voters filed for divorce, believing that party leaders had been too solicitous of black demands.

Second, it is likely that black turnout in the state fell off. In 1994, when Republicans won five statewide offices, blacks cast only 16 percent of the votes statewide. Four years later, Republican gains ceased when blacks accounted for 23 percent of the votes cast as three African Americans sought to become the first blacks to win state constitutional offices. In 2002, while two of the African Americans sought reelection, their continuation in office was never in doubt. Moreover, in 1998, the candidates at the top of the Republican ticket had made comments that the black community interpreted as racist. The Democratic Party disseminated these comments to black voters in a mail out.[2] Finally in 1998, Congresswoman Cynthia McKinney's machine turned out black voters. In 2002 after the controversial congresswoman lost renomination—which she blamed on lack of support from Barnes—people appeared on street corners in her district urging motorists to "Support Cynthia by Not Voting."

A third general factor, and one that reduced the gender gap and promoted higher white participation, was the attention given the state by President George Bush. Most surveys conducted during 2002 showed the President's popularity in the state above 70 percent. With Georgia on the direct route between Washington and Florida where the President frequently campaigned to reelect his brother, and with a hotly contested Senate seat, Georgia received multiple visits from the Chief Executive, Vice President Dick Cheney, and former New York City Mayor Rudy Giuliani. Appearances by the president in Atlanta and Savannah on the Saturday before the election spurred turnout and stirred up Republican activists, busloads of whom went from the Atlanta rally to canvass neighborhoods.

The presence of two candidates from the part of Georgia that often feels ignored politically and economically by the Atlanta power elite stimulated turnout in the southern half of the state. Eric Johnson of Savannah, Republican leader in the state Senate, summed up anger about Barnes' redistricting, education reform and flag change initiatives. "There is someone up in Atlanta trying to tell you who you're going to get to vote for, how to teach our children and what flag to salute." South Georgia voters expected Perdue, who comes from just south of Macon, and Chambliss, from further south, would be more responsive than the Atlanta-based Democratic incumbents.

A fourth factor that may have influenced turnout was the weather. Tuesday saw heavy rains in much of the state, especially in metro Atlanta, where black turnout has frequently been strong.

GUBERNATORIAL ELECTION

Within these general trends, specific factors influenced the outcome of individual contests. The gubernatorial election became a referendum on Roy Barnes, who had alienated numerous groups during his activist first term. An Atlanta columnist said of the governor, "He played power politics so relentlessly that even some Democratic supporters recoiled. There was just *so much money*, so much propaganda, so much negative research."

Barnes attributed his defeat to changing the state flag to remove the

Saint Andrews Cross that had graced the Confederate flag. In response to threats from black leaders that retention of the flag would lead to a boycott similar to the one in South Carolina, Barnes pushed a new flag through the legislature. While major corporations and the hospitality industry applauded the change, it alienated many rural white voters. Protestors waiving the old flag shadowed the governor as he campaigned, put up yard signs calling for a referendum on the flag and implored voters to "Boot Barnes." Black newspaper publisher Alexis Scott observed that, "Black voters forgot about the flag but whites didn't." Barnes saw the flag change as even more significant. "It became a symbol for everything that anybody didn't like— about Atlanta, about any change that had occurred," he explained. "It energized and helped the surge."

Others see the flag as but one of Barnes' problems. His education reforms touched off a reaction among teachers, a group that had traditionally been strongly Democratic, who believed Barnes unfairly labeled them as incompetent and uncaring before he eliminated tenure for new teachers.[3] Television ads boasting that Barnes' reforms reduced class size did not ring true with many parents. While elementary class sizes had been reduced, enrollments in middle and high school classes increased since resources were not available to hire the teachers and build the classrooms necessary to achieve smaller classes throughout K–12. Moreover, the latest SAT scores showed Georgia to have slipped to dead last nationally, thereby undercutting the governor's claims that his education reforms were producing higher achievement.

In northern metro Atlanta, where many affluent suburbanites supported the flag change, Barnes lost support for backing the Northern Arc, a major highway project. Even though the governor backed off the Northern Arc during the campaign, Arc opponents saw this as nothing more than an election ploy.

Barnes participated actively in redistricting, and since Democrats no longer commanded majorities among legislative voters statewide, the only prospects for continued Democratic rule required ignoring traditional practices of using county boundaries and compactness. Rural voters whose counties had never been split were outraged by the new plans that divided even small counties among as many as four state house districts.

The perception that the governor had unchecked power fit with the Perdue characterization of "King Roy." These perceptions also cost Barnes support among local officials and law enforcement officers and supporters of video poker.

Barnes, who delivered on most of his 1998 campaign promises, realized that his activism stepped on toes. One of his advisors explained that the governor raised so much money—more than $20 million—because he knew he had a hard sell. In all, the incumbent spent more than $15 million on television, going up in April even though he had no primary challenge and remaining on the air non-stop until November. Barnes' aggressive fundraising tapped lawyers, lobbyists and corporate leaders, 450 of whom gave the $10,000 maximum. Underdog Perdue struggled to raise less than one-sixth what Barnes acquired, with only 25 giving the challenger $10,000.

With scant funding, Perdue emphasized grassroots efforts. He directed the second staffer hired to build an organization in all 159 counties. The organization had a county chair and four other individuals each responsible for a specific constituency such as veterans, educators and religious communities. Each county had a targeted number of votes to produce and a campaign staffer reports that all but 35 met their goal. More than 30 Democratic county chairs endorsed Perdue and Democrats filled Perdue leadership positions. After the election, some leading Democrats criticized the Barnes campaign for investing too much in television advertising and doing too little to nourish the grassroots.

Seventy counties that had voted for the reelection of Senator Paul Coverdell (R) but also backed Barnes in 1998 held the key to Perdue's success. Perdue's grassroots efforts succeeded in winning all but five of these counties, most of which are in south and middle Georgia. The heavy turnout in south Georgia stunned the Barnes camp and invalidated the models they had used when analyzing their tracking poll results. Barnes' vote in south Georgia fell 40,000 below 1998 while Perdue ran 80,000 votes ahead of the 1998 GOP nominee. Perdue lost metro Atlanta with only 46 percent of the vote, but more than compensated with 56 percent of the vote in the remainder of the state.

Perdue carried ten rural counties that had not previously voted for a Republican below the presidency and helped Chambliss in rural Georgia, leading the Senate nominee by 13,000 votes in the 120 non-metropolitan counties. Chambliss's television advertising enabled him to outpace Perdue by 43,000 votes in urban counties for a 30,000-vote lead statewide (see table 15.1).

U.S. SENATE

Being a Georgia senator used to be a career. Walter George served from 1922–1957 and his successor Herman Talmadge served until 1981. Richard Russell held the other Senate seat from 1933 to 1971, and following an interim appointment made upon Russell's death, Sam Nunn served four terms. Since the departures of Talmadge and Nunn, Georgia Senate seats have become revolving doors. In 2002, Nunn's successor, Vietnam veteran

Table 15.1 Selected Results from Georgia's General Election, 2002

Republican	Votes	Percent	Democrat	Votes	Percent
U.S. Senator Saxby Chambliss	1,068,813	52.8	Max Cleland	928,790	45.9
Governor Sonny Perdue	1,039,035	51.4	Roy Barnes	933,802	46.2
Public Service Seat 1 Doug Everett	1,005,109	52.5	Earleen Sizemore	909,768	47.5
Public Service Seat 4 Angela Speir	916,861	47.5	Bubba McDonald	908,192	47.1
U.S. House, District 11 Phil Gingrey	69,413	51.6	Roger Kahn	65,007	48.4
U.S. House, District 12 Max Burns	77,443	55.2	Champ Walker	62,878	44.8

Source: Georgia Secretary of State
Note: Percentages that sum to less than 100 indicate the presence of Libertarian candidates.

and triple-amputee Democrat Max Cleland tried to retain the seat. Challenger Saxby Chambliss had served four terms in the House where he chaired the subcommittee dealing with homeland security.

Despite widespread popularity and a personally compelling story, Cleland was vulnerable, having initially won with a 30,000-vote plurality. As he faced reelection, Cleland's weaknesses stemmed from the temptations that have brought down other Southern Democrats. After winning as a moderate, Cleland voted with his party more than 80 percent of the time. This posed problems for Cleland, since the Democratic Party's Northern leadership no longer reflects the concerns of the moderate-to-conservative wing once anchored in the South. During his first four years in office, Cleland voted with the liberal Americans for Democratic Action 82.5 percent of the time while his average support for positions taken by organized labor was 75.5.[4] In contrast, he averaged 8 percent support for the American Conservative Union and 8.25 percent support for the Christian Coalition.

Cleland's support for the national Democratic Party became more lethal in 2000 when Senator Coverdell died unexpectedly. Governor Barnes appointed his Democratic predecessor Zell Miller to the vacancy. Miller quickly resurrected the role of the traditional Southern Democrat, sometimes voting with the northern wing of his party but frequently siding with Republicans. Miller became the Bush administration's favorite Democrat. He supported the nomination of John Ashcroft for attorney general and

President Bush's tax initiative and education reform. He frequently appeared in the Georgia press in the company of native Georgian Senator Phil Gramm (R-TX). On selected, high-visibility issues, Miller's support for the administration placed him at odds with Cleland who stood with the Democratic Party. Many conservatives, who saw in Miller the legacy of Nunn and Russell, concluded that Cleland had abandoned his Georgia values.

The Chambliss campaign hammered away at policy differences with Cleland. Television ads noted that Cleland had not embraced the President's homeland security proposal. In charges that can be damning in a right-to-work state, ads attacked Cleland for putting the demands of labor unions for job security ahead of national security. Chambliss also castigated Cleland for not fully embracing the President's tax reduction package and for voting against the Boy Scouts.

Although Miller and Cleland did not present a united front on the floor, Miller enthusiastically supported his colleague's reelection. Miller appeared in Cleland television ads promoting Cleland as the "conscience of the Senate" and asserted that he and Cleland voted together 80 percent of the time. In response to an ad criticizing Cleland for not supporting the President's homeland security bill that began with pictures of Osama Bin Ladin and Saddam Hussein, it was Miller who called Chambliss a liar and angrily denounced him for attacking Cleland's patriotism.

Cleland's campaign suffered from the same inadequacies as the Wyche Fowler (D) reelection effort a decade earlier. Both senators did little to define themselves. Rather than aggressively staking out positions, the incumbents hung back, waiting to counter-punch once attacked. The incumbents' passivity allowed the challengers to make the legislators appear unacceptable to most Georgians as they castigated Cleland and Fowler as too liberal for Georgia. To drive home the point, a Chambliss mailer juxtaposed Cleland with Ted Kennedy and Hillary Clinton, thus blunting Cleland's protestation that he supported President Bush.

The Chambliss victory largely duplicated Perdue's which, in turn, bore a strong resemblance to George Bush in 2000. The Republicans swept north Georgia except for three counties in metro Atlanta and the home of the University of Georgia. The key was the Republicans' ability to wrap up a number of middle and South Georgia counties that historically voted Democratic. Democrats took all the major urban areas and held on to a number of black belt counties distributed diagonally just below the middle part of the state.

OTHER STATEWIDE OFFICES

A GOP surge, more than individual successes, is apparent in Public Service Commission outcomes. Candidates for this body spend little money and voters know little about them or the positions they seek making these state-wide contests where voter choices often reflect party identification. Republicans unseated incumbents in both contests. Especially notable is political novice Angela Speir who had no television, radio or newspaper ads but upset Bubba McDonald who had spent a lifetime in politics with a career that included almost two decades as a state legislator and a 1990 gubernatorial bid. Speir was so unknown that some newspapers had no file photos of her. Her victory suggests that more Republicans than Democrats turned out which would be unprecedented.

CONGRESSIONAL ELECTIONS

Democrats who controlled the state legislature and governor's office crafted maps intended to ensure the dominance of their party for the rest of the decade. Their plans were designed to give Democrats 7 of the 13 congressional districts and to yield a gain of 5 state Senate seats and 15 state House seats. None of these goals, however, came close to realization.

While no congressional districts were designed to be competitive—the most competitive district based on past electoral performance, the 11th, had a projected 56 percent Democratic vote—ultimately, three of the districts drawn for Democrats became competitive and Republicans made off with two after the primaries saw flawed Democrats nominated. Democrats drew the 40 percent black population 12th district to elect Champ Walker, son of the Senate majority leader. The father helped his son and namesake to adequate funding and was the primary factor in the son's nomination, but was also was a major impediment to his election. Since he lacked a well-established persona, the son was tainted by the hint of scandal swirling around the father. The senior Walker's campaign was assessed a large fine for campaign finance problems, and although a report by the state's Democratic auditor found no wrongdoing on the father's part, voter concerns were not fully dissipated.[5]

Despite these problems, Republicans rarely win districts 40 percent black and so while Walker had no political experience, observers initially expected him to prevail. Political scientist David Lublin, an expert on black-white elections, wrote an op-ed piece in *The Washington Post* projecting Walker's victory. If Walker secured the 95 percent of the black vote that a black Democrat usually gets against a white Republican, he could win with a mere quarter of the white vote.

Max Burns, the GOP nominee, immediately began attacking Walker. His mailings and advertising reported that the Democrat had been arrested numerous times for a variety of offenses, including disorderly conduct and shoplifting. A Web site posted Walker's mug shot. Burns also gained traction as Walker regularly ducked joint appearances, giving the Republican candidate the entire televised debate on public television to himself. In a debate held at the University of Georgia, Walker showed up after Burns had had the stage to himself for over forty-five minutes. By the time he arrived, most of the crowd had long since left. These problems raised serious concerns about the capabilities of the Democratic nominee.

Toward the end of the campaign, the national Democratic Party became concerned that what was supposed to be a sure pickup was slipping away. The DCCC sent outsiders in to help, and in the closing days Representatives Nancy Pelosi (D-CA) and Martin Frost (D-TX) visited the district. While these would be prime attractions at a Georgetown cocktail party, they provided scant assistance in the 12th District. Pelosi is too liberal for Georgia moderates and Frost came to Athens during the Georgia/Florida football weekend when the student body and many of the residents migrate to Jacksonville for what is billed as "The World's Largest Outdoor Cocktail Party."

Walker failed to attract white voters and became one of the few Democrats to lose in liberal Athens. Burns won an improbable victory with 55 percent of the vote. If he wants to serve more than a single term as congressman, he will need to work aggressively to develop a broad base of support.

Across the state in the 11th District, another Democratic primary produced the wrong nominee. Buddy Darden, who had represented parts of this district until defeated by Bob Barr in 1994, tried a comeback. In the primary Darden faced Roger Kahn, a wealthy liquor distributor who had retired to Florida, where he became active in Republican politics, before returning to Georgia to become a gentleman farmer. Kahn spent millions in 2000 before being drubbed by Barr, but from that experience learned how to savage an opponent in television ads. Darden found his experience held against him as Kahn charged him with being hostile to the needs and concerns of the elderly, as well as being a pawn of special interests.

In the general election, Kahn focused his high-spending campaign on state Senator Phil Gingrey. After some positive, get-acquainted ads, Gingrey released a humorous attack on his Democratic opponent, painting him as a wealthy dilettante who was running for Congress to fill a void in his life. As in 2000, all of Kahn's money proved insufficient and Gingrey received 51.6 percent of the vote in a district expected to elect a Democrat with a 10-point margin.

CONCLUSION

When asked to explain the power shift in Georgia, Chambliss's chief consultant exclaimed, "People got tired of dancing with the devil!" Concerns about Cleland's voting record and Barnes' expanding power triggered an avalanche of opposition in rural Georgia that ended generations of Democratic loyalty. Four Republican statewide victories—three of which were unforeseen—punctuated the end of Democratic dominance in the Empire State of the South.

Ripples from November 5 continue to expand. As noted earlier, the GOP secured a state Senate majority when four Democrats changed parties. If Republicans redraw Senate districts, as they say they will, they could control the chamber for the remainder of the decade. Currently, the fate of the state House is up in the air. Even though Democrats won 106 of the 180 seats, the unsuccessful hopeful for the Democratic nomination for the speakership is exploring the possibility of a coalition with Republicans that would make him speaker, name the GOP leader the speaker pro tem and anoint Republicans as chairs of some committees. Should this come to pass, Democratic dominance will not simply be under assault, Democrats could teeter on the verge of minority status in the legislature from which they might not emerge for years. Loss of control of both chambers and the governorship might stimulate further defections to the GOP and make Democratic candidate recruitment more difficult.

Change in party control has already occurred in three Southern states (Florida, Texas and Virginia). In those states, however, the process was more gradual and Republican victories were widely anticipated. The shifts in Georgia were largely unexpected. The Perdue victory was the biggest shock, but the Public Service Commission wins also came as a surprise as were the events that gave Republicans control of the state Senate. In a decade the GOP has gone from having no constitutional offices, one congressional district and 20 percent of the Senate seats to control on all three fronts. If Perdue governs from the center and uses the resources of his office judiciously, Republicans may become the majority in the state, but they are certainly not likely to win the governorship for fifty consecutive elections.

NOTES

1. Georgia's 26 percent population increase during the 1990s netted the state two more congressional districts.

2. Georgia is one of five states in which registration records indicate the race of the voter making it relatively easy for the Democrat to target the households of the black electorate.

3. The Barnes camp does not see teacher alienation as a major cause of defeat and claims that polling showed teachers evenly divided between Barnes and Perdue. Even if accurate, a 50 percent share of educators' votes is poor for a Democrat.

4. This mean is calculated using the scores compiled by the American Federation of State, County and Municipal Employees.

5. Although running in a majority-black district, the older Walker also fell to a white Republican in 2002.

16

California Governor

Don't Vote, It Will Only Encourage Them

MARK Z. BARABAK
Los Angeles Times

On a February morning twelve days before the California primary, Garry South was on a pay telephone at Los Angeles International Airport, talking to Governor Gray Davis and the rest of his political brain trust. It was not an opportune time for South to be headed out of town; his travels forced the cancellation of a morning conference call between Davis and his political team, a rarity in the more than five years the daily bull sessions took place. But South's mother was gravely ill back in Montana and needed her son's immediate attention. So did the governor. Just a day earlier, Davis had decided to pull a last batch of negative ads targeting former Los Angeles Mayor Richard Riordan, the leader in the Republican gubernatorial primary.[1] Davis, a Democrat fighting his own troubles, had taken a risky gamble, crossing over and meddling in the GOP race by dumping millions of dollars into an anti-Riordan campaign aimed at weakening him in advance of the general election. The strategy had paid off; Riordan was badly wounded and Davis—who was unopposed on the Democratic side—decided to end the campaign on a positive note, finishing with ads aimed at polishing his own tarnished image. But Paul Maslin, the governor's pollster, had seen something startling in fresh survey data that morning and he called South at home, catching the governor's chief strategist just before he left for the airport. "We might have just zigged when we should have zagged," Maslin told South. "This guy looks like he's going down."[2]

It would have seemed improbable even a week earlier. Riordan, a multimillionaire who enjoyed the backing of the George W. Bush White House and virtually the entire California Republican Party establishment, was a commanding front-runner against two weak opponents, the badly underfunded Secretary of State Bill Jones and the little-known Bill Simon Jr., a Los Angeles financier making his first try for public office. But Riordan, who had run an extraordinarily ham-handed campaign, was sinking with astonishing speed under the weight of Davis's advertising assault. As South waited for his plane, standing at a bank of pay phones at the United Airlines gate, he convened an emergency strategy session, tying in the governor and the rest of Davis' campaign advisors for an impromptu conference call. "Why are we re-litigating this case?" the governor demanded. "Because, governor, we've turned up some new evidence," Maslin replied. A decision was made to reverse the earlier one: Davis would continue his negative ad blitz to the end, hammering Riordan in hopes of not just wounding his candidacy, but driving him out of the race and delivering Davis his preferred November opponent, the rookie Simon.

Twelve days later, the move was vindicated: Simon beat Riordan in an 18-point landslide. In November, after a general election campaign widely derided as the worst ever run by a candidate for California governor, Simon lost to Davis even though six in ten of those casting ballots disliked the incumbent and more than half said the state was heading down the wrong track.

It was a remarkable feat and one that proved many of the truisms that have made campaigns today so off-putting to so many people: it showed the power of money, the advantage of incumbency and the reward for ruthlessness. It demonstrated—as a whole succession of failed millionaire businessmen candidates can attest—that, in California at least, a run for governor is no place for on-the-job training.

And it underscored that, no matter what people might think, politics is not necessarily about popularity but simply getting one more vote than the opposition. "We don't have to make Gray Davis into the sweetheart of the rodeo," said South, as he prepared an ad campaign that would annihilate Simon in the fall just as Riordan was laid to waste in the winter. "Gray Davis is not going to be judged against himself. He will be judged against his opponent."

After the race, with victory in hand, South put it more tartly, describing the contest as a choice between "damaged goods versus defective product." So the governor and his strategists "bludgeoned Simon with a blunt object," South added, unapologetically. "It was not a pretty sight." ·

A career politician, Davis had won election in 1998 in a 20-point landslide over another middling opponent, then–state Attorney General Dan

Lungren. His first eighteen months or so in office were relatively quiescent, thanks to a roaring economy and the spectacular dot-com run-up. At one point, a gushing *Time* magazine hailed Davis as "the most courageous" governor in America thanks to, among other achievements, a bipartisan healthcare reform package he signed into law. But the adulation died about the same time the economic good times ended. Davis, who approaches politics with all the warmth of a Customs inspector, had never enjoyed a deep reservoir of personal regard among Californians. When money grew tight and the state faced a major energy crisis starting in late 2000, attitudes toward the incumbent quickly soured.

Confronted with a dysfunctional electricity market, Davis dithered as the wholesale price of electricity skyrocketed, the state's biggest utility tumbled into bankruptcy and California suffered through its first mandatory blackouts since World War II. Eventually, the market would stabilize, thanks in part to federal intervention from a reluctant Bush administration and a series of long-term contracts that ended the wild gyration in spot prices. But not before Davis had suffered indelible damage which, for a time, made him Republicans' Number 1 target in the nation.

Back in Washington, at the White House, political strategists were searching for a credible candidate to face Davis and, ideally, capture the statehouse and give the president a toehold in politically inhospitable California. Bush had campaigned hard in the state but still lost badly in 2000, despite outspending then–Vice President Al Gore by roughly $20 million-to-nothing. Jones might have been a natural choice. He was the lone statewide GOP officeholder—withstanding a Democratic tide in California in 1998—and had performed admirably as the state's chief elections officer. But Jones made a politically fatal miscalculation, switching his support from Bush to Arizona Senator John McCain after Bush lost the 2000 New Hampshire presidential primary. The president, who places loyalty above all virtues, never forgave Jones and word from the White House dried up contributions and effectively killed his candidacy before it started.[3] Jones would finish a distant third in the March 2002 primary.

Improbably, the White House found its bright hope in the 71-year-old Riordan, an affable non-ideological Republican who left office on a wave of good feeling after two prosperous terms. In May of 2001, Bush placed a phone call to Riordan wishing him a happy birthday and, according to the mayor, urging him to consider a run for governor. Others in the state GOP establishment soon piled on the proverbial bandwagon. For many, Riordan's moderate stance on social issues and his appeal to women and minority voters in Los Angeles suggested a different brand of Republicanism that could overcome the state party's angry image. Encouraged by those blandishments, Riordan jumped into the governor's race and began running

against Davis from the start, treating the GOP primary as a mere technical-
ity. He never even used the word "Republican" during his announcement
tour, until a questioner brought it up on the second day. He ignored the
jabs of his opponents and, worse from the perspective of the faithful, almost
seemed to go out of his way to antagonize GOP loyalists. Riordan not only
touted his support for legal abortion, but also lectured Republicans on the
need to adopt his views or face extinction as a party.

He showed up at events featuring gay rights activists and honored
Representative Barbara Lee, the Oakland Democrat who cast the lone vote
in Congress opposing the use of force after the September 11 terrorist
attacks. While many Republicans—eager to win back the statehouse—were
willing to make some accommodations, Riordan "ran around sticking his
finger in the eyes of conservatives," said one disgusted supporter, who
helped recruit the ex-mayor into the race. "By saying to people, 'Change or
die' it's inherently saying to them, 'You're wrong' and it was too negative
an approach."[4]

But the pivot point in the race may have come at the end of January
2002, when Davis launched his first attack spot. The 30-second television
ad criticized Riordan, a devout Catholic, for his prior support of anti-abortion candidates and causes. The Riordan camp responded that same night
with a generic ad—filmed weeks earlier—that expressed his disappointment
at Davis' tone but did not dispute the facts. Strategists for Riordan wagered
that in a post–September 11 environment, voters would have little appetite
for the sharp-elbowed advertising of the past. But Davis persisted. He
pounded Riordan on abortion and the death penalty—the GOP hopeful
having expressed ambivalence about the latter—and also assailed his record
as mayor. The GOP front-runner's lead, once as high as 40 percentage
points, began eroding. That convinced the wealthy Simon, who had hus-
banded his resources, to foot the kind of multimillion dollar ad campaign
that is needed to get voters' attention in a diverse state with 15 million registered voters and 23 widely scattered media markets.

Simon had been the first candidate to announce his intentions to run
for governor, forming an exploratory committee in February 2001. He
entered the contest with the encouragement of Riordan, a friend and fellow
parishioner at St. Monica's Catholic Church in Santa Monica, whose own
candidacy was still months from conception. Simon ran the West Coast
office of his family's investment firm and had only lived in California for 12
years. He was largely unknown in GOP circles, despite his namesake father,
a member of President Richard Nixon's cabinet and a sometimes cruel task-
master who would terrorize his seven children with "the water treat-
ment"—waking them on Saturdays by dumping buckets of water over their
heads.[5] It was the approach of Simon's 50th birthday, as well as dismay at

the state of one of his children's schools, that spurred him into running for office. Some suggested the novice candidate aim for a lesser job, such as state treasurer. But in late January 2001, Simon flew to Sacramento for a series of meetings with consultant Sal Russo, a political veteran of more than 25 years. During those sessions, Russo told Simon that there was no point in running a down-ticket race. "You can't win a lower constitutional office unless you have the top of the ticket," Russo told Simon. With only Jones in the race for governor at that point, Russo figured there was plenty of room for an alternative. So by the time he left Russo's office, Simon had decided to explore a run for governor.

He proceeded cautiously. There would be no final decision until summer, after seeing whether Simon could attract donors, staff, and supporters. At one point, Simon and Russo went to visit Riordan at his home in Los Angeles's elegant Brentwood neighborhood. Arnold Steinberg, a pollster then working for Riordan, recalled that Simon kept asking the mayor whether he was going to enter the governor's contest. Riordan gave no clear answer. "I walked away feeling that Riordan had lost an opportunity to persuade Simon to withdraw from the race," Steinberg later said. So Simon kept traveling the state, speaking wherever a handful of Republicans gathered. He outlined plans to address the state's energy problems, water, and transportation, called for tax cuts and touted himself as "the candidate of ideas." Simon finally took to the television airwaves in late January 2002 with a spot featuring former New York City Mayor Rudolph Giuliani. Simon had served as an assistant U.S. attorney for a few years under Giuliani. Seeing one of the heroes of September 11 on their TV screen was enough to make voters pay attention. Simon triumphed at a February straw poll at the state GOP convention—after Riordan boycotted the popularity contest—and built on his momentum by expanding his meager TV advertising campaign. More important, he consolidated the conservative GOP base and established himself over Jones as the alternative to the more centrist Riordan. On March 5, Simon easily captured the GOP nomination—a surprise even to many of his own strategists who were busy in the days before the primary looking for new jobs.

Few knew at the time, but the upset would prove the high point of Simon's campaign. He entered the general election with no strategy and a good deal of skepticism among fellow Republicans, starting with the White House. Within weeks, state party insiders were grumbling about Simon's failure to capitalize on the momentum from his primary win. The state's major Republican donors sat on their wallets. National party leaders began bad-mouthing the campaign. Internally, the Simon camp split into rival factions. On one side were friends, family members, and Simon's original set of strategists who believed that one of the candidate's strongest assets was his image as a congenial conservative. They discouraged Simon from attacking Davis, even as the Democrat began pounding his challenger with a barrage of negative ads that would not cease until Election Day. On the other side were new strategic recruits, pressed on the Simon campaign by the White House and the national GOP, whose leadership wanted to fight back measure for measure. The result was dysfunction and a campaign at constant war with itself.[6]

Davis, meantime, enjoyed the services of a finely tuned campaign team together since before his own upset primary victory in 1998. They took care of the mechanics while Davis provided the fuel: the astonishing $70 million he started raising before he even took office. Throughout his career, Davis had been an unabashed fundraiser, infamous for crashing other politicians' events and even working the pews at funerals. But he took his money-raising efforts to audacious new heights. On one occasion he even stunned shock-proof political insiders by asking a teachers' union leader for $1 million while discussing education policy.[7] Although the solicitation was not illegal, it damaged Davis's image and fueled attacks on him as a "pay-to-play" governor, as Simon frequently put it.

A series of revelations suggesting links between Davis's fundraising and official action kept the issue alive throughout the campaign. But Simon proved a deeply flawed messenger. His own controversial actions in the business world, including dealings with a failed savings and loan, badly undermined his credibility, particularly in the toxic atmosphere created by the collapse of Enron, Global Crossing, and other corporate high fliers. In the midst of a national backlash against executive greed, Simon suffered a devastating blow in July when a jury in Los Angeles returned a $78 million fraud verdict against his family's investment firm. Although the verdict was overturned weeks later, it sent the Simon campaign reeling and scared off many Republicans for good.[8]

But Simon himself did the most serious damage to his campaign. During an early October debate, he intimated Davis had broken the law by raising funds on state property back when he was lieutenant governor. Pressed for proof, Simon released a photograph that purported to show Davis standing in his Capitol office accepting a $10,000 campaign contribution from a law enforcement political action group. It turned out Simon was wrong. The check had been turned over at a private residence; no one on his staff bothered to check the locale until it was too late. The candidate was forced to retract the charge and apologize, and his campaign never regained its balance.[9]

Still, despite Davis's enormous advantages in money, political resources and experience, he never could put the contest away—a testament to his enduring unpopularity. He won the election 47 percent to 42 percent, a much closer finish than expected. Turnout hit a record low, about 50 percent of the registered voters and 30 percent of all adults, and the phrase "lesser of two evils" became the unofficial state motto during one of the most thoroughly uninspiring, content-less elections in California history. While many stayed home, others who felt obliged to vote skipped the governor's race or cast their ballots for one of the minor candidates, who collectively received the highest third-party vote in more than 60 years. Michelle Allman, a 26-year-old homemaker from Bloomington in San Bernardino County, summed up the attitude of many. "All I cared about was voting for someone besides Davis or Simon," she said while waiting at an Inland Empire car wash on Election Day. "I saw their names, skipped right past them and went to the other ones, and then I did an 'eeny, meeny, miney, mo.' I don't even remember the name of the guy I voted for. Because it didn't matter."

NOTES

1. Author interviews with Garry South, 12 November 2002; 10 November 2002.

2. Author interview with Paul Maslin, 14 November 2002.

3. George Skelton, "Jones' Catch-22," *Los Angeles Times*, 4 February 2002.

4. Mark Z. Barabak and Nicholas Riccardi, "Riordan's Bid Plagued By Missteps," *Los Angeles Times*, 7 March 2002.

5. David Ferrell, "Simon Forged His Future In Father's Formidable Past," *Los Angeles Times*, 15 October 2002.

6. Mark Z. Barabak, "Simon Camp Fears Loss Of Momentum," *Los Angeles Times*, 22 April 2002. Mark Z. Barabak, "For Simon, Naughty Or Nice Race," *Los Angeles Times*, 15 June 2002.

7. Dan Morain, "Davis Fund-Raiser Is A Last Hurrah," *Los Angeles Times*, 10 November 2002.

8. Michael Finnegan, "Records Outline Simon's Role In Collapsed S&L," *Los Angeles Times*, 13 June 2002.

9. Mark Z. Barabak, "Simon Won't Apologize, But GOP Strategists Are Left In Sorry States," *Los Angeles Times*, 10 October 2002.

17

Florida Governor

Three Elections in One

SUSAN A. MACMANUS
University of South Florida

Florida's Election 2002 was three elections rolled into one: presidential election 2000, the governor's race, and presidential election 2004. From the beginning, it was cast as a highly competitive race because of the incredibly close 2000 presidential election, decided in Florida for George W. Bush by just 537 votes. Even the White House's own political adviser worried that Florida's governorship was a "Possible D Pickup."

Winning the Florida governor's race became the primary goal for both Democrats and Republicans once Democratic National Committee Chairman Terry McAuliffe identified "defeating Jeb Bush as the Party's No. 1 priority."

Some saw the governor's race as a surrogate grudge re-match between George W. Bush and Al Gore—a chance to prove once and for all who really won Florida in 2000. Both the current president and former vice president visited the state a number of times.

Inside Florida, most saw the election as a fight over the direction the state would take in the next four years. Republican Governor Jeb Bush, 49, and Democratic nominee Bill McBride, offered Floridians clear choices on everything from education to taxes to adoptions by gay couples.

For both parties, the race signaled the opening of the 2004 presidential season. Both wanted the "bragging rights" and organizational advantages associated with controlling the governorship of this battleground state. Before the Democratic primary was even over, Democratic presidential "wanna-bes" like U.S. Senators John Kerry of Massachusetts, John Edwards of North Carolina, and Joseph Lieberman of Connecticut were courting the attention of Florida's Democrats. Most chose to attend the state Democratic Party Convention in Orlando and returned to campaign for Democratic candidates.

THE DEMOCRATIC PRIMARY: MCBRIDE UPSETS RENO

The Democratic Primary attracted three contenders: the well-known former U.S. Attorney General Janet Reno, 64, the little-known state senator Daryl Jones, 47, an African American from South Florida, and the totally unknown McBride, 57, from Tampa, former CEO of Holland and Knight, the state's largest law firm. The September 10 primary ended as a photo finish between Reno (44 percent) and McBride (44.4 percent) that was not resolved for several days. It was also the first year in which Florida had no runoff election—a winner-take-all primary.

McBride's upset led many to label him the "giant slayer" and gave Democrats across the United States hope that Jeb Bush could be beaten. Campaign contributions rolled in to the McBride campaign, just in time because he had whittled his $3 million campaign treasury down to $60,000. (In contrast, the Bush campaign still had more than $5 million in the bank.)

Outside Florida, Reno had been virtually anointed as the nominee. But inside the state it was a different story. Many party leaders feared that Reno was too liberal to attract Florida's conservative Democrats or independents. Some voiced concern about her health and age.

McBride was the last of the major party candidates to file for the race. A folksy party insider, he had been interested in the governor's race for some time. A *Washington Post* reporter described him as "a promising novice candidate with a Bronze Star, a football injury and a drawl." His big break came when the state's teachers' union, the Florida Education Association (FEA), decided to throw its weight—and money—behind him. He, in turn, pledged to make education his number one priority.

The FEA and the Democratic Party invested millions in a TV ad campaign that stressed his military service, his brief football stint at the University of Florida, his volunteer efforts as Little League coach, his children's attendance at public schools, and his overriding commitment to investing more in Florida's education system. It was clear that the ads were aimed not just at women voters, but also at men voters, who had been slipping away from the Democratic Party in recent elections.

The first FEA-sponsored ad quickly drew controversy. A *St. Petersburg Times* editorial pointed out that the association "is walking an extremely fine line in maintaining that its 30-second spots address an 'issue,' as federal and state laws permit, rather than promoting McBride's candidacy." Republican Party leaders filed a formal complaint with the Florida Elections Commission against the ad, which led the FEA to replace it with others. However, the close connection with the FEA remained an issue throughout the campaign.

In contrast, Reno, who didn't have the money for TV ads, ran a grass-roots campaign, driving her red pickup truck from one end of the state to the other—an approach that yielded considerable free press coverage. Unfortunately, her advance team was not able to generate large crowds at many stops, which became the second half of the stories. It was not until a week or so before the primary that Reno agreed to let the state Democratic Party run TV ads for her. By this time, polls showed her lead slipping away to McBride.

Reno cast her lot with South Florida, and particularly with older voters and African Americans. She also gambled on the time-tested assumption that a large percentage of the state's *high turnout* Democratic primary voters reside in Miami-Dade, Broward, and Palm Beach counties. Her strategy? Win big in vote-rich South Florida and capture senior and minority votes in the rest of the state . . . and stress issues like prescription drugs and the environment, as well as education, while criticizing Bush's handling of problems with the state's child welfare agency.

McBride's primary strategy, on the other hand, focused on North and Central Florida, including the I-4 corridor. His campaign assumed that he, as the most moderate of the three candidates, would have considerably more appeal to the state's conservative and moderate Democrats outside South Florida. His strategy? Win big in North and Central Florida and capture some of the South Florida vote . . . and stick with education.

Both strategies were sound. After all, just 0.4 percent separated the two in the final vote tally. Had Jones not been in the race, Reno might have won. As it was, he siphoned off a sizeable number of African-American votes.

THE DEMOCRATIC DEBATE:
A LOVE FEST AND A MAVERICK

At the outset, the three candidates agreed to avoid attacking each other. McBride quipped: "I want you to like Janet Reno and Daryl Jones. I just want you to like me a little bit more."

Only one televised debate, held in West Palm Beach August 27, featured all three candidates. Jones, an eight-year veteran of the Florida Senate and Air Force fighter pilot, persuaded the nonpartisan sponsoring group that he deserved a spot, despite his low standing in the polls. Once in, Jones launched a few barbs at his opponents—it was his only shot at gaining press recognition and he had no money to buy sufficient TV time. In the debate, while Reno and McBride spoke in generalities, Jones offered specifics. His performance captured the attention not just of African-American voters, but also of moderate white voters outside South Florida—a fact never sufficiently recognized by Democratic leaders.

McBride's message was that *he*, not Reno, was the one who could beat Jeb Bush. This was the same message that party leaders and the FEA had been touting for months. After McBride lost to Jeb Bush, many Reno supporters argued that she might have beaten the governor because *she* would have generated higher turnout than McBride in South Florida. (McBride supporters argued just the opposite.) Both campaigns agreed, however, that the regional fissures that perennially divide the party contributed to McBride's loss. Florida Democrats continue to be a regionally fractured party that even Humpty Dumpty would have trouble putting back together.

A MESSY PRIMARY ELECTION
DAY AND POST-PRIMARY

In the vote-rich South Florida counties of Miami-Dade and Broward, primary Election Day turned out to be a mess. Polls didn't open on time, poll workers didn't show up as promised, and some of the new voting machines malfunctioned and/or were foreign to ill-trained poll workers. Even Reno was unable to vote at her precinct when she appeared with national media in tow because it was not yet open! By midafternoon, Secretary of State Jim Smith asked Governor Jeb Bush to issue an executive order keeping polls open an additional two hours, which he did, although some poll workers never got the message and closed at 7:00 p.m.

Late that night while it appeared McBride had won, the state's voters once again went to bed uncertain of the winner and grimaced as the nation dusted off its "Flori-duh" jokes. Miami-Dade and Broward counties began recounting ballots. Reno refused to concede until satisfied that every vote was counted. Three days after the primary, she demanded a statewide recount, a request denied because her numbers were not high enough to authorize it under Florida law. The day before, McBride, anxious to move ahead, declared himself the victor, even though the official certification was not until September 17.

The unanticipated anger among Reno's South Florida senior and African-American supporters over this "premature" declaration never substantially diminished, likely costing McBride a considerable number of votes, maybe even the November 5 election. A black South Florida Democrat warned of the situation's sensitivity, noting that McBride "needs to communicate to people that he is a fair person who didn't steal or take anything from Janet."

THE GENERAL ELECTION CAMPAIGN: FROM DEAD HEAT TO LANDSLIDE

McBride survived the primary with his image of giant slayer intact. But unbeknownst to many, he had fired his campaign manager the day after the primary and replaced her with "people from the state teachers union and related organizations who had little campaign experience and none running against a political machine as formidable as the Bush family's." The decision boiled down to personality conflicts—but it became increasingly controversial as the contest between McBride and Bush heated up.

THE "TAPS" TV AD

The Republican TV ad campaign against McBride had actually started during the *primary*. A 30-second ad pictured just the feet of a woman, then a man's, tap-dancing, and asked viewers: "What do you get with Reno and McBride? A song and dance." The ad accused Reno and McBride of being evasive on issues like the death penalty and the use of standardized test results for grading schools. The ad continued to run while McBride's name recognition and approval ratings kept rising. The Republicans also ran an ad describing McBride as a "corporate lawyer who cut health care benefits and froze wages for support staff in order to increase profits for each partner by $50,000."

McBride seized on the ads as proof that the Jeb Bush campaign feared running against him more than Reno. Soon Republicans began criticizing the ads, lamenting they were fueling the McBride campaign.

Eventually the party pulled the ads, but in the end, they probably helped Bush more than McBride. The tap dancing ad in particular had planted a seed in the minds of undecided voters that the Democrat's plans lacked specifics. Jeb Bush amplified this theme so that by the third, and most watched, debate, it was *the* message. This demonstrates what ad professionals know—namely, that judging an ad's impact at a single point in time is not necessarily wise. It ignores the fact that ads run during a campaign are often coordinated with stump messages—and with subsequent ads.

A DEAD HEAT FOR MOST OF OCTOBER: EDUCATION THE ISSUE

The race between Jeb Bush and McBride remained a statistical dead heat until the third gubernatorial debate on October 22. The McBride campaign was able to keep it tight by hammering Bush on the shortcomings of his educational policies. McBride's TV ads cited Florida's low rankings on SAT scores, graduation rates, class size, and per-pupil spending relative to other states. On the stump and at the first two debates (September 27 and October 15) McBride roundly criticized grading public schools from A to F based on results of the state's FCAT test—a standardized test used to measure achievement of students in grades three through ten. He proposed instead that the FCAT be used as a diagnostic tool.

McBride also roused audiences when he pushed for the adoption of a constitutional amendment that proposed to reduce class sizes for pre-K through high school. However, up to mid-October, few Floridians had paid much attention to the class size issue or to the nine other proposed amendments on the ballot. That soon changed.

Meanwhile, Jeb Bush began running ads proposing his own plans to build more classrooms and improve teacher pay and training. The ads also highlighted the improvements made during his first administration (rising student reading scores, especially among minorities, $3 billion in new school spending, and greater accountability requirements for individual schools). Other ads focused on his efforts in such areas as crime, jobs, the environment, and prescription drugs for seniors.

Just prior to the third debate, as press coverage of the various constitutional amendments began to intensify, the Bush camp began running an ad challenging McBride to explain how he would *pay* for all his proposals. Would it be with a property tax, a sales tax, or an income tax? The McBride campaign cried "foul" because an income tax is prohibited under the state constitution. McBride emphasized that the only tax he was proposing was a 50-cents-a-pack tax increase on cigarettes. Nonetheless, the question stuck and the stage was set for the third debate—and what many believe was the campaign's turning point.

FOCUS SHIFTS FROM EDUCATION TO POCKETBOOK

Tim Russert of NBC's "Meet the Press" moderated the final debate, televised across the state on NBC stations. Among his questions, Russert asked about the cost of the class size amendment. When McBride responded that it was "somewhere in between" the usually cited $8 billion and $27 billion range, the audience laughed. It got worse. He was also forced to acknowledge that his 50-cents-per-pack cigarette tax increase could not pay for all the programs he supported.

After the debate, Republican ads successfully recast McBride as a liberal big spender who would raise taxes. One ad featured a cash register ringing warnings: "If McBride gets the job, you'll get the bill." By the time McBride got around to running a direct response ad, it was too late. The polls began showing a widening gap. The last major poll (MSNBC/Zogby) of likely voters conducted October 31 to November 2 predicted Bush to win by a 57 percent to 42 percent margin. The actual vote was Bush 56 percent, McBride 43 percent.

As a novice candidate, McBride did not heed advice to prepare for the debates with a knowledgeable, hard-hitting sparring partner as had Jeb Bush. A senior member of the McBride staff said, "It was just something he didn't want to do. He thought he could just go in there and wing it."

Important lesson: Florida has always been an anti-tax state to a large degree, primarily as a consequence of its unique age and racial/ethnic demographics. The state's (and the nation's) struggling economy made the anti-tax message resonate all the more.

Ironically, the class size amendment passed, although by a slim margin, leaving Jeb Bush with few desirable choices about how to pay for it.

NO EASY STREET FOR BUSH:
POLITICAL AND PERSONAL PROBLEMS

The campaign wasn't all easy street for Jeb Bush. Problems at the Department of Children and Families (DCF)—specifically, losing track of 5-year-old Rilya Wilson and other children—revealed an agency out of control. Democrats quickly reminded the governor of his pledge to fix the problems in 1998. The DCF secretary resigned midway in the campaign, and the governor quickly appointed a successor only to have his choice attacked. Revelations of the new secretary's authorship of ultra-conservative materials put pressure on the governor to rescind the appointment. The controversy died down, but embarrassing statistics on DCF kept seeping out during the campaign. After the election, some Democrats wondered aloud why McBride never made more of the DCF issue.

Another setback and personal heartache for Jeb Bush occurred when his daughter, Noelle, was arrested for writing an illegal prescription for Xanax, an anti-anxiety drug. While in rehabilitation, she was caught with crack cocaine and sent to jail for ten days. The McBride campaign stayed away from the issue, but Bush was criticized for not going to court with his daughter as she was being sentenced. The governor explained that he feared it would give the false impression of trying to influence the judge's decision. To Florida's voters, it was a non-issue; 95 percent said the incident would have no bearing on their decision.

Perhaps Jeb Bush himself made *the* most embarrassing campaign miscue. He remarked in a reporter's presence that he had "devious plans" for dealing with the class size amendment should it pass. He later said it was a sarcastic remark, but McBride used it in all his subsequent speeches as well as some TV ads.

None of these situations was enough to defeat Jeb Bush. Republicans simply bested Democrats at the turnout game.

How bad was it? In Miami-Dade, Broward, and Palm Beach counties, average turnout was down 17 percent from 1994—when Democrat Lawton Chiles barely beat Jeb Bush in Bush's first attempt at the governorship. In Broward County, historically Florida's Democratic stronghold, turnout dropped from 60 percent in 1994 to a dismal 45 percent in 2002. McBride did not spend a day in Broward County until four weeks after the primary, and he paid dearly for it.

GET-OUT-THE-VOTE EFFORTS: REPUBLICANS RULE

Republicans were far more successful than Democrats in getting their supporters to the polls. Tactics that worked:

- They invested huge sums to encourage Republicans to vote absentee. Their absentee ballots outnumbered Democratic ones by 160,000.
- Jeb Bush toured the Panhandle and Central Florida by bus, an approach he used successfully in 1998. (Turnout rates in these counties are traditionally higher than those in the larger, more urban counties of South Florida.)
- Republicans spent millions on direct mail pieces that contrasted the candidates on key issues and prominently featured Jeb's popular brother, the president.
- The GOP heavily targeted the state's burgeoning Hispanic population, especially the non-Cuban Hispanics, in Central Florida. More than $1.5 million worth of ads ran on Hispanic cable television and radio; Bush made repeated visits to Hispanic neighborhoods and campaigned in Spanish. In contrast, Democrats did not run a

Spanish-language TV ad until 13 days before the election. As a result, Orange County, which went for Gore in 2000, went heavily for George W. Bush in 2002 (a likely advantage for the president here in 2004).

- George W. Bush appeared in key metropolitan areas, like Tampa, which bolstered turnout among suburban Republicans. In addition, appearances of former Republican New York Mayor Rudy Guiliani in South Florida's retirement communities helped splinter the senior vote—a vote once "owned" by Democrats.

Historically, Democrats have outdone Republicans in get-out-the-vote (GOTV) efforts. Early in the campaign, Reno stressed that Democrats would have to turn out voters at a presidential election level and appeal to the party's base constituencies—blacks, Jews, women, and seniors. The party did not focus on absentee ballots, primarily because it did not have the money (each absentee ballot costs $2 to $3) and because, according to one report, "many elderly and minority voters—likely Democrats—distrust the notion of voting by mail." Instead they prefer early voting (new under Florida law this election cycle).

In the campaign's closing days, Reno and Jones worked hard to mobilize these key bases; McBride, too, concentrated on South Florida. Former President Bill Clinton and former Vice President Al Gore, Senator Joe Lieberman, Reverend Jesse Jackson, Al Sharpton, and numerous Democratic luminaries came in to help as well. A *St. Petersburg Times* editorial said the last-minute appearances were an "unwelcome intervention [that] helped to turn a close gubernatorial race into an easy victory for Bush."

But the bottom line is that the Democrats spent less time and money on GOTV efforts than in presidential election 2000—and paid the price. A poll of 29 heavily black precincts in nine large counties estimated that black turnout fell from 72 percent in 2000 to just 43 percent in 2002. (Even so, black turnout was higher in 2002 than in 1998 when it was a paltry 27 percent.)

Disgruntled Democrats began to complain of stale, outdated GOTV techniques. Some questioned the wisdom of focusing on black churches or using local black political leaders as intermediaries. Henry Crespo, president of the Miami-Dade Democratic Black Caucus, said: "Clearly, what [McBride] did was to go to a couple of chiefs to get their approval and expect us to come out and vote for him with a promise for a piece of the pie when historically we only get crumbs. The black electorate is smarter than that." State Representative Chris Smith, a Democrat from Fort Lauderdale, lambasted the party for delay in getting GOTV funds into the field: "The money [$44,000 for Broward County] didn't get here until the Friday before the election. What the hell do you expect?"

Others criticized McBride's single-issue campaign that never excited senior voters. Turnout in key South Florida retirement communities like Sunrise Lakes, Century Village Pembroke Pines, and Century Village Deerfield Beach ran 10 to 20 points below the 56 percent statewide rate. Longtime Century Village Democratic leader "Trinchi" Trinchitella noted: "McBride is a good man, but he didn't get the message across down here in South Florida." He also pointed to changing demographics. Younger retirees, unlike the Great Depression generation they are replacing, are not as solidly Democratic.

Criticisms of McBride's choice of running mates also resurfaced. Some disappointed and angry Democrats believed he should have chosen a woman or a minority like Daryl Jones as a running mate. Instead, he selected Senate Minority Leader Tom Rossin, D-Royal Palm Beach, a 69-year-old white male hardly known outside of his south Florida district.

MONEY: REPUBLICAN PARTY RULES

Democrats point to the disadvantage in campaign cash. McBride and Bush raised $8.2 million and $10.4 million respectively in their campaigns, but the Republicans clearly had the edge in soft money—$52.5 million to the Democrats' $30-plus million. The GOP used the advantage to pay for most of the campaign's television ads (permitted when an ad mentions at least two other Republican candidates—Florida's "three-pack" rule).

Although the primary nearly emptied McBride's campaign chest, he benefited from renewed interest inside and outside Florida after beating Reno. The Florida Democratic Party raised around $15.7 million after the primary, more than the Republican Party's $14.7 million, and the national Democratic Party sent $4.4 million in soft money into Florida during the final two months of the campaign. In addition, the FEA spent millions running TV ads supporting McBride's education plans. National labor unions and lawyer groups closely linked to the party provided at least $2.9 million during the last two months.

Some Democrats complained that too much was spent on TV ads ($10 million of the $15.7 million raised in the final weeks) and not enough on GOTV efforts. They argued that "TV ads . . . fail to effectively motivate specific target groups in the party base such as black voters, women, Jews, and seniors, who are better reached through phone calls, mail, and the radio." For some, the failing provided further evidence of the inexperience of the campaign managers brought in after the primary.

Campaign spending differentials aside, the state's major newspaper endorsements split evenly: 12 for Bush and 12 for McBride.

A CLEAN SWEEP BY REPUBLICANS

When the polls closed November 5, Florida heaved a collective sigh of relief—no voting problems. Reporting of results by county supervisors went so quickly that by 9 p.m. most of the television news networks had declared Bush the winner.

He won in a landslide, carrying 55 of 67 counties and receiving 656,619 votes more than McBride. One reporter said McBride's defeat was "the worst showing of a Democrat running for governor since 1868."

The governor's, and arguably George W. Bush's, coattails were long. For the first time in Florida's history, Republicans control the governorship, all three cabinet posts, 18 of 25 Congressional seats, 26 of 40 state Senate seats, and 81 of 120 state House seats. Democrats' only remaining comfort was their grasp of the two U.S. Senate seats, held by Bob Graham and Bill Nelson.

An analysis of Bush's victory, based on a Zogby post-election survey of 600 registered voters who voted on November 5, revealed the following:

- More Democrats crossed over to vote for Jeb Bush than Republicans for McBride. The independent vote tipped slightly for Jeb Bush (45 percent to McBride's 43 percent).
- Florida's baby boomers and seniors voted for Jeb Bush, while McBride carried only the 18- to 29-year-old group.
- Jeb Bush received 62 percent of the white vote and 53 percent of the Hispanic vote, while McBride got 92 percent of the African-American vote.
- Jeb Bush did well among Catholic voters (64 percent) and Protestants (57 percent), while McBride won the Jewish vote (56.8 percent to Bush's 35 percent). The Jewish vote for Bush was higher than is typical for a Republican candidate.
- Male voters overwhelmingly supported Jeb Bush, while the female vote was nearly evenly split between the two (Bush—49.5 percent; McBride—48.0 percent).
- McBride carried South Florida, but Jeb Bush carried the rest of the state. Jeb Bush carried the small city, suburban, and rural vote, while McBride barely won the large city vote (48.2 percent to Bush's 47.5 percent).

Perhaps the most telling statistic is that less than one-third of the voters identified education/schools as the "*one issue* that was most important" in determining their vote for governor. Nor were taxes and the economy the overwhelming issue. Actually responses were spread over a wide range of issues. Running on a single issue in a large, diverse state like Florida is a dangerous strategy. Many voters, especially older voters, base their decisions on an individual candidate's qualities.

Voters also tend to stick with a "known" incumbent during periods of uncertainty. This is especially true when a challenger, like McBride, fails to show he could do a markedly better job than the incumbent.

FLORIDA STILL A BATTLEGROUND STATE IN 2004

Florida continues to be seen as a critical battleground state on the road to the White House. It now has 27 Electoral College votes, having gained two more congressional seats after the 2000 Census.

In spite of the lopsided victory by Jeb Bush, the results of the race should not be interpreted as a sure-fire prediction of Florida's leanings in 2004. The dynamics of the 2002 race—poor Democratic turnout, especially among African-American and elderly voters, and the swing of independent and older voters to Bush—will be hard to replicate in a higher turnout presidential contest.

In addition, Florida's voters are nearly evenly divided on partisan lines: 43 percent are registered Democrats, 39 percent, Republicans, 2 percent are registered with minor parties, and the remaining 16 percent are independents (no party affiliation). The Democratic-Republican registration figures are actually even closer. Democrats in the Panhandle, the state's most conservative and rural region, often vote Republican in presidential contests.

The challenges facing Florida's Democratic Party are formidable, but not insurmountable. The 2002 race clearly demonstrated a need to revamp the party's get-out-the-vote and minority outreach strategies. Party officials need to work on melding Democrats across regions and move beyond the problems in the 2000 presidential election. According to an election night poll by two Florida think tanks, less than 1 percent of Floridians who stayed away from the polls November 5 did so out of anger with the 2000 fiasco.

The state's Republican Party faces its own challenges. Party leaders know the fate of the Bush brothers will remain inextricably intertwined in 2004 just as it was in 2002. The party must deal with the realities of changing demographics in a fast-growing state, most importantly the growing minority populations and the ever-rising number of independent voters.

In the end, the voter registration figures in Florida tell the tale: the Democratic-Republican playing field is more level than the 2002 governor's election results suggest. Florida will once again be at the center of what promises to be a tough fight for the presidency. In the words of one analyst, "Florida almost certainly will be the most-contested state in the country because it is the most populous one considered to be in play." The White House's own pollster agrees, "I don't know how you win without Florida."

NOTE

Michael B. Greenman, a graduate student in USF's Master of Public Administration program, contributed to this chapter.

18

Illinois Governor

It Was More Than the Ryan Name

PAUL GREEN

Roosevelt University

In 1972 Dan Walker, a combative lawyer and unorthodox Democratic politician, was elected Illinois governor. Few political observers at the time would have predicted that it would take the Democrats 30 years to win this office again. But it did.

Starting in 1976 Illinois Republicans put together a seven-election gubernatorial winning streak. Two factors drove this remarkable political run. First, legendary Chicago Mayor Richard Jim Daley in 1970 agreed to a constitutional change that after 1976 all state constitutional offices would be contested during the off year and not presidential year elections. It was one of "Hizzoner's" few political errors because low-income voters in his party's Chicago base were less likely to turn out in non-presidential year elections. Second, there was the quality of the candidates. Except for the 1990 battle (Republican Jim Edgar and Democrat Neil Hartigan), GOP gubernatorial nominees out-fundraised, out-organized, and out-campaigned their Democratic rival in every one of the other six contests.

THE PRIMARY CAMPAIGNS: HARD-NOSED PARTY BATTLES

All of the above history was duly noted by a young and ambitious Democratic Chicagoan, Congressman Rod Blagojevich. The son of Serbian immigrants, Blagojevich is a political paradox. A product of the Democratic organization and married to the daughter of a powerful Chicago Democratic alderman/ward committeeman, Blagojevich has enjoyed enormous support from traditional liberal elements within the party and the city. As a state representative and congressman he maintained his dual power sources, and prior to the 2000 Democratic National Convention made it known to both support groups that he was running for governor in 2002.

For nearly a year an uncontested Blagojevich put together a statewide organization unmatched in recent Democratic history. And he would need all of it. Two late challengers with far better name recognition than Blagojevich turned the March 2002 Democratic gubernatorial primary into a three-way shoot out.

Longtime African-American Democratic office-holder Roland Burris (former state comptroller and attorney general as well as second place finisher in the 1994 and 1998 gubernatorial primaries) once again sought the governorship. Burris' entrance wiped out Blagojevich's game plan to win black primary support.

The other contender was Paul Vallas, the former Chicago Public School CEO who had gained national attention for improving the city's public schools. Vallas, despite limited funds and a questionable campaign organization, quickly became a media favorite and the darling of suburban voters.

On primary day Blagojevich eked out a two percent victory over Vallas (25,469 votes) despite finishing last in vote-rich Chicago and coming in second to Vallas in suburbia. Blagojevich won the primary by crushing his opponents in downstate Illinois. Here his carefully crafted organization headed by Democratic county chairmen and union leaders held firm, and many pundits joked that it was hard to believe a name like Blagojevich would run so well in rural and small town Illinois. Nonetheless, Blagojevich insiders worried about their candidate's dismal showing in Chicago and its suburbs.

If Democrats stressed about the November 2002 gubernatorial election, the Illinois GOP put themselves on a "political suicide watch." Seldom in the state's rough and tumble history was there a tougher or meaner primary than the 2002 fight for the Republican gubernatorial nomination. Why?

In 1998 then–Secretary of State George Ryan won the state mansion for the GOP in a close contest with Democrat Glenn Poshard (then a congressman). On taking office, Governor George Ryan, a consummate politician from the old school, dazzled Illinoisans with new programs and a grandfatherly demeanor. Then the roof fell in.

A scandal stemming from his term as secretary of state broke wide-open turning Governor Ryan politically into damaged goods. Dozens of his former employees were charged and convicted of participating in a "license for bribes" scandal. It involved selling licenses to unfit drivers (especially commercial truckers) who paid off secretary of state employees. Worse yet, many employees admitted that some of the bribe money went to pay for tickets to George Ryan's fundraisers. And even worse, one of the illegal licensees had a tragic truck accident that killed six children of a south suburban Chicago family.

Though not personally implicated in this sordid mess, George Ryan in the summer of 2001 announced he could not and would not run for reelection. Into this political void came three prominent Republicans espousing different philosophies, unique personalities, and genuine animosity against each other and Governor George Ryan.

Jim Ryan, a two-term Illinois attorney general, had informed Governor George Ryan even before the latter's "no second term" speech that he was running for governor. (The coincidental same last name of both men would be an ongoing campaign issue through Election Day.) Jim Ryan was never close to George Ryan and he had his own power base in DuPage County—Illinois Republicans' best vote-producing area. A pro-life conservative, Jim Ryan was slightly to the right of his more moderate Illinois GOP governor predecessors, but many believed he was still in the electoral mainstream. His two rivals did not.

On the right was State Senator Patrick O'Malley who accused Jim Ryan of being a "soft" conservative. He "out righted" Jim Ryan on every issue as he appealed to the state's Christian right and diehard Republican conservatives. Most important his campaign was well financed which allowed him to use television ads early and often as he attempted to link Jim Ryan with George Ryan's troubles.

On the left was Lieutenant Governor Corrine Wood who called both Jim Ryan and O'Malley political extremists. Attempting to become the state's first female governor, Wood, a pro-choice/somewhat anti-gun candidate, aimed her campaign directly at moderate voters in both parties. Like O'Malley, she had plenty of campaign funds to spread her positive message and political attacks in the media throughout the state.

When the Republican primary dust cleared, Jim Ryan had a somewhat surprisingly comfortable win over both of his vocal and hardworking foes (Jim Ryan—45 percent, O'Malley—28 percent, Wood—27 percent). Numerically, his victory was far more impressive than Blagojevich's in the Democratic Party. However, politically and philosophically the Illinois GOP was in disarray as lingering scandals and bitter political feelings left a large chunk of the party angry and demoralized.

THE GENERAL ELECTION CAMPAIGN:
AN ORGANIZATION TALE OF TWO PARTIES

Illinois Democrats rallied quickly behind Blagojevich. Both of his primary opponents immediately endorsed him and his own political and fundraising operations and operators energetically spread out through the state.

Illinois Republicans were a far different story. Neither of Jim Ryan's primary foes endorsed him, and the party's nominee was forced to spend several crucial months rewinning the nomination. In fact, from his March primary victory through Labor Day, Jim Ryan campaigned against his fellow Republicans as much if not more so than he did against his Democratic opponent. Why?

Three simple words: scandal, philosophy, and energy.

Scandal. Governor George Ryan's approval ratings were mired in the "political dumps" as Blagojevich pounded the Ryan name with his "time for a change" theme throughout Illinois. Moreover, Illinois GOP party chairman and House Minority leader State Representative Lee Daniels, (also from DuPage county) was forced to resign his party post due to a federal investigation into the conduct of his legislative office. For weeks Illinois Republicans sought a new state party chairman (a figurehead position) with more vigor than they could muster for the gubernatorial campaign. Undoubtedly, the "scandal here/scandal there" media mantra left Jim Ryan totally on the defensive for the campaign's first five months.

Philosophy. The conservative O'Malley argued he would endorse Jim Ryan only if he agreed to support certain principles key to O'Malley's *losing* primary campaign. Jim Ryan refused O'Malley's offer and O'Malley refused to endorse Jim Ryan. Wood gave a boilerplate general endorsement of the state GOP ticket but given her all out pro-choice primary stands, an exuberant pro–Jim Ryan endorsement would have appeared hypocritical.

Energy. Jim Ryan had courageously fought serious illness for many years and whether his ongoing battle against cancer or the depressing state of Republican Party affairs caused him to appear somewhat listless on the campaign trail, will probably never be known. But one thing was for certain, the 45-year-old Blagojevich was a political dynamo whizzing through the state putting in very long campaign hours.

Campaign Strategy

Geographically, Illinois is composed of four voting regions: the city of Chicago; the thirty suburban Cook County townships that surround the city; the five collar counties that surround suburban Cook; and downstate—the state's remaining 96 counties. In recent elections, the first three regions *each* voted about 20 percent of the statewide vote while downstate cast the rest.

Politically, Chicago is overwhelmingly Democratic and the collars strongly Republican; downstate leans Republican while suburban Cook is the crucial swing vote area. In the seven previous gubernatorial races, the GOP candidate carried suburban Cook by at least 109,000 votes. Yet this demographically and politically changing area heavily supported the Democratic presidential candidates in 1992, 1996, and 2000.

Print and electronic media polls from late spring to early autumn saw Blagojevich holding a commanding lead in suburban Cook. This factor coupled with his unified Chicago support and general statewide GOP political ennui gave Blagojevich high double digit leads in most reputable polls.

Jim Ryan's advisors recognized early that Chicago was going to be a disaster, thus he had to use issues of personal character and ethics and the old Republican "go to issue" fear of the Chicago political machine to energize his collar county base, downstaters and most important suburban Cook voters.

One of the few things working early for Ryan was the near geographical homogeneity of the Democratic statewide ticket. Except for U.S. Senator Dick Durbin, the entire Democratic ticket was made up of Chicagoans with many of them having family connections to long-time city politicians. However, with the southern part of suburban Cook undergoing racial change and with his pro-life position hurting him among affluent north suburban residents, Jim Ryan had a huge hurdle to overcome in the critical suburban Cook region.

Campaign War Chests and the Important Economic Issues

For the first time in over 40 years the Democratic gubernatorial nominee was outfundraising and outspending his Republican foe. Not only were traditional Democratic donors, labor unions, and trial lawyers contributing more than usual but Blagojevich also was getting dollars and endorsements from traditional Republican business associations including the Illinois Medical Society. Though not without resources, Jim Ryan was clearly running as the financial campaign underdog to his Democratic opponent.

On the key issue of the campaign, both candidates tiptoed on the state's looming budget crisis. Both pledged to veto any increase in the state income or sales tax (62 percent of the general revenue fund) and both claimed they could manage the budget with the existing revenue. Both also said the budget mess could be solved by setting new state priorities and eliminating wasteful spending. And as expected, both candidates agreed that education was the number one issue in the state, but gave little specifics on how to increase funding.

On several economic issues, the candidates disagreed. Blagojevich supported raising the state's minimum wage from $5.15 an hour to at least $6.50. Jim Ryan did not. Blagojevich endorsed many other pro-labor positions including reinstituting the so-called Scaffolding Act (provide additional rights for workers hurt on a construction job) that a GOP controlled Illinois legislature abolished in 1995. Jim Ryan did not.

Jim Ryan stressed hi-tech jobs and economic development as his reason for his opposition to Blagojevich's labor agenda.

He promised a deputy governor for technology and economic development who would serve as a facilitator between the private sector and state government.

In all honesty, both candidates' critical economic platforms were little noticed by the average Illinois voter. What interest there was in the campaign centered on Jim Ryan's relationship to Governor George Ryan and who really was this guy with the different name of Blagojevich.

The Illinois State Fair

Traditionally in election years, the annual late summer state fair in Springfield jumpstarts candidates' ten-week run to Election Day. Each party has its special day as candidates mingle with party workers amid old-fashioned outdoor rallies highlighted by pork sandwiches, cold beer, and over the top rhetoric. In 2002, the state fair did not work as a positive for either gubernatorial candidate, as strange things happened to both men.

Historically, the party controlling the mansion has their day called Governor's Day—but not in 2002. In order to separate himself from Governor George Ryan, Jim Ryan had the day renamed Republican Day. At a lunchtime rally for the state GOP ticket, the governor's photo was conspicuous by its absence among the other pictures. Moreover, Jim Ryan spoke out as to how he and not his opponent had the experience and character to clean up the Springfield mess. Later, Governor George Ryan had a separate rally at which only one statewide GOP candidate attended and where the sparse crowd of George Ryan's GOP loyalists were bitter, if not angry at their own ticket.

Bad press indeed. However, one day later the Democrats had their turn to show some disunity (it would be the only chink in a professionally put together campaign chain). Blagojevich criticized a budget item pushed through by House Speaker and state party chairman Michael Madigan—a man considered the state's shrewdest politicians and whose daughter was running for state attorney general. Madigan responded to media questions about the criticism by saying he would not comment on that or mention Blagojevich's own "past indiscretions."

What indiscretions was the howl from the media, but Madigan refused to specify and Blagojevich claimed he had no idea what his party leader was talking about. The Democrats tried quickly to dismiss this extraordinary development but it did give a bruised Republican Party and its gubernatorial candidate a potential opening to go on the offensive.

The Final Weeks: Jim Ryan Closes the Gap

Turning the tables on the Democrats Jim Ryan focused his campaign stretch drive on the character and ethics of his opponent and Madigan. Jim Ryan claimed only he could be trusted to clean up Springfield's corruption mentality that had been created by both parties.

In mid-October at a statewide-televised City Club of Chicago debate, Jim Ryan's campaign hit its high point. Blagojevich, near the end of a dry debate, created a sensation, claiming that on "Election Day 1994 two things happened. Both Ryans—George and Jim—got elected and a tragic accident occurred. Neither George Ryan nor Jim Ryan did anything to change that failed system. And as every day passed, the corruption continued."

At that point, Jim Ryan exploded—pointing his finger directly at his opponent, he shouted "Have you no shame, Rod? Have you no shame? Are you talking about those Willis children (the six children who died in the accident)?" After months of lethargy Jim Ryan looked angry and alive and Republican Party stalwarts throughout the state rejoiced at the confrontation.

Jim Ryan pushed his argument that his opponent would do and say anything to win until Election Day. Though most polls still showed Blagojevich with a high single-digit lead, a *St. Louis Post Dispatch*/Zogby weekend poll before the election actually showed Jim Ryan nudging ahead of Blagojevich.

Was Zogby an aberration or was Jim Ryan's surge of support turning into a tidal wave? One thing was for certain, Illinois is a state where Election Day field operation is critical and if Jim Ryan was indeed neck and neck, then ground troops getting out the vote would decide the election.

THE RESULTS

Election night gave Blagojevich a comfortable victory over Jim Ryan (52 percent to 45 percent). Clearly, the Zogby poll was wrong, as Blagojevich's campaign-long lead held firm. And he won the battle of political field organizations, especially in his vote base.

The key to Blagojevich's victory centered in Cook County. In the city of Chicago, he demolished his opponent by over 418,000 votes while winning 49 of 50 wards. His margins in African-American wards were massive to staggering, and Blagojevich also ran well throughout the rest of the city.

Equally important to his statewide victory was his ability to win suburban Cook County. Aided by huge victories in heavily black and liberal suburban townships, Blagojevich defeated Jim Ryan by over 51,000 votes (remember, in the previous seven gubernatorial contests every GOP candidate carried this region by at least 109,000 votes).

In the state's other 101 counties, Jim Ryan cut Blagojevich's 469,000 Cook County margin in half, but unlike the 1998 U.S. Senate race when Republican Peter Fitzgerald devastated Senator Carol Moseley Braun outside of Chicago, Blagojevich remained competitive, if not always triumphant, in most regions of the state. In short, given Blagojevich's Chicago and suburban Cook margins there were simply not enough GOP voters elsewhere to overcome the Democratic vote mountain in Cook County. Why?

Two reasons:

First, in Illinois like many other Midwestern states, *potential* Democratic and independent voters are moving into once solid Republican suburban outer counties (in Illinois these are so-called collar counties—DuPage, Kane, Lake, McHenry and Will). And though Democrats at the local level have difficulty winning anything in these counties, statewide and national Democratic candidates have made serious inroads. Thus, while the Democratic Chicago base remains solid, cracks have formed in Illinois bedrock GOP counties.

Second, the influence and prestige of Chicago Mayor Richard M. Daley. Not mentioned until now, the "Mayor" has achieved a bigger political presence than that of his father, former Mayor Richard J. Daley. By nearly unifying all voting blocs in Chicago under his banner, his endorsement carries significant weight in turning out city Democrats for statewide elections. Moreover, his no-nonsense and straight-talk political style (similar to President George W. Bush) has given him standing in inner as well as outer Chicago suburbs. His moderate political philosophy has also made him attractive to these voters and though he will *never* run for statewide office, he has become an incredible weapon for other Illinois Democratic candidates.

Final point: given all of the above, it still takes a candidate to win an election. Blagojevich in 2002 won two tough races by being the most focused, hardest working, financially secure and politically able politician in the field. He broke the Democrats' seven-election gubernatorial losing streak by parlaying old-fashioned Democratic support (unions and party chairmen) with the desire for change and reforming government in Springfield. Given the sour economy, he will need all of his campaign skills to satisfy hungry Democrats seeking support for favored programs while he governs a state with huge fiscal problems.

19

Iowa Governor

Vilsack Gets an Encore

DAVID YEPSEN
Des Moines Register

When the campaign of 2002 opened, Iowa's Democratic governor, Tom Vilsack, was considered vulnerable. His first election in 1998 was a bit of a fluke, the state historically elects Republicans to the governorship, and the economy and state finances were in the tank. In the end, Vilsack won a second term by a comfortable margin. He won by running a superior campaign, by helping with a sophisticated Democratic voter turnout program and by successfully making his opponent the issue in the campaign. A little Iowa history helped, too. But his victory has few national implications. It gives the Democrats something of a base to use in keeping the state in the Democratic column in the 2004 presidential election. It may position Vilsack for higher office, although he doesn't seem inclined to want to do that. The most important national implication of the race is the Democratic voter turnout program he used (see also Chapter 6 on Senator Tom Harkin's re-election). As Democrats around the country look for ways to recover from their losses in 2002, the Iowa system may provide a cure.

Vilsack came out of nowhere in 1998 to become Iowa's governor. A former small-town mayor and a state senator, he was unknown when his gubernatorial campaign opened. Former Congressman Jim Ross Lightfoot, who had only narrowly lost a bid for the U.S. Senate to Tom Harkin in 1996, was the heavy favorite. Early in the race, Lightfoot led Vilsack by about 30 points in early polls and few gave Vilsack much of a chance. But Lightfoot proved to be a poor candidate who ran an abysmal campaign. Vilsack, an articulate trial lawyer, seemed more conversant in state issues than the former congressman. Vilsack also was an aggressive campaigner while Lightfoot tried to sit on his lead. Lightfoot also gave his wife too much of a role in the campaign, a decision that upset numerous Republicans who felt she was making strategic decisions that were out of her depth. For example, she insisted on running poor-quality attack ads criticizing Vilsack for once supporting "totally nude dancing" in Iowa as a state senator. The ad lacked credibility and backfired. On Election Day 1998, Vilsack became the first Democrat to win Iowa's governorship in 32 years. Democrats were jubilant and Republicans stunned about Lightfoot's inept campaigning.

During the first two years of his term, Vilsack's popularity soared. He embarked on an aggressive program to expand spending on education and awarded handsome pay raises to state workers, who had supported him in his campaign. However, the honeymoon ended about midterm. He angered Republicans, who controlled the legislature, by waging a highly-partisan effort to capture control of the General Assembly from them in the 2000 election. That effort failed, but made him look far more partisan and less gubernatorial. The downturn in the national economy collapsed Iowa's tax revenues, and he was left to make painful budget cuts that alienated traditional Democratic constituencies. Also, his call for more immigrants to increase Iowa's workforce and population backfired. Iowa is 96 percent white, and many voters objected to any suggestion that the way out of the economic doldrums was to lure more Latino workers into the meat packing plants. Organized labor, which provided important help to Vilsack in the 1998 campaign, objected to the plan, and Vilsack was forced to beat a quick retreat. Finally, Vilsack's effort to extend civil rights protections to gays and lesbians who worked for the state government was struck down by a court. Vilsack's job approval rating dropped to 57 percent. The numbers of Iowans who saw the state headed in the right direction also dropped while those who said the state was headed in the wrong direction soared. By 2001, the right-track, wrong-track numbers were about even.

Republicans, who felt Vilsack was in office largely because of their own inept candidate in 1998, began to see the governor as a liberal, fiscal incompetent who could—and should—be defeated. While Vilsack was unopposed for renomination, the Republican primary featured three contenders: State Representative Steve Sukup, a small-town lawmaker and businessman; Bob Vander Plaats, a Sioux City businessman; and Des Moines lawyer Doug Gross, who entered the race late after many party insiders said they didn't think the other two candidates could defeat the Democratic incumbent. Gross, 47, a former chief of staff for Iowa Governor Terry Branstad, had never run for office before. He had spent his career in private life building one of Iowa's largest law firms and was well connected as a result of his political and legal experience. But Gross's firm had also represented large livestock confinements in Iowa, a highly controversial and unpopular form of raising hogs. Sukup pounced on the opportunity and criticized Gross for being a Des Moines hog lot lawyer who did not understand rural Iowa. However, Gross won the primary by the narrowest of margins. He got 35 percent of the vote, Sukup received 32.4 percent and Vander Plaats got 31.7 percent. (Iowa law requires a candidate to win at least 35 percent of the vote in a primary to win a party nomination outright.) It meant Gross entered the fall contest with two big strikes against him: Two-thirds of the GOP rank and file having voted against him in the primary and the Sukup-inflicted wounds still fresh. Vilsack wasted no time. He started running attack ads against Gross before the GOP primary, a tactic borrowed from California Governor Gray Davis who ran ads attacking one of the GOP candidates prior to the primary in that state. Vilsack's ads played on the same themes Sukup used—that Gross is a corporate hog lot lawyer from Iowa's largest city. While Vilsack wasn't successful in knocking out a foe the way Davis was, he stained Gross' image. In the first poll taken after the June Republican primary, GOP leaders were jubilant. Vilsack led Gross, 43–41 in the *Des Moines Register*'s Iowa Poll. (The survey had a four point margin of error.) Only one other Democratic governor—Jim Hodges of South Carolina—was in a weaker position.

At this point in the campaign, Vilsack's larger war chest came into play. During the summer, the governor was able to pound Gross with more attack ads than Gross could fire back. Gross also was slow in releasing position papers detailing just what he would do as governor. Although his primary victory had clearly tweaked public interest in him as a candidate, he was slow in defining himself and just what he wanted to do with the job. Vilsack's continuation of Sukup's attack defined Gross before Gross was able to define himself. By Labor Day, Vilsack had opened an eight to ten-point lead in most polls and held onto that position throughout the campaign. By the end of the campaign, 51 percent of voters said they had an unfavorable opinion of Gross while 56 percent had a favorable view of Vilsack.

Vilsack had three important pieces of Iowa history working on his behalf. First, Iowans like to keep incumbents in office. The state's voters have not thrown out a sitting governor since 1962. Iowa has had only three governors in the past 34 years. Voters haven't even given the boot to a sitting U.S. Senator since 1984. Second, Iowa's rural voters don't like candidates from Des Moines. Only one governor in Iowa history—Bob Ray—came from Des Moines. There is a rural-urban split in Iowa, and it means candidates from larger communities like Des Moines can have difficulty with rural voters who often don't think these "urbanites" understand their problems. Gross may have been born and raised in a small town, but he never was able to shake the reputation of being a Des Moines lawyer. It enabled Vilsack, a small-town lawyer, to eat into what should have been a good Republican margin in the state's rural counties. Third, Iowa voters don't elect unknowns to be governor. Most governors in modern times have either run for or held a major public office before becoming governor. Gross had done neither. He was an unknown in the eastern half of the state, where most of the voters reside.

On Election Day, Vilsack won 52.7 percent to 44.5 percent for Gross. Final unofficial totals were Vilsack, 540,757; Gross, 457,250; Green Party candidate Jay Robinson, 14,652; and Libertarian candidate Clyde Cleveland, 13,031. According to the final pre-election Iowa Poll taken by the *Des Moines Register* in the week leading up to the November 5 election, Vilsack's victory was pretty much across the board. Vilsack won 87 percent of the Democratic vote in that pre-election poll while Gross got only 76 percent of the Republicans. Vilsack won independents 58 percent to 32 percent; men, 48 to 44 percent; and women, 56 to 37 percent.

The Iowa governor's race highlighted two national implications. First, Vilsack himself could become a player in national Democratic affairs although he's shown no desire for that. He has said he is not interested in running for president, vice president, or U.S. Senator (against Republican Charles Grassley) in 2004. Vilsack also has said he would only serve two terms in office, meaning he leaves office in 2006, giving him time to run for the Democratic presidential nomination in 2008, if he's so inspired— something his backers are beginning to tout and encourage with him. A second implication of the Iowa results is in the Iowa party's get-out-the-vote operation. One reason Vilsack and Democratic Senator Tom Harkin were able to buck a national tide against Democrats in 2002 was this voter turnout program. The Democrats spent about $3 million contacting an estimated 170,000 voters. Most traditional get-out-the-vote programs focus on making sure the party faithful show up at the polls. Democrats did some of that but less of it than in the past. Instead, the party focused time and resources on the thousands of Democrats who vote in presidential elections but not in nonpresidential years and on independent voters who lean Democratic in their voting habits. Paid students and volunteers canvassed those voters in key precincts for two summers leading up to the election. They recorded their interviews on Palm Pilots, which were then downloaded each night into computers at party headquarters. If the worker ascertained the voter was likely to vote Democratic, an application for an absentee ballot was filled out and signed by the voter. One top Democrat said his party would ultimately spend $3 million on the effort and would distribute

80,000 absentee ballot requests. He expected the effort to net 130,000 more absentee votes for Democrats by Election Day. Republicans countered late with a similar program but Democrats probably bested the GOP by 2–1 in absentee ballots on Election Day. Since Vilsack only won by a margin of 84,000 votes, that absentee ballot program may have been what reelected him. It also helped Harkin, who won by 103,000 votes. Consider that along with what Georgia Republicans did with their get-out-the-vote campaign that wrested the state from the Democrats. One lesson for both parties is clear: An old-fashioned, shoe-leather ground game—enhanced with the latest in computer technology—can provide the margin needed for victory. In Iowa, it seemed especially pivotal at a time when many voters find the blizzard of political television commercials to be an intrusive nuisance. Just imagine. A real human being showing up to ask someone's views and for their support. What's next, torch-light parades and food baskets at Christmas?

20

Maryland Governor

The Close of Camelot

DANIEL LEDUC
The Washington Post

Maryland's governor's race upended more than three decades of one-party rule, destroyed the fledgling career of a daughter in America's most famous political dynasty, launched a possible national career for the almost unknown, young Republican winner and radically altered the terms for debate on a host of issues, from taxes to transportation to legalized gambling.

If some apathetic voters believe elections don't matter, Maryland in 2002 proves them wrong. But then very few analysts—this writer included—predicted it would turn out the way it did.

U.S. Representative Robert L. Ehrlich Jr., who had won office in the 1994 Republican wave, defeated Lieutenant Governor Kathleen Kennedy Townsend—eldest daughter of Robert F. Kennedy and widely seen as the rising star in her family's new generation—by a surprisingly comfortable margin of four points.

Maryland is one of the most liberal, Democratic states in the nation. Registered Democrats outnumber registered Republicans two to one. Abortion rights have been upheld in statewide referenda. Polls show such strong support for gun control that one recent survey found half of all Marylanders would ban handguns. Environmental protection—the Chesapeake Bay is a state treasure—is enormously popular. There is, it seems, no such thing as too much government regulation in a state where the most populous region is a bedroom community for Washington bureaucrats.

Two-term Governor Parris N. Glendening, a Democrat, was prevented from seeking a third-term. The primary campaign for his potential successor began almost immediately after his decisive 1998 victory over Ellen R. Sauerbrey, a conservative former state legislator.

On the Democratic side, Townsend was Glendening's handpicked successor. He had plucked her from near-obscurity (or at least as obscure as a Kennedy family member can be) to be his running mate in their first campaign in 1994. Inexperienced and an awkward public speaker during the first term, Townsend became Glendening's savior in their 1998 reelection bid. Personally unpopular, Glendening was in trouble and polling showed that most Marylanders found Townsend likable. She began appearing in all his television commercials and together their ticket in 1998 defeated Sauerbrey by ten points.

Still, it was difficult for Townsend to shake her image as ill-prepared and unable to govern. During her second term as lieutenant governor she began to assert herself on crime-fighting and economic development. But she faced problems on those fronts. The most serious came when the *Baltimore Sun* exposed beatings and abuse of young inmates by corrections officers at Maryland's juvenile boot camps—one of Townsend's areas of supervision. Glendening took responsibility but Townsend took the political hit.

Three adversaries for the 2002 Democratic gubernatorial nomination lined up: the Baltimore County Executive, C.A. "Dutch" Ruppersberger; the Montgomery County Executive, Douglas M. Duncan and the newly-elected Baltimore Mayor, Martin O'Malley. Without Townsend in the race, a contest between the three would have been spirited.

But, as is becoming increasingly clear in American politics, primary campaigns are more about fundraising than attracting voters. Using her family connections, Townsend was a powerhouse. Eleven months before the primary, she had raised more than all of her potential rivals combined and had $3.3 million in the bank. Most of the money came from state contributors. Duncan—who heads Maryland's largest jurisdiction—announced he'd seek reelection rather than run for governor. Ruppersberger, who was term-limited, said he'd run for Congress. (He went on to win.) O'Malley—the wunderkind of state politics at age 39—kept everyone guessing until the summer. But in the end, he too decided not to run, leaving the field wide open for Townsend.

Among Republicans there was only one choice: Ehrlich. Though he had been considering a run since 1998, he was unsure if he wanted to give up his relatively safe House seat in the Baltimore suburbs. GOP loyalists pleaded with him to run. But he was skeptical the party would have the cohesion necessary for him to win. In December 2001, he admonished the GOP state convention: "We lack the discipline . . . the understanding of what it takes to win. To the extent that there is intramural fighting among you, stop it, now, please. I am really tired of it."

Party activists took heed. While some—the staunchest abortion foes, for example—declared he was not conservative enough for their support, most eagerly signed on. Without him, the GOP had no alternative with a chance of winning. In March, after major party contributors promised their best efforts, Ehrlich finally decided: He was in.

The settings for the formal announcements illustrated the themes for the candidates.

Ehrlich spoke from the front stoop of the tiny red brick rowhouse where he grew up, emphasizing his roots in Maryland and his working class upbringing. He hit Democrats for profligate spending and said, "I was taught in this place you pay your bills."

Townsend spoke from the front steps of the State House in Annapolis. She appeared the powerful incumbent and invoked her family tradition of lofty rhetoric. "I pledge to you today that I will dedicate myself to make sure that every Marylander reaches her or his indispensable destiny," she said. The phrase struck many as confusing—no one seemed quite sure what "indispensible destiny" was. Townsend soon dropped the phrase. In hindsight, it was an ominous sign.

The contrast remained for the rest of the campaign. Ehrlich offered few substantive proposals other than legalizing slots at Maryland's horse racing tracks to help pay for education (the revenue comes nowhere close to filling the need). But he was likable and engaging with the press. His top campaign staffers were Maryland political veterans. One strategist, Paul Schurick, had been chief of staff to former Democratic Governor William Donald Schaefer, still an icon in state politics.

Ehrlich also had friends in the legislature—many of them Democrats. Sauerbrey, the GOP standard bearer four and eight years earlier, had served in the legislature and annoyed many lawmakers with a resolute conservatism. Ehrlich, on the other hand, was known for consensus-building. Democrats had even tried to recruit him to their side. Those friends said they'd back Townsend out of party loyalty but wouldn't criticize Ehrlich. They predicted Townsend would try to demonize Ehrlich as too conservative for Maryland and said it wouldn't work. They were prescient.

Going into 2002, Townsend had devoted much of her energy into her formidable fundraising. It had served her well in keeping out primary opponents but some close advisors and top Democrats began expressing concern that she was not adequately tending to her base voters—African-Americans,

union members, and environmentalists. She, in fact, alienated some environmentalists with her first break from Glendening administration policy when
she threw her support behind plans for a new commuter highway in the
Washington suburbs—a proposal Ehrlich had been calling for for some
time.

Townsend's campaign was run by her state house chief of staff, Alan
Fleischmann, who was young, affable, and devoted to his candidate. But he
had never run a campaign before and never earned the trust of many of the
state's leading Democratic operatives and strategists.

Townsend's failure to solidify her base voters was most glaringly
apparent with her selection of a running mate. African-American leaders
had lobbied Townsend hard to select a black. Apparently confident she
had enthusiastic black support, she instead turned to Charles Larson, a
respected, retired admiral who had run the Naval Academy in Annapolis
and who had been a Republican until switching parties only days before her
announcement of his selection. The initial reviews were terrific: Larson len-
ded Townsend gravitas. He made her palatable to the many conservative
military personnel who call Maryland home. He was an innovative, fresh
face.

Within days, however, there was a near-mutiny by Townsend's African-American supporters. "I think the Democratic Party is failing African
Americans here," a black legislator, Anthony Brown, told *The Washington
Post*. "It's a real problem." It took Townsend weeks to mend fences and
eventually, black turnout on Election Day would be less than expected.

Ehrlich made a clumsy, public attempt to recruit the state school
superintendent, who is a longtime Democrat, but failed. On the eve of the
filing deadline, he selected Maryland GOP chairman Michael Steele—the
only African-American state Republican chairman in the nation—as his
running mate. Initially, the choice received poor reviews: Steele would not
motivate conservative white voters (Ehrlich needed every one of them). And
he had personal financial troubles that could undermine Ehrlich's contention that Democrats were mismanaging state finances. (The state GOP paid
Steele a "consulting fee" after his nomination—in effect, paying him to be
their candidate.)

But as the campaign wore on, Steele's presence innoculated Ehrlich
against any veiled attempt to paint him as a racist. (A similar Democratic
effort in 1998 had cost Sauerbrey dearly.) And it enabled the Republicans
to reach out to African-American voters in an aggressive way that the Maryland GOP had never done before. Steele appeared in television ads and on
Election Day, Ehrlich's campaign placed life-sized posters of him at 1,000
polling places in the largely African-American enclaves of Baltimore and
Prince George's County. (In the end, Townsend still received 87 percent of

the African-American vote, but black turnout was down from the 1998 election.)

The impact in the polls of these developments was steady through the year with Townsend's support slowly declining. The surveys showed a subtle but important message from voters: They knew who she was. But many were willing to consider an alternative to her for governor.

During her last legislative session she attempted to start carving out a greater role for herself. But it was a calculated, Rose Garden–type strategy that never appeared to resonate with voters. She advocated drunken-driving legislation that was already a priority of legislative leaders. She came out of the session looking unsure of herself.

Townsend also came out of the legislative session with some heavy political baggage thanks to Glendening. She owed her position to him and both had spent most of the last four years using the term the "Glendening-Townsend administration." But Glendening's popularity was plummeting. He had sought a $350,000 a year position as chancellor of the state university system for when he left office. The regents who make the selection were all appointed by him—and Glendening was forced to retreat after criticism that the arrangement appeared unethical.

He also divorced his wife of 25 years and married an aide 24 years younger than him in a secret ceremony at the governor's mansion that was not publicly announced until three days after it occurred. The aide was pregnant at the time and gave birth to their daughter in August, just as the fall campaign was getting underway.

At the same time, state revenues began to plunge. Glendening had consistently boosted state spending during his eight years as governor and said he would not make any major cuts during the campaign.

Townsend studiously avoided appearing with the governor. But Ehrlich's fall television campaign ads frequently pictured the two together.

Glendening injected himself into the scene during the summer when he paid for advertising supporting his secretary of state who was challenging Schaefer for the job of state comptroller. Schaefer, the former governor, and Glendening had never gotten along. Glendening's efforts—despite Townsend's pleas to him not to—exacerbated divisions among Democrats.

Townsend's verbal gaffes continued as well. At the Preakness Stakes— Maryland's premier national sporting event—she called the winning horse "War Monger" rather than its actual name "War Emblem." At her introduction of Larson as her running mate, she referred to him as "Lawson." And at a campaign event she referred to the retired admiral as "ambassador."

In July, a Gonzales/Arscott Research & Communications poll showed Townsend's lead over Ehrlich had slipped to only seven points, 48 percent to 41 percent. The same pollster had showed her with a 15-point lead in January. More troublesome for Townsend was the finding that the portion of voters saying they had a favorable opinion of her had slid precipitously, from 53 percent in September 2001 to 41 percent. She had virtually universal name recognition—97 percent—which meant voters knew her but didn't like her.

In August, former Governor Schaefer went public with his concern, telling *The Washington Post*, "The thing that has worried people is: Can she do the job? And she hasn't projected that she can."

The poll results seemed to ignite Ehrlich's fundraising. He had long said he would never match Townsend's war chest. By midsummer he was sometimes raking in $250,000 a day. By campaign's end, he had raised $10.5 million to her $9 million.

The campaign's dynamic froze one month before Election Day when news of the race was shoved aside by the Washington sniper case. The electorate was riven by fear and Maryland's major media outlets—in print and on television—offered blanket coverage. The candidates all but disappeared.

The case could have done great damage to Ehrlich. He has opposed many gun control initiatives. Gun control advocates were the first to come out aggressively against him early in the campaign. It was, even his aides acknowledged privately, his greatest vulnerability.

Instead of hurting him, however, the case seemed to lock in the horse race at a time when Ehrlich was steadily gaining. By the final week of October, a Potomac Survey Research poll put the Republican in front by four points—outside the poll's margin of error.

Maryland has long been split politically between what is known as the Big Three jurisdictions (heavily Democratic Montgomery and Prince George's counties, which are the core Washington suburbs, and Baltimore) and the rest of the state, which is more Republican. But the Big Three represent 41 percent of the state's likely voters. Glendening had won office in 1994 by winning the Big Three and losing the rest of the state. He had won in 1998 with the Big Three and only two other counties.

In the Big Three, Townsend was ahead 64 percent to 28 percent. In the rest of the state, Ehrlich was ahead 62 percent to 29 percent.

But more telling were the answers to two other poll questions.

Asked if "Bob Ehrlich is too conservative for Maryland," only 32 percent agreed while 53 percent disagreed. And half of voters agreed with the statement, "Kathleen Kennedy Townsend would just continue the policies of the Glendening administration. It's time for a change." Only 38 percent disagreed.

On election night, Ehrlich won 52 percent of the vote.

Ehrlich's victory ran counter to the national trend that saw Democrats making gains in governorships. And it was all the more notable because his victory marked the first time a Republican governor was elected since Spiro T. Agnew won in 1966.

The race came down to turnout and Ehrlich clearly was able to rally his supporters in a way that Townsend was not. The number of voters who cast Republican ballots was up significantly in nearly every region of the state over 1998. The number of voters who cast Democratic ballots was down in nearly every region.

In Central Maryland—the city of Baltimore and the counties of Anne Arundel, Baltimore, Carroll, Harford, and Howard—Townsend received 46,886 fewer votes than Glendening did in 1998. In that same region, Ehrlich received 113,450 more votes than Sauerbrey did four years earlier.

In the all important, populous Washington suburban counties of Montgomery and Prince George's, Ehrlich actually won 3,964 fewer votes than Sauerbrey did in 1998. But Townsend won only 331 more votes than Glendening did four years before.

Townsend had "one of the worst-run campaigns in the country," Glendening told *The Washington Post* on election night. "She had a very small group of advisers and they put on the oddest campaign for governor anybody has ever seen. You have to remember your base and they did not."

But one enormous factor was Glendening himself. Ehrlich tied Townsend to the unpopular governor and voters noticed. The state's mounting financial woes—Maryland was facing a $1.7 billion shortfall on Election Day—and Glendening's divorce and remarriage left voters looking for a change. (Exit polls showed the state's budget the number one issue for voters.)

But Townsend's other mistake was her failure to solidify her support among core Democratic voters—women, liberal activists, and African-Americans who make up the majority of Maryland voters. Townsend's decision to pick a Republican as her running mate and run a centrist campaign appeared based on the assumption she had her base firmly with her. In fact, many Democratic activists felt ignored and stopped campaigning for her.

Turnout in liberal Montgomery County was high but not dramatically so on Election Day. It was depressed in majority black Prince George's County and Baltimore. "Nobody knew [Larson]. He was a Republican until two weeks before she picked him. How do you trust that?" Carl Williams, a community development executive in Prince George's said in *The Washington Post*.

In a closely watched congressional race in Montgomery County, Democrat Chris Van Hollen was able to defeat popular longtime incumbent Republican Constance Morella. In Baltimore County—an Ehrlich stronghold—voters picked Ruppersberger for Congress over a Republican and elected another Democrat as County Executive. That would indicate that voters weren't anti-Democratic, just anti-Townsend.

That seems clearly the case among women voters who would be expected to be strong Townsend supporters. She favored gun control and would have been Maryland's first female governor. But exit polls showed Ehrlich won 61 percent of white women while Townsend won only 38 percent. In the past two governor's races, white women split equally between the Republican and Democratic candidates.

Ehrlich not only energized voters in traditionally Republican regions, but also made an effective appeal to crossover Democrats and to Maryland's many voters not affiliated with a party.

The Republican won 50 percent of the vote of those who described themselves as moderates and 55 percent of unaffiliated voters. It was the first time in at least the last three Maryland elections that the Republican gubernatorial candidate won such large support from moderates.

Some analysts have suggested that the election represents another shift in power in Maryland—from the populous Washington suburbs to the growing, more conservative swath of Central Maryland. It is too early to say that is true.

It is clear that the election was Townsend's to lose and she did, much by her own hand. The existing Democratic organization in Maryland remains powerful and formidable—and capable of winning if properly motivated.

What happened in Maryland in 2002 is that lightning struck and ignited a spark. It is now up to Ehrlich and Maryland's Republicans to see if they can keep it burning.

21

Minnesota Governor

The End of the Ventura Interlude

HOLLY A. HEYSER
St. Paul Pioneer Press

The 2002 governor's race in Minnesota began with one big question: Wrestler-turned-governor Jesse Ventura—would he or wouldn't he seek a second term? With him, the race promised to be a national spectacle of rock n' roll, feather boas and outrageous remarks; without him, Minnesota stood to fade into the drab wallpaper of Ds and Rs that stretched across the rest of the country.

On June 18, he bowed out. But almost in the same breath, he anointed an eminently electable successor—former congressman Tim Penny, a conservative Democrat—to carry the Independence Party banner in his place. Penny vaulted almost immediately into neck-and-neck status in public polls, and it became clear that Minnesota would remain a busy laboratory of political hypotheses.

The race promised to be phenomenal, not only because of the three-way tie, but because there were four major-party candidates: Ralph Nader's 5 percent showing in the 2000 presidential election in Minnesota had secured major-party status for the Greens. With the post-Jesse lineup set, three major questions hung over the race:

- Could Green Party candidate Ken Pentel—the only one of the four who had run a statewide campaign—bring home enough votes to

233

keep major-party status for the Greens? It was a crucial challenge: In Minnesota, major-party status means not only easier access to the ballot, but vital public financing.

- Could Tim Penny secure a second consecutive term in the governor's office for the Independence Party, proving that there was more to the party than the decreasingly popular Jesse Ventura?
- Could the Republican and Democratic-Farmer-Labor parties effectively respond to a third-party challenge after failing to recognize the legitimacy of and respond to Jesse Ventura's candidacy in 1998?

NOMINATION CONTESTS

Minnesota politics features both endorsement contests waged at party conventions May through July and primary elections in September. In recent elections, serious candidates had challenged the endorsed candidates in the primary, but there were no major challengers this time, and endorsed candidates coasted to victory on September 10. The candidates were:

Roger Moe, 58, Democratic-Farmer-Labor Party. In the first convention of the year, Moe, Senate majority leader in the state legislature, beat two women seeking the nomination: state Senator Beckey Lourey, a Paul Wellstone–style liberal, and Judi Dutcher, the young state auditor and a former Republican. His victory disappointed many in the party who had been waiting for a woman to lead the ticket, but women would be relegated to the running-mate spot in all four major parties this year.

Moe was a formidable power in the legislature, a 32-year veteran. But to the public, he was the quintessential Norwegian politician: low-key and charisma-deficient. Much like Bob Dole, Moe never showed the public what insiders saw in him.

Ken Pentel, 41, Green Party. Pentel was exactly what the Greens needed—a party-builder. He won easily in his endorsement contest in May and started campaigning diligently, using major-party status to give an amplified voice to Green ideals. It was clear from the start that his goal was to win at least 5 percent of the vote in November—enough to keep major-party status.

Tim Pawlenty, 41, Republican. The gregarious, quick-witted, young state House majority leader was planning to run for the U.S. Senate in 2002, but the day he was going to announce his run, Vice President Dick Cheney called Pawlenty's cell phone and asked him to step aside because the White House wanted St. Paul Mayor Norm Coleman to run for that seat instead. Pawlenty held his press conference as planned, but announced he would run for governor.

Later, major party backers tried to dissuade him from running for governor, saying they favored the self-financed, conservative entrepreneur Brian Sullivan. This time, though, Pawlenty stayed in the race. Though Sullivan would ultimately lose, he had a big impact in the endorsement contest, forcing Pawlenty to take strong stands against new taxes and gay rights.

Tim Penny, 50, Independence Party. Propelled into the race by Ventura's decision not to seek a second term, Penny was instantly an appealing replacement. Like Ventura, he disdained party politics and didn't mind bucking the tide, but he didn't share Ventura's propensity for shooting off at the mouth (for example, Ventura saying in a 1999 interview with *Playboy* that he'd like to be reincarnated as a 38DD bra). Penny was a Democrat with a conservative bent, pro-life while he was in Congress, a fiscal conservative who worked for the libertarian Cato Institute after leaving Congress.

In 2002, the Independence Party was clearly the party of the disaffected moderates. Penny said he probably wouldn't have entered the race if the DFL had endorsed the more moderate Judi Dutcher. For a running-mate, Penny chose a pro-choice Republican state senator who had lost her endorsement battle to a pro-life challenger. Party-builder Dean Barkley (who would become the state's interim U.S. Senator after Paul Wellstone died) declared the ticket a "dynamite team: a Democrat who is too conservative, and a Republican who is too liberal." Washington insiders who had watched Penny in Congress cooed appreciatively, and voters flocked to him in the polls, giving him early credibility that Ventura never had. But Moe warned that they would be "fishing from the same pond" for voters.

Others. Three more candidates entered the race. Lawrence Aeshliman of the Constitution Party, a pro-life Christian who often toted a large religious portrait wherever he went; Kari Sachs of the Socialist Workers Party who ran for governor of New Jersey in 2001; and Booker T. Hodges IV, a young independent who maintained the highest visibility of the three, often complaining that the major-party candidates were a "Geritol fest." None would get more than 10,000 votes.

MAIN ISSUES

A race that's tied three ways is a minefield for candidates who rightly fear that attacking one opponent could drive voters to the other opponent. That fear translated into a tepid beginning for all but Pentel, who boldly touted Green positions against expanding freeways and for raising taxes on polluters.

Even when candidates were ready to take stronger stands on their issues, it was tough for them to be heard: Campaign spending limits eviscerated their ability to advertise on TV, where candidates for the U.S. Senate and House were already making a lot of noise. Their most consistently available venue for reaching the public would be nearly 30 debates, many of them broadcast statewide on television or radio. The key issues that emerged were:

1. *Abortion.* Republican Pawlenty was pro-life; DFLer Moe and Green Pentel were pro-choice. Penny, on the other hand, was tougher to figure out. Always pro-life in Congress, he had undergone a transformation after leaving office: He still opposed abortion, but he wanted to find middle-ground solutions. When pressed, he promised he would veto any abortion restrictions passed by the legislature.

This was immediately a sticky situation. Penny had betrayed his former pro-life allies, and pro-choice groups still didn't trust him. The issue didn't command a lot of media attention once the initial hubbub of Penny's candidacy settled down, but it lay in wait for him. Interest groups on both sides had the ability to deliver votes to their chosen candidates, and neither side chose Penny.

2. *The budget.* The looming state budget shortfall was clearly the biggest challenge awaiting the winner. In the fall, it was expected to reach $3 billion, or about 10 percent of the state's general fund. It was obvious that there would be budget cuts, but the candidates consistently steered clear of saying what they would whack, despite relentless media pressure.

On the taxing side, however, they were more willing to talk. Minnesota is a high-tax state, traditionally willing to pay what it takes to offer top-notch services, so it wasn't shocking when Moe, Penny and Pentel admitted that they might need to raise taxes in addition to making cuts to balance the budget. But Pawlenty pledged not to raise taxes, setting himself apart from the others.

Penny also had the chance to set himself apart. As majority leaders in their respective bodies of the legislature, Moe and Pawlenty bore significant responsibility for the impending shortfall; they had balanced the budget that year using reserves and accounting shifts, delaying the tough choices and leaving a significant gap in the next budget.

3. *Guns.* Minnesota is a key battleground in the nationwide effort to loosen restrictions on concealed weapons permits for law-abiding citizens. Gun rights advocates had fallen short of their goals by just one or two votes in recent sessions of the legislature. As expected, Pawlenty supported expanded access to concealed weapons permits, and Moe and Pentel opposed it.

But Penny straddled a middle ground that subjected him to accusations of vagueness and waffling. In Congress, he opposed the Brady Bill, but supported the assault weapons ban. In Minnesota, he talked of "compromise" on the issue. He said he would support expanded access if police could conduct accurate criminal background checks, but said he couldn't support the bill that Pawlenty had voted for and Moe had voted against that year.

It went over like his abortion position: The interest groups wouldn't go near him, and he didn't win any points for staking out the middle ground. Concealed Carry Reform Now, the group backing wider access to permits, maintains that Pawlenty is "the only choice for gun owners."

4. *Terrorism.* There was only one issue, and initially, the candidates only talked about it when asked: identifying temporary visitors to the country as such on their driver's licenses. That year, the legislature had deadlocked a proposal to put visa expiration dates on foreign visitors' driver's licenses. Among the candidates, only Pawlenty supported the plan, but the issue wasn't stirring voters. At least, not until Pawlenty touted his position in the boldest television ad of the session.

KEY STRATEGIES

Roger Moe, Democrat-Farmer-Labor. Moe suffered from a bad start. All summer long, his campaign was geared to go up against the bigger-than-life Ventura. It unveiled a leased Chevy Monte Carlo stock car that the candidate wouldn't drive, and commissioned 5,000 Chinese-made Roger Moe bobblehead dolls for sale—cute, but not in keeping with Moe's Norwegian reserve and dignified 32-year history in the state legislature.

The campaign spent a whopping $600,000 before Labor Day—a vast sum in a state where candidates face a $2.2 million spending limit in exchange for public financing. Behind the scenes, Democrats were upset about the mounting bills and worried because phone bank workers were finding a lot of voters who supported Democrat Paul Wellstone in the U.S. Senate race and Tim Penny in the governor's race. Moe got a new campaign manager and things changed right away. At the state fair in August—an important campaign venue for candidates in Minnesota—the campaign yanked the Moe bobblehead dolls from the candidate's booth.

A leaner campaign continued with a clear goal: winning as many Wellstone voters as Moe could get. He didn't even need all of Wellstone's supporters; in a three-way race, 34 percent could mean the key to the governor's office. So he linked himself to Wellstone and focused on core Democratic issues—education and the social safety net. He would win 36 percent of the vote on Election Day, which might have been enough if it had remained a three-way race to the end.

When Wellstone died in a plane crash on October 25, the conventional wisdom initially was that the sympathy vote would carry his replacement to victory in the Senate race. But the campaign had lost its partner, and everyone knew that the sympathy vote wouldn't necessarily accrue to Moe.

Tim Pawlenty, Republican. Pawlenty stood out on the key issues of the race—abortion, budget, and guns—and because there was no need to win the vast middle of the electorate in a three-way race, he could sell these positions unabashedly to Minnesota's Republican base. Early in the campaign, he highlighted his opposition to tax increases. He didn't need to bring up abortion and guns because the interest groups were already working for him on those issues.

He stood out in other ways, too. At 41, he was the youngest of the three front-runners, still playing hockey, a beloved sport in Minnesota. Over the summer, he started taping material for TV ads targeting a younger audience, using jerky video that left room for "pop ups" that would point to where he grew up, the car he drove and the supermarket where he "learned to work hard and be accountable." He also told the camera that when his dad lost his job, the family had to tighten its belt, and Minnesota should too. One resulting ad would use that opening to point out that Pawlenty had a 34-inch waist. The messages were drenched in youth and vigor.

The resulting ads became a big campaign issue, not because of the content, but because of how they were produced. Pawlenty's campaign sold the tapes to the Republican Party of Minnesota, which produced and broadcast ads including a biographical piece with the pop-ups and a comic book–style piece parodying Moe and Penny as "the dynamic tax-raising duo." With Pawlenty addressing the camera in them, they looked like campaign ads, not party ads, but Pawlenty hadn't spent a dime of his $2.2 million spending limit to get them on the air. The Independence Party complained that Pawlenty and the GOP had coordinated illegally to produce them, bolstered by statements from someone on the camera crew who happened to be an Independent Party candidate for the legislature.

The state campaign finance board held hearings on the complaint and in early October, ruled against Pawlenty and the Republicans on two of the ads, fining Pawlenty $100,000 and deducting $500,000 from his spending limit. It was a significant blow financially, and a potentially lethal outcome in a state hypersensitive to scandal. Outraged GOP backers wanted Pawlenty to fight the ruling, but the next day, Pawlenty held a press conference to accept responsibility, saying that while he disagreed with the ruling, he would cooperate with the board. (He was also characteristically quick on his feet. When a cell phone rang in the audience at his press conference, he quipped, "That's not Dick Cheney, is it?" It was wit and humor that voters wouldn't see much in Moe and Penny.)

The other candidates weren't at all assuaged by Pawlenty's failure to embrace guilt. But it went over just fine with the public, which never latched on to why it was wrong for the party to promote its candidate in this case when parties advertise in elections all the time. The scandal was out of the news in six days.

Less than two weeks later, Pawlenty launched his toughest attack, an ominous television ad warning that "terrorists are in Minnesota." Remember, this is the state where alleged September 11 terrorist Zacarias Moussaoui took flying lessons. Pawlenty's ad highlighted his support for putting "foreigners'" visa expiration dates on their driver's licenses. Moe, Penny and Pentel reacted with outrage, Moe invoking the memory of "Willie Horton." But Republicans kept smiling. The ad was wildly popular in focus groups, and it appealed to what one Republican called "the bubba vote" in suburban Anoka County, a Ventura stronghold that would be crucial to Tim Penny.

Tim Penny, Independence Party. Penny's motto from the start was "the sensible center," and he set out to tell voters about the alternative to the political dogma of the left and the right. Starting the fall with such a prominent poll position, he envisioned a campaign that would highlight all that was wrong in politics, with Moe and Pawlenty as poster boys. But the strategy never really took hold.

In September, he found himself on the defensive—a lot. The Minneapolis-based *Star Tribune* published an article about Penny's writings for the libertarian Cato Institute, many of which ran counter to Minnesota's tradition of progressive social services. His response was essentially that it was a job, and he didn't necessarily believe in everything he put his name on. The respected newsletter "Politics in Minnesota" reported, "Most political folks we know were stunned by Penny's answer. One called Penny's retort the 'I'm not really a nut, just a whore' defense." Also in September, the *St. Paul Pioneer Press* wrote about his position on concealed weapons, which was far less absolute than Pawlenty's or Moe's. And the Republican Party of Minnesota launched a gimmick that made people laugh: Waffleman, a guy dressed as a waffle who planned to follow Penny around Minnesota. The word "Waffleman" started showing up in GOP tracking polls.

While Penny had the benefit of major-party status, the Independence Party as an institution was almost non-existent. There was no apparatus to attack his opponents, no one to spend money on his behalf, no network to turn out supporters wherever he went. At the same time he was polling as a front-runner, he was making campaign stops where just a few supporters would show up. After five easy reelection bids for Congress, Penny's campaign for governor wasn't going how he had envisioned it. He wasn't having a good time, and it was showing on the campaign trail, where he sometimes snapped at critics publicly.

Ken Pentel, Green. Pentel kept his eye on the magic number—5 percent—and traveled around the state talking to any gathering of people willing to listen. His approach is unapologetically Green: He appealed to the faithful, and launched a low-budget ad campaign on the fronts of city buses, based on his signature fluorescent orange laundry detergent box that touted his "refreshingly clean politics."

POLLING TRENDS

Through most of the race, Ken Pentel was having a hard time getting more than 3 percent in public polls. But once Ventura put Penny's name out, the former congressman was a contender. Through mid-October, most public polls showed Moe, Pawlenty and Penny each with support ranging from the mid- to high-20 percent range. Taking into account margins of error, most were deemed three-way ties. Even the campaign finance board's ruling against Penny didn't break the logjam.

By the end of October, though, most public polls showed Penny in a dramatic slide, and none could pinpoint exactly what had happened to him (see figure 21.1). Penny, who shunned polling, contends it was the death of Wellstone on October 25 and the subsequent disastrous memorial-turned-political rally on October 29 that drove his voters to Republicans (see chapter 7 on the Minnesota Senate race). But most other polls don't bear this out:

- St. Cloud State University released a poll in late October showing Penny still in a three-way tie, but it had been conducted over 13 days—October 14 to 27.
- A one-day poll conducted by the *Star Tribune* on October 28—after Wellstone's death but before the memorial/rally—found Penny down to 19 percent, 10 to 14 points behind Moe and Pawlenty, respectively.
- Democrats say they saw Penny start to slip in internal polls in late September, when his "sensible center" was starting to look more like a mushy middle, but this contradicts all public polls from that period.
- Republicans contend it was the "terrorists" ad that started running October 22 that did the trick. They say that in internal polls, Penny dropped down to the low 20s after the ad came out, then to 19. After that, they didn't even bother attacking him anymore.
- A *Star Tribune* Minnesota Poll conducted before and after a televised October 21 debate showed Penny plummeting among a small sample of viewers. The sample was small and skewed toward

Republicans—not as reliable as a normal poll—but it documented a poor reaction to Penny's debate performance by viewers.

The upshot: Penny's fall began in the dark, and the strobe light of public polling never showed clearly what tripped him. The Sunday before the election, polls published in the *Pioneer Press* and *Star Tribune* found opposite results in the U.S. Senate race—the *Pioneer Press* showed Coleman leading; the *Star Tribune*, Mondale—but they agreed in the governor's race: Penny was at 16 percent, and Pawlenty was in the mid-30s, leading Moe by a few points.

TV AND OTHER ADVERTISING EFFORTS

With the exception of the brutally stoic Roger Moe, the candidates (or in Pawlenty's case, his party) all waged clever ad campaigns. Pentel touted his refreshingly "clean politics" on the laundry detergent boxes and produced

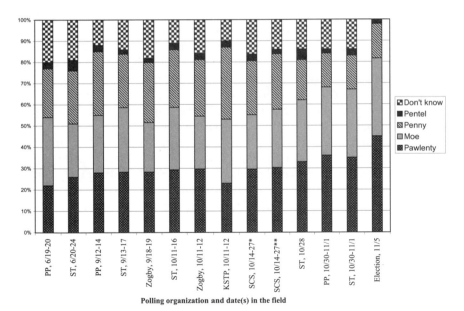

*all respondents
**likely voters
Notes: PP = *Pioneer Press,* St = *Star Tribune,* SCS = St. Cloud State.
Paul Wellstone died October 25.

Figure 21.1   Polling in Minnesota Governor Race, 2002

1950s-style TV ads in October that featured him and running mate Rhoda Gilman debunking myths about the Greens—including the idea that a vote for Pentel would be a wasted vote. In one ad, Pentel argued that Greens aren't trying to tell people how to live. "The Green Party is about giving you more choices on how to live," Pentel says in the ad. "Now eat your broccoli and vote for me." Pawlenty was the hero taking on the "dynamic tax-raising duo" in GOP ads, the local boy with the 34-inch waist. Penny put up a deadpan piece showing two children on a teeter-totter without a fulcrum. The point? Without a center, politics just doesn't work. Moe played it straight, talking to the camera about his key Democratic themes—education and the safety net—showing himself with his elderly parents and with children and educators.

But cleverness—and even Pawlenty's controversial "terrorists" ad—could go only so far when they were drowned out by an incessant, Washington-driven blast from the U.S. Senate race and two particularly bitter U.S. House races. With strict spending limits in place, candidates for governor couldn't keep up with the congressional blitz until the final cacophonous days of the race.

But the subterranean campaigns of interest groups were playing a critical role in breaking up the three-way tie. Minnesota Citizens Concerned for Life (MCCL), an anti-abortion group, kept up a steady drumbeat against Penny to make sure none of its followers thought he was still on their side. Pro-choice groups touted Moe. Penny was trying to appeal to the middle, but he had no real party, only a primitive mailing list and not a single interest group on his side to make his case. An MCCL exit poll found that 27 percent of voters recalled receiving one of the group's mailings, while 8 percent recalled getting mail from Planned Parenthood.

Advertising went silent for a few days after Wellstone's death, and even after it resumed—with less than a week to go before Election Day—substantive, critical media coverage had shifted largely to the newly constituted Senate race. In the final days, when Penny was clearly out of contention, the GOP cut loose with TV and radio ads smacking Moe's record on crime, just like an old-fashioned two-party race. The media scarcely noticed.

MONEY/CAMPAIGN FINANCE

The money race is not the issue in Minnesota that it is in other states, but lack of money is.

Major-party candidates who want public financing—which ranged from $240,000 to $418,000 in 2002—agree to strict spending limits of about $2.2 million apiece. All four candidates accepted the money and the limits, which profoundly leveled the playing field and constrained the candidates' television ad campaigns. This was why it was so controversial, at least in political circles, that the GOP was putting out ads that looked like they came from Pawlenty way back in September—he got the benefit without having to pay up.

In fundraising, Pentel brought in a fraction of what he could have spent, but it was enough to get some TV ads on the air. Penny topped the $1 million mark without taking PAC money—an impressive accomplishment given the Independence Party's flimsy foundation. And as expected, Moe and Pawlenty approached the maximum. And each took a financial hit because of campaign mistakes, but none proved fatal. Pawlenty's $600,000 penalty from the campaign finance board ($100,000 in fines, $500,000 deducted from his spending limit) didn't hamper him—he had no problem running the "terrorists" ad in late October. Moe overspent early in the campaign, but even if he had more money to spend on advertising in October, the content of the ads he did run couldn't attract attention like the "terrorists" ad.

VOTE TOTALS

Come Election Day, the results couldn't look more different than the polls that dominated the first four months of the campaign. Pawlenty skated to a comfortable win with 44 percent of the vote (and ever vigorous, he woke up the next morning and went roller-blading for 45 minutes before reporting to the Capitol for a press conference). Moe pulled 36 percent—a number that easily could have been a win had the three-way race held to the end. And Penny landed exactly where the last polls left him: 16 percent.

On election night, it appeared an equally devastating blow had hit Ken Pentel—with 2.3 percent, he received fewer than half the votes the Greens needed to retain major-party status. The Green candidates for auditor and secretary of state did better, but not well enough. But after the election, when the secretary of state was preparing to send notice to the Green Party that it had lost its position, someone remembered a state law passed in 2001 that confers major-party status for four years after it is won. The Greens didn't know about it because it was the work of the Independence Party's Dean Barkley, who wanted to ensure that the party survived 2004, when it was highly unlikely that an IP candidate would surface for the only statewide election of the year—the race for president. The state attorney general concluded on the last day of the year that the law applied to the Greens' status earned in 2000. "Sweet!" exclaimed Pentel when he heard the news. "Now we just have to see who the Greens run for president in 2004."

HIGHLIGHTS OF EXIT POLLING

Post-election polls in both the *Pioneer Press* and the *Star Tribune* showed that abortion ("social/moral issues" in the *Pioneer Press* poll) was the biggest single reason people voted for Pawlenty, and people concerned about education delivered the most votes to Moe. Pawlenty also won the vast majority of people concerned about taxes in the *Star Tribune* poll, and the *Pioneer Press* poll showed that his voters were the most inclined to believe that Pawlenty and the legislature would balance the budget without raising taxes.

The *Pioneer Press* poll revealed other factors: More than half of the people who voted for Ventura in 1998—people who could have become Penny's base of support—turned to Pawlenty in 2002. Pawlenty did better with his base than Moe, winning the votes of 91 percent of GOP voters, compared to Moe's 73 percent showing with DFL voters. Among voters with no party affiliation—again, Penny's potential pool—Pawlenty scored just under half, while Moe and Penny split the remainder.

Voters who flirted with the idea of voting Green or Independence Party but voted for Moe or Pawlenty instead cited three reasons for changing their minds in the *Pioneer Press* poll: 38 percent said they were more impressed with another candidate; 36 percent said they didn't want to waste their vote; 15 percent succumbed to loyalty to the GOP or DFL.

ANALYSIS

For the second governor's race in a row in Minnesota, the Democratic-Farmer-Labor and Republican parties faced a serious third-party threat. This time, though, they recognized it and shifted strategies. The typical election calculus requires Republicans and Democrats to appeal to their extreme elements in primaries, then tack to the center in the general election. But in a three way race, because they only need a hair over one-third of the vote, they realized they could stick closer to their bases. Moe talked relentlessly about core DFL issues—education and the social safety net—and reminded voters that he was the solid pro-choice candidate. Pawlenty did the same, saying he was the only candidate who wouldn't raise taxes, and by the way, he opposes abortion and supports gun rights. Neither needed to temper his positions on controversial issues to appear moderate.

Then there's Penny. He started the race strong, and stumbled badly before the finish line. But was it GOP strategy that wiped him out? Or Wellstone's death? Or did the former congressman implode on his own? The answer is most likely a combination of the three.

Voters clearly wanted to like Penny in the beginning. There really was a thirst for someone who shuns political dogma. But as they got to know him, they started to see a man who didn't take a strong stand on any particular issue, who disavowed major positions of a think tank he used to work for and who sometimes looked irritable on the campaign trail. The contrast Pawlenty offered was vivid: firm positions, accepting responsibility for the wrongdoing of his campaign and an engaging personality. The seeds for defeat were all there when Pawlenty launched the "terrorists" ad and siphoned off some of Penny's potential supporters. When Wellstone's plane crashed, the senator's death started driving more Democratic voters back home. And when Wellstone's memorial turned into a political rally, Republicans and fence-straddlers who were appalled by the spectacle rushed to the GOP. Point, game, match.

CONCLUSION

Minnesota's third parties failed to crack the GOP and DFL dominion over state politics in 2002.

To maintain major-party status in the next governor's race, the Greens may have to come up with a compelling presidential candidate in the 2004 election. In the meantime, though, the Green Party will continue building from the bottom, waging its battles in non-partisan local races, where it has already started making inroads.

The Independence Party must decide whether it's a political party or a passing fad that shone brightly only when a loud former wrestler took up the cause. Penny says he'll stay involved in the party, but that he won't take a leadership position. It's unclear who the Independence Party's candidate will be in 2006, but with the GOP and DFL having demonstrated that they can respond more effectively to a three-way race, he or she will have a much tougher job to do.

The Democrats are not in good shape themselves. They lost the governor's race, gave up a seat in the U.S. Senate and lost ground in the state legislature as well. With the death of the party's most charismatic figure, the DFL needs to find a compelling leader who can bring it back.

And the Republicans are in charge in Minnesota, holding the governor's office, commanding a larger majority in the state House of Representatives and narrowing the gap in the DFL-controlled Senate. Now all the GOP has to do is govern judiciously enough to hold onto power next time around.

22

Pennsylvania Governor

Philadelphia Gets a Governor

THOMAS FITZGERALD
Philadelphia Inquirer

Ed Rendell seemed an unlikely governor that February day in Erie, Pennsylvania, with no coat, leaning his balding head into the northerly wind howling off the lake as he tromped through snow toward a news conference.

He was nobody here, 427 miles from Philadelphia. Back home, he was "America's Mayor" and had a hoagie sandwich named for him, a hero credited with bringing a once-proud American city back from the brink of bankruptcy. Polls showed he was trailing badly in the race for the Democratic nomination, to the son of the party's last governor.

Nobody was at the Avalon Hotel when Rendell arrived. Eventually, a couple of TV cameramen set up their equipment to grab some B-roll for a routine "candidate for governor visits town" mention on the evening news. A print reporter ambled in.

"If there's one person, I still have to give my presentation," Rendell said.[1]

And so he did, offering his version of the Philadelphia Miracle, how he erased a budget deficit, went on to cut taxes, cleaned up the downtown streets and launched a hotel building boom, turning job losses into job gains. Pennsylvania, he said, faced huge problems—it ranked near the bottom in economic growth—and he was the man to turn things around. He promised billions in bond money to help cities like Erie attract investment, all-day kindergarten everywhere, reduced property taxes, and in general, an activism to shake off the traditional torpor of a cautious state government.

Rendell would wind up traveling 49,000 miles by the end of the campaign in a luxury bus covered with a shrink-wrapped image of his face, delivering much the same message. He rarely varied it, filling every room he entered with a torrent of words, optimistic promises. Rendell saturated the TV airwaves with ads, too, but he made a point of visiting nearly every county, letting people see and touch him, learning that he was not the citified devil, but a regular, backslapping guy. And that he cared enough to come in person.

Nine months later, Rendell was elected governor of Pennsylvania, defeating Republican Attorney General Mike Fisher 54 percent to 45 percent. His winning margin of 332,684 votes qualified as a blowout by the standard of open-seat gubernatorial elections in the state.

But the real surprise was that he had made it at all, since Rendell was the first former Philadelphia mayor to be elected governor since 1906, when state politics was dominated by the city's GOP machine, and the first city resident of any stripe to win the job in 88 years.

Analysts credited Rendell's personality—his charisma, stunning in its comparison to the stiffness of most Pennsylvania leaders—with overcoming the state electorate's historic loathing of Philadelphia, long considered the rat hole down which much of their tax money is poured. His relentless campaign of personal persuasion must have played a part. How else could a cultural liberal, a supporter of gay rights, gun control, and unrestricted access to abortion, crush a conservative Republican in what is, essentially, a conservative state?

He would go to a potentially hostile audience in the hinterlands and say, "How many of you think you don't get enough money from Harrisburg?" Hands would pop up around the room. "Well, it wasn't Philadelphia governors who did that to you, there hasn't been one since 1914." Invariably, the audience would chuckle.

Rendell's victory did conform to one political trend, however. Every eight years since 1946, the two major parties have swapped the governor's office. This time, it was the Democrats' turn.

For all his cultural liberalism, Rendell governed Philadelphia as a pro-business centrist bent on achieving consensus—and that was the image he projected most during the campaign for governor. Despite launching a crusade to sue gun manufacturers for the cost of street violence, for instance, Rendell spoke often about his respect for hunters and hunting.

There was little national significance to his victory, except that it provided a bright spot on the night Democrats lost control of the U.S. Senate.

"Make no mistake about it, people all over Pennsylvania voted for change tonight," Rendell told a ballroom of delirious supporters on election night. "Tomorrow morning . . . the campaign for change begins."[2] He thanked hundreds of thousands of voters from outside the Philadelphia area for their decisions "to give me a fair chance."[3]

They did, and change may yet come to Pennsylvania. But it was clear that Rendell managed to overcome the state's historical regionalism only on the strength of regionalism. He had an unassailable base in the southeastern part of the state. For the eight years of his mayoralty during the 1990s, Rendell had been burned into the public consciousness with almost nightly appearances on television stations reaching about 44 percent of the state's voters. He was a celebrity, and people liked him.

Rendell won 69 percent to 30 percent in the Philadelphia DMA (Designated Marketing Area), the election returns showed, and his margin in the city alone was almost enough to guarantee him victory. It seemed that he had become the mayor of a region—people in the suburbs admired the city's turnaround—and he carried all of the traditionally Republican suburban counties, even Chester County, the Republicans' most reliable suburban bastion since the Civil War. "That was our firewall," said Alan Novak, the state GOP chairman.[4]

A map of the returns showed a deep gash of Rendell red in the east, a dab in Allegheny County around Pittsburgh, and in a handful of southwestern counties near West Virginia. The rest of the state was solid Fisher blue. It was the Pennsylvania equivalent of the national electoral map in the 2000 presidential race, when Al Gore swept the population centers on both coasts.

"He was a product that people felt they had come to know," said John Brabender, Fisher's media consultant, describing Rendell's regional appeal. "It was like Coca-Cola. You can't take a Coke drinker and tell them all sorts of things to stop drinking Coke because they've been drinking it for years."[5]

Fisher himself said he has come to the conclusion that he couldn't have done much of anything to change the outcome because of his rival's hold on the southeast. Registered Republicans there just deserted him, and never came home.

"It was like campaigning against Santa Claus at Christmas time," Fisher said. "No matter what we said about him or about ourselves, the people there loved him—he was giving them presents—and they were going to vote for Santa Claus regardless."[6]

It didn't help that they were outgunned. Rendell burned his way through $42 million, for both the general and primary, while Fisher, unopposed for the GOP nomination, spent $13.8 million. That would have been a state record for a single candidate, but Rendell blew him away, raking in so much money that he was able to outspend Fisher three to one. The margin was eleven to one in the final three weeks of the campaign.

All told, three major candidates for governor raised $71 million this year, according to campaign-finance reports—a record, nearly double the previous mark of $36.6 million raised in 1994 by former Governor Tom Ridge and a half dozen rivals.

Pennsylvania is among a dozen states with no ceiling on the amount that individuals or political action committees can give to candidates, though donations cannot be drawn on corporate accounts.

The spending disparity was the key in the fall, both campaign managers agreed. "We took a knife to a gunfight," said Kent Gates, who ran Fisher's campaign. "We could throw three counterpunches on TV for every punch we took," said David Sweet, the Rendell campaign manager.

Fisher withdrew his ads in the Philadelphia market four weeks before the election, allowing Rendell to concentrate his fire elsewhere and keep him from gaining any traction. There was an opening for Fisher—Rendell had made so many promises, it seemed inevitable he would have to raise state taxes to pay for them; the former mayor said he wouldn't rule out raising taxes, especially for an infusion of $1.5 billion for education that he claimed could be done by legalizing slot machines and cutting unspecified government waste.

As time wound down, Fisher honed his message down to one point: Rendell would raise your taxes. The Republican also raised fears that Philadelphia would get the lion's share of the new state education money Rendell promised, according to the state aid formula. But few people could hear the message because Fisher was outspent on television. Rendell turned the attack on the city around, proclaiming his outrage in order to juice up turnout in Philadelphia. His biggest potential enemy in the last days was ennui from supporters who might stay home, thinking he had the election won.

"It was working," Gates said of the tax-and-spend attack message, "but we didn't have enough money . . . We were able to match him in the Pittsburgh DMA for the last two weeks, but it was too little too late."

Republicans were not blown out, though; the party actually increased its margin of control in both houses of the state legislature, an indication that voters agreed the GOP was doing a pretty good job in Harrisburg. A little gerrymandering in the decennial redistricting process didn't hurt, but there was no real groundswell for Rendell's party or ideology. (In fact, he boasted of transcending both.) It was evident that suburban moderate Republicans voted for Rendell at the top of the ticket, then fell back on their partisan inclinations when voting for legislative candidates.

As a transcendent figure, Rendell's victory contained a central contradiction: he stressed that Pennsylvania needed fundamental change, and he was uniquely qualified to lead it, yet the public was not clamoring for change. Voters expressed concerns about the future, true, but they were not angry.

One respected public opinion poll found that 52 percent of voters in September believed that Pennsylvania was headed in the right direction, a respectable number—down slightly from the 55 percent who said so in June, and the 62 percent who thought the state was on the right track at the beginning of the year. (Of course, that was after months of Rendell ads told them the state was in crisis.) [7]

A competing poll in June found that 68 percent of voters statewide were somewhat or very satisfied with the state's direction, though dissatisfaction was the highest in the southwestern part of the state, an economically depressed coal region, the one area outside of Philadelphia Rendell would sweep.[8]

Even though Fisher was the status-quo candidate who promised a continuation of eight years of Republican control of the governor's office, he was not the incumbent, and voters did not see him as the heir to popular administrations of former Governor Tom Ridge and Governor Mark Schweiker, said Berwood Yost, director of the Center for Opinion Research at Millersville University.

One survey in September found that Schweiker, had he decided to run for governor, would have been leading Rendell, 47 percent to 29 percent.[9] The incumbent had been the lieutenant governor, and took over when Ridge left in October 2001 to head the nation's homeland security effort. Schweiker decided not to run, citing family reasons.

The promises and prescriptions for problems that Rendell spewed out were really just "symbolic rhetoric" that established his bona fides as a leader, in case things got worse, Yost said. It does not necessarily mean voters endorse the specifics of that agenda, or even expect to see them enacted.

"There was no incumbent to truly benefit from those 'right track' numbers," Yost said. "There is some concern about the future—where the stock market is going, the state budget—and Rendell did a credible job of describing the uncertainty. He offered a vision of the leadership he would provide, and that is what voters responded to."

And like so much else with Rendell, his vision of leadership comes from his first days as Philadelphia mayor in 1992, when the city had a $250 million debt and was dodging creditors. The city "stands on the brink of disaster," Rendell said in his inaugural address. He had plenty of help—a state authority floated $256 million in bailout bonds and the state raised the sales tax in Philadelphia—but to get the help he had to cut wasteful spending in the city government. He cracked down on city unions, forcing benefit and work-rules concessions. He privatized some city services. Eventually, the rising tide of the national economy lifted Philadelphia, and Rendell was a tireless promoter, putting together deals that built eleven hotels in the city and revitalized its tourism industry. Plenty remained undone—the schools are horrible and the state took them over last year—but most people consider the Rendell years a time of renewal. People like to be seduced.

The irony is that Rendell earned his credibility as a leader calling on people in Philadelphia to sacrifice for the common good. But as a candidate for governor he promised the sun, the moon, and the stars—with absolutely no pain. He said the state must change but did not make it sound threatening. He did win a mandate, but it was for pie in the sky. Harrisburg insiders are muttering that it's just a question of when he'll raise taxes, which taxes they'll be, and by how much.

So Rendell's victory may have raised more questions than it answered. Can he keep people happy? Will the public allow him to skate away from his promiscuous promises, or will it get angry and blame him when the promised land—school-funding equity and property-tax relief, for example—turns out to be much, much harder to achieve than Rendell ever let on?

Already, Rendell has been laying the groundwork to postpone some of his more expensive promises, selling the idea that there is going to be a budget deficit of nearly $1.8 billion next year because of softening tax collections and some one-time revenue sources used to patch holes in the last budget.

"He gets to play it both ways—but let me defend that," said Jack Hanna, a member of the state Democratic Committee from Indiana, Pennsylvania. "People want to hear about optimism, and vision, and that's what leadership is all about. Part of the reason he did so well is that Fisher was not even able to articulate a vision at all."

Rendell, in an interview the day after the election, was not worried about pulling it off. He plans to fire up the campaign bus to travel the state and sell, sell, sell.

"It is deja vu all over again," Rendell said. "Remember, in my first year as mayor, I had to disappoint a lot of people. I had to say no to a ton of very legitimate requests for more money for parks, more money for libraries, more money for recreation centers . . . but my message was 'Look, we can't do it now because there just isn't any money, but if we do this thing right, we'll be able to grow our economy and reduce the cost of the operation of government—we're going to be able to get there.' And that's my same message [now]. I think I have a little bit more of a stronger position to deliver that message because it worked."[10]

NOTES

1. Tom Infield, "His frantic pace makes Rendell strong across Pa.," *The Philadelphia Inquirer,* 28 April 2002.

2. Thomas Fitzgerald, "Rendell Rules—Phila. area propels him to victory," *The Philadelphia Inquirer*, 6 November 2002.

3. Tom Infield, "Rendell's appeal went beyond Phila.," *The Philadelphia Inquirer*, 6 November 2002.

4. Ibid.

5. Ibid.

6. Personal interview with author, 3 December 2002.

7. Keystone Poll, Center for Opinion Research, Millersville University. 26 September to 29 September 2002.

8. Quinnipiac University Polling Institute, 5 June 2002.

9. Keystone, September 2002.

10. "Rendell: the people voted for change," *The Philadelphia Inquirer*, 7 November 2002.

23

Texas Governor

The Democratic "Dream Team" Bites the Dust

PEGGY FIKAC
San Antonio Express-News

Texas Governor Rick Perry—who as lieutenant governor stepped up to the state's highest post when George W. Bush resigned in 2000 to become president—won election to the job in his own right when he beat South Texas businessman Tony Sanchez by a wide margin in a rough, expensive battle that illustrated the ascendancy of the Republican Party in Texas and pointed to the state's political future.

True to form, the fight didn't end easily between George W. Bush's Republican successor and the man Democrats had hoped would make history and help them regain a foothold in statewide office. Perry declared victory at about 10:00 p.m. on election night, but with ballot-counting problems plaguing two big counties, Sanchez wasn't ready to give up. He proclaimed that Perry's announcement "literally reminds me of 1948," when Republican Thomas E. Dewey was wrongly credited in a famous headline with victory over Democrat Harry S. Truman. "He needs this message: I am going to give them hell and fight like hell until the last vote is counted," said Sanchez, who didn't concede until the next day. Perry got 57.8 percent of the vote to 40 percent for Sanchez[1] in a race that also offered a Libertarian, a Green Party candidate and two write-in candidates.

The Texas-tough race broke spending records as the major-party candidates in campaign speeches and in statewide television advertising questioned each other's ethics in the most negative terms. Sanchez accused Perry of selling the power of his office for campaign contributions, and Perry sought to link Sanchez to drug traffickers who killed a U.S. Drug Enforcement Administration agent. The latter commercial particularly outraged Sanchez, who called it a lie and said its ugliness would be Perry's legacy. Each candidate defended his own record as honorable, and each spent big to point out what he saw as the other's weaknesses, with Sanchez's massive investment quickly setting a new state record. A multimillionaire whose interests included oil and gas and banking and who was an early investor in Blockbuster, Sanchez spent $64 million through October 26, the last reporting period before the November 5 election. Most of it was his own money, from a fortune estimated at $600 million. Perry, his campaign fueled by donors including two national Republican groups and outgoing U.S. Senator Phil Gramm, had spent $25 million by the same time. The previous record for a Texas race for governor was set in 1990, when eight candidates spent more than $45 million.[2]

Despite the huge spending and a much-ballyhooed get-out-the-vote effort, turnout was just 36 percent of the state's 12,563,459 registered voters,[3] short of the 40 percent that had been predicted by Texas Secretary of State Gwyn Shea.[4] Although voter-registration efforts were launched with ambitious goals, a smaller percentage of Texas's voting-age population registered than in either 2000 or 1998.[5] Some blamed negative campaigning for dampening voter enthusiasm. "I think the negative campaigning has taken a toll and created some serious apathy," said Democratic Representative Pete Gallego of Alpine, head of the House Mexican American Legislative Caucus.[6] State Senator Eddie Lucio, D-Brownsville, said the negative tone was bad for both sides at a time when Texas along with the rest of the country was still living with the memory and fallout of the September 11 terror attacks. "If I would have to pinpoint a factor in the campaign that has hurt both sides, it's the negative campaigning, without a doubt. After 9/11, people from all walks of life have come together in our state and our country, and they're tired of the division that has been at hand in Washington. They don't want the same type of thing happening in Texas," Lucio said.[7]

Perry, 52, drew support from President Bush—the Washington resident whom Texans claim as a favorite son and to whom they, along with the rest of the country, looked during the terror attacks and the war-talk-filled aftermath. With the battle in his home state drawing national attention, the president campaigned for Perry as well as for U.S. Senate candidate John Cornyn, whose bid more directly affected Bush's national agenda. A campaign sign that sprouted before the election sought to draw the line in the sand: "Support President Bush. Vote Republican." Perry's career itself was an example of the GOP's ascent in Texas. A former Democratic lawmaker, Perry switched to the GOP before winning his first statewide office of agriculture commissioner in 1990. Using a favored GOP line, he had said he didn't leave the Democratic Party but that "the party left me." He cited his public-service experience as he campaigned to stay in the Governor's Mansion against the outsider challenge by Sanchez, who suggested it was time for a governor who was something other than a "professional politician."

Sanchez, 59, described himself as a steadfast moderate and had been a big contributor to Bush, who as governor appointed him to the University of Texas System Board of Regents. Despite that support, Sanchez strongly defended his credentials as a Democrat and noted that he also had given generously to Democratic candidates. A supporter pointed out that Sanchez had been "one of many, many Democrats who supported Bush." The University of Texas post was one of two state appointed posts in which Sanchez had served; he had been appointed to the first by a Democratic governor.

The 2002 race was Sanchez's first bid for elected office, and he made it as part of a Democratic "dream team" ticket that also included U.S. Senate candidate Ron Kirk, an African-American former Dallas mayor, and lieutenant governor candidate John Sharp, a former state comptroller who is Anglo (see also chapter 14 about the Texas Senate race). "It is our time," said a sign at rallies by Democrats, shut out of statewide office for years. If he had won, Sanchez would have been Texas's first Hispanic governor since it joined the United States. The Democratic combination was seen as a potential way to increase minority turnout, but Sharp said the candidates' main attraction lay not in their diversity but in a centrist message. "I think the first priority of the ticket was that it not be seen by Texans as something on the far left," said Sharp, acknowledged as key architect of the ticket.[8]

Sanchez used both themes. He trumpeted the benefits of having a businessman-governor, and he called the Democratic ticket "an historic opportunity to change government so that it looks like Texas. Texas is a diverse state, but we have not had a diverse government." Perry also reached out to Hispanic voters, running Spanish language advertising, campaigning in South Texas and early on supporting a ballot measure to pave roads into poverty-stricken neighborhoods known as colonias in the heavily Hispanic border region. That move won him praise from some border officials even though he had earlier angered some border interests by vetoing several measures they supported.

The effort to attract the Hispanic vote was acknowledged as key by both parties because the group is a growing part of Texas's population, predicted to become the majority in the state by 2035 and perhaps earlier.[9] The William C. Velásquez Institute, which tracks Latino voting trends, said its exit polling found that 87 percent supported Sanchez and 10 percent voted for Perry. It found that Latinos turned out at a rate of 39.9 percent, which institute president Antonio González called a record high for an off-year election.[10] The institute's assessment of Hispanic support for Sanchez was disputed by Perry pollster Mike Baselice, who said his tracking found Perry had support from 35 percent of Hispanic voters. He also said Perry was supported by 72 percent of Anglo voters and 15 percent of African-American voters.[11] Regional director Ricardo Castañon of the Southwest Voter Registration Education Project, which works with the institute on voting issues, said institute pollsters interviewed 838 people leaving polling places in 15 Texas counties, including large population centers and some border counties. Baselice said his numbers were based on tracking polls Sunday and Monday before the election in which 1,008 people were surveyed by telephone, including 172 Hispanics. It was a random-dial survey that included the majority of Texas counties.[12]

Whatever the voter breakdown, it was a knockdown loss for the Democratic Party. Ben Barnes, a former state lieutenant governor and national fundraiser for Democrats, said the party's failure up and down the ticket was a result of Democrats not adequately selling a message. "It's not the end of the Democratic Party, but . . . its candidates have got to tell the people of Texas why they should vote for them. The Democrats did not get a message out there this time," Barnes said. In contrast, he said, "The president and Karl Rove, his political strategist, did a wonderful job. . . . They convinced the American public [that] if you're for the president and national security and for a safe homeland, you need to vote Republican."[13]

Despite the loss, Sanchez still made Texas history by becoming the first Hispanic to win a major-party nomination for governor in the state. To do so, he beat another Hispanic—former state attorney general Dan Morales—in the Democratic primary race. Morales challenged Sanchez on issues in his business background that later were raised by Perry. The primary also served to focus attention on ethnicity, as Sanchez took a strong stand in favor of affirmative action and insisted on debating Morales in Spanish as well as in English. Morales, who took a primary drubbing, later endorsed Perry. The primary fight may have taken a toll, said political science professor Andy Hernandez of St. Mary's University in San Antonio. "The first thing that white voters hear about Tony Sanchez is affirmative action," Hernandez said. "He had to have a stronger message—not just to white voters, but to voters, period."[14]

Perry, who traveled the state extensively after becoming governor, was spared a primary fight, but the general election soon was in fast-and-furious mode. Sanchez's television advertising included accusations that Perry—whose actions as governor included a record 82 vetoes of legislation in 2001—sold out to big campaign contributors such as insurance interests.

Perry took $1.24 million on contributions from various interests between the time the 2001 legislative session ended and the deadline for vetoing bills, and he got $888,782 from insurance interests alone from 1997 through June 2002.[15] Perry said he was not swayed by contributions. Sanchez also targeted the fact that Perry took over the state's top job without benefit of election with the refrain, "We didn't elect him. We don't have to keep him." Not long before Election Day, a Sanchez ad used video of Perry showing impatience at a traffic stop when he was lieutenant governor and his driver was stopped and given a warning for speeding. The videotape showed Perry asking the trooper, "Why don't you just let us get on down the road?" The ad went on to say, "We didn't elect him. Let's just let him get on down the road."

Perry's advertising included a jibe at Sanchez's admittedly spotty voting record and commercials focusing on alleged drug-money laundering in the 1980s at Sanchez's failed Tesoro Savings and Loan of Laredo. In his hardest shot, Perry sought to link Sanchez to drug traffickers who tortured and killed U.S. drug agent Enrique "Kiki" Camarena in 1985. A former DEA agent in the ad said, "The same drug dealers who killed Kiki laundered millions in drug money through Tony Sanchez's bank."

The subject arose because the federal government in 1984 suspected two Mexican men with ties to Miguel Felix Gallardo, leader of a drug cartel, had laundered almost $25 million in drug money through Tesoro. Gallardo later was implicated in Camarena's murder.[16] Sanchez repeatedly said thrift officials fully cooperated when told of suspect deposits and noted that no charges were filed. He said he was cleared by two judges and by testimony from representatives of the DEA, U.S. attorney's office and Internal Revenue Service. The testimony from those representatives came during a libel lawsuit.

Sanchez called Perry a liar in denouncing the ad concerning Camarena's murder, and some saw racism in the effort to tie a prominent Hispanic candidate to drug-money laundering. "Against Hispanic candidates, the racial coding is you can't trust 'em and you insert crime and drugs in some form. . . . It's like a code to the scared white voter," said González.[17] Perry's camp defended its efforts as factual and as bringing out the record of a man running on his business experience.

While the negative hits drew most of the attention, there were serious issues begging to be addressed, including a revenue shortfall that the state comptroller estimated would be $5 billion to meet commitments in the upcoming two-year budget period. Neither candidate offered a specific plan to deal with the prospect. "I think that it's irresponsible to talk about new taxes before we have an opportunity to go in and find the inefficiencies in our government," Sanchez said. "I think if we're given that opportunity,

especially with people from the private sector, we will find a lot of ineffi-
ciencies and waste." Perry said, "Obviously we'll set our priorities in the
state of Texas. And with the right kind of leadership, I feel very confident
that we'll have a budget that's balanced with no new taxes."[18] Each cited
education as a top priority, with Sanchez calling for changes in the state's
high-stakes student testing program and Perry contending with support
from U.S. Education Secretary Rod Paige that Sanchez's proposal was a bad
plan[19] and that the state instead should build on successes of the existing
program.

One issue seemed tailor-made for a challenger: Homeowners saw their
insurance rates skyrocket even while comprehensive coverage became less
available. Sanchez blamed Perry for not acting more quickly to head off a
problem, calling it a prime example of him bowing to big campaign donors.
Sanchez offered a plan for addressing rates and urged Perry to call lawmakers into a special legislative session to address the problem, because Texas
lawmakers only meet in regular session in odd-numbered years. Sanchez
even floated the idea that if elected, he would ask the state attorney general
to call for a "court of inquiry to look into the criminal activity of office-
holders, former office holders, lawyers, lobbyists and consultants."[20]

But Perry acted quickly as well, announcing his own plan to deal with
the matter while refusing to call lawmakers into a pre-election session on
the volatile issue. Perry touted a state investigation of top insurers, and a
lawsuit and administrative cease-and-desist order against Farmers Insurance. The company said it had done nothing wrong, and the state action
resulted in Farmers announcing plans to leave Texas. Perry used the action
as a demonstration that he was not influenced by campaign donations. He
also sought to turn the insurance issue around on Sanchez, because a subsid-
iary of his International Bank of Commerce sold insurance policies. University of Texas-Pan American political science professor Jerry Polinard said
about two weeks before the campaign that he opened a "beautiful flier"
concerning insurance expecting it to be from Sanchez. It was a Perry mailer.
"That's an example of a very effectively managed campaign. You take an
issue that should put you on the defensive and actually use it against your
opponent," Polinard said.[21]

The advertising blitz was part of massive spending that drew attention
even in a state in which there are no limits on the amount candidates can
raise and spend. One newspaper's review of contributions and expenditures
through September 2002 found that Sanchez spent more than twice as much
on payroll as Perry's campaign. It showed $2.1 million was paid to 934 peo-
ple who worked for Sanchez at one time or another over 14 months. Perry,
by comparison, spent $809,400 on 41 paid staff members. The analysis
found that even though television ads generally eat up the lion's share of

campaign budgets, Sanchez had spent more on expenses other than television than Perry had spent on his campaign overall to that point. Sanchez had spent $5,323 on confetti alone, leading one former political consultant to say, "It would be cheaper just to shred money" and to assess the Sanchez effort this way: "It's not a campaign, it's a cruise ship."[22] Sanchez, pressed on the expenses, explained them as necessary to catch up to an opponent with nearly two decades as an officeholder under his belt. "I know every penny that was being spent in this campaign, believe me," he said. "I've had to catch up in seven months to what my opponent has done in 18 years. He's been campaigning most of his adult life."[23]

The difference in spending ability could be glimpsed even in such trappings as the campaign buses. Perry's bus was big and comfortable, with perks including box lunches prepared at the Governor's Mansion—food that was paid for by the campaign or personally, according to Perry's staff. But Sanchez's bus had bells and whistles including satellite TV and a sound system that broadcast music to herald his arrivals and departures. Perry called his vehicle a "poor boy's bus" by comparison but added, "It gets the job done."[24] And so it did.

But Sanchez, in an e-mail addressed, "Dear Fellow Texan" and sent shortly after the election, suggested he did an important job as well. "We may not have been victorious, but we fought long and hard to make Texas a better place—and Texas will be a better place as a result of what we have done."

NOTES

1. Texas Secretary of State Web site, unofficial election results, http://204.65.107.70/02novgen.htm.

2. W. Gardner Selby, "Governor's race nears the $89 million mark; Perry outspends Sanchez in past month for 1st time," *San Antonio Express-News*, 29 October 2002.

3. Texas Secretary of State Web site, http://204.65.107.70/02novgen.htm.

4. Texas Secretary of State press release, 31 October 2002.

5. Peggy Fikac, "Voter registrations in downward slide, Total is up, but is lower percentage of eligible," *San Antonio Express-News*, 19 October 2002.

6. Gallego Interview, 18 October 2002.

7. Peggy Fikac, "Races now in homestretch; Latest polls favor Perry, Cornyn; Demos hope new voters turn tide," *San Antonio Express-News*, 3 November 2002.

8. Sharp interview, 5 November 2002.

9. Texas State Data Center, "New Population Predictions for Texas Show a State Growing Extensively, Diversifying Rapidly and Aging Substantially in the Coming Decades," 18 December 2001.

10. "Massive Latino Vote in Texas Gives Support to Democrats," News Release, 7 November 2002.

11. Peggy Fikac, "Democrats asking selves, 'What now?'" *San Antonio Express-News*, 7 November 2002.

12. Rebeca Rodriguez, "Hispanic voting profile disputed," *San Antonio Express-News*, 9 November 2002.

13. Peggy Fikac, "Democrats asking selves, 'What now?'" *San Antonio Express-News*, 7 November 2002.

14. Peggy Fikac, "Errors in strategy by Sanchez cited," *San Antonio Express-News*, 10 November 2002.

15. Figures compiled by Texans for Public Justice.

16. George Kuempel, "Sanchez sets stage to make Texas history; Democrats target businessman for gubernatorial candidate, R. G. Ratcliffe" *Houston Chronicle*, 3 March 2001; Pete Slover, "Sanchez expecting political foes to revisit money-laundering case; Banker cleared in '80s S&L inquiry says it shouldn't be an issue in campaign," *The Dallas Morning News*, 5 August 2001.

17. Interview, 30 October 2002.

18. Dallas debate, 25 October 2002.

19. Peggy Fikac, "Education chief raps Sanchez testing proposal; Paige calls it 'significant undoing,'" *San Antonio Express-News*, 22 June 2002.

20. Houston debate, 9 October 2002.

21. Peggy Fikac, "Errors in strategy by Sanchez cited," *San Antonio Express-News*, 10 November 2002.

22. Wayne Slater and Pete Slover, "Cash flow now a flood," *The Dallas Morning News*, 13 October 2002.

23. Dallas debate, 25 October 2002.

24. Peggy Fikac, "Some races didn't need a starting gun," *San Antonio Express-News*, 1 September 2002.

24

A Final Look in the Rearview Mirror for 2002

The Midterm Map of America

LARRY J. SABATO

University of Virginia Center for Politics

Bulletin: There was no national election in November 2002, whatever you may have read to the contrary. No, there was no coup, and terrorism or bad weather didn't force a postponement. The truth is much more simple: there was not enough competition to qualify November 5 as anything other than a patchwork of party battles in widely scattered parts of the United States.

Just like a presidential election, we tend to think of a midterm as "national," since all 435 seats in the U.S. House of Representatives are on the ballot, plus 36 of the 50 state governorships, and about a third of the U.S. Senate seats. In no midterm year is there anything as leavening as the presidential contest, which every state lists on the ballot. Still, with the layering of contests for state executives and federal legislators, most midterms feature multiple close races in about two-thirds of the states.

Not so in 2002. Just 16 of the 34 Senate contests and a shockingly low four dozen of 435 House seats could be termed competitive. The governorship elections provided some relief with 24 out of 36 registering as competitive. ("Competitive" is a somewhat subjective designation here, covering any contest that attracted substantial press, party, and donor attention and whose result was at least partly in doubt before November 5.)

Yet nearly half of the states had no intense fights for either of the top statewide offices. Some of these states—such as Connecticut, Indiana, Kentucky, Mississippi, Nevada, Ohio, Utah, Washington, and West Virginia— had just a House seat or two on the political radar screen, hardly enough to gain the attention of an entire state's electorate. And five states had not a single close, competitive election for governor, senator, or U.S. representative: Alaska, Delaware, Idaho, Nebraska, and Virginia.

The varying state schedules for electing governors and senators account for some of this, but so does the strongly pro-incumbent redistricting that took place after 2000 in all but a handful of states. Incredibly, there was but a single close House contest in each of the mega-states of California (53 total seats), Illinois (19 seats), Ohio (18 seats), and New York (29 seats)—4 seats out of 119. Of the fifty states, only Iowa had even as many as four close House elections on tap.

So where did political junkies migrate for the autumn of 2002? The Midterm Election Map of American gives directions. A state was assigned ten points for any very competitive Senate race; ten for a large-state governorship contest of the same variety; eight points for a very competitive medium- or small-state governorship; six points for a second-tier competitive race for the Senate anywhere or a governorship in a large state; four points for a second-tier governor's contest in a medium or small state; two points for each competitive House seat; and, of course, no points for uncompetitive contests.

Based on this scale, each state was expanded or contracted to represent its real significance in the 2002 midterm elections (see figure 24.1).

Election aficionados flocked to two states in the South (Georgia and Texas), and two in the Midwest (Iowa and Minnesota). In all four states, voters were treated to marvelous Senate and governor match-ups, plus solid House races, yielding "competition scores" of 24 to 26. Three other states, New Hampshire, South Dakota, and Tennessee, rounded out the top seven with 20 points each. Fierce jousting for both senator and governor took place in each state, plus a hot House race. Two small states, South Carolina (18 points) and Maine (16 points), ranked relatively high on the competitiveness scale, especially when one considers that the average score for a state was less than 8 points.

Regionally, the West was by far the least competitive region in 2002; the proof is in its shrunken visage on the map. All other geographic regions were home to at least one state with 20 points or more on the competition scale.

Still, the overall impression left by the rankings on the Midterm Map is the country's need to refocus the political parties and the public on the need for greater competition. Yes, in a nearly split Senate and House, just a

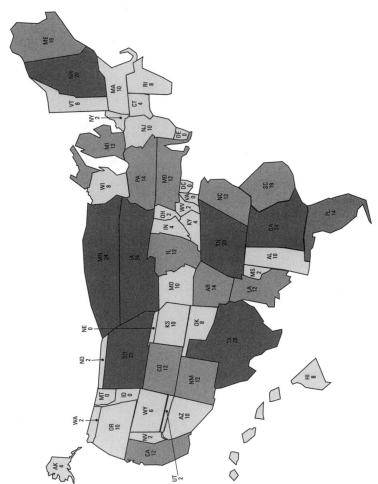

Figure 24.1 The Midterm Map of America, 2002.

© Larry J. Sabato, University of Virginia Center for Politics, 2002. Designed by Chester + Hound, Inc., and revised by Adam Blumenkrantz, University of Virginia Center for Politics.

few contests were needed to create drama and affect control of the Congress. But excitement in a few places, like scattered thunderstorms in a draught, is not good enough, despite the pyrotechnics.

The Midterm Map of America ought to more closely resemble the geographic map of the United States. And it only takes a quick glance at this year's concoction to see how far we have to go. Hope springs eternal: perhaps the next set of midterm contests in 2006 will yield a more representative picture.

Index

Note: A "t" indicates a table and an "m" indicates a map.

abortion, 102, 236, 244
Adams, Michael, 51
Adelphia, 8
Aeshliman, Lawrence, 235
AFL-CIO, 129, 140
AFLAC, 62
African Americans: and Florida politics, 199, 203; and Georgia politics, 178–79, 184–85; as governors, 27; and Maryland politics, 228; North Carolina voting by, 140; in Senate, 172; voter turnout by, 11, 12
agenda-setting, 8
Agnew, Spiro T., 231
Alaska, governor's race in, 28
Alexander, Honey, 162
Alexander, Lamar, 15; background of, 156–57; 2002 campaign of, 157–65
Alexander, Rodney, 68
Allard, Wayne, 39
Allen, Diane, 106–7
Alliance for Better Campaigns, 51, 53
Allman, Michelle, 193
American Airlines, 98
American Association of Health Plans, 12
American Conservative Union, 182
American Red Cross, 139
Americans for Democratic Action, 182
Americans for Job Security, 131
Americans with Disabilities Act, 81
Arctic National Wildlife Refuge, 128

Armistead, Bill, 80
Arthur Anderson, 8
Ashcroft, John, 91, 95, 99, 182
AT&T Wireless, 131
Atlanta Journal-Constitution, 51
attack ads: free airtime and, 54; on Internet, 62; in Iowa, 78, 80, 220, 221; in South Dakota, 147; in Tennessee, 160, 164, 165; in Texas, 256, 258–59
Ayres, McHenry and Associates, 12
Ayres, Whit, 156, 164–65

Baghdad 3, 40
Baker, Howard, 157, 162, 164
Bali bombing, 49
Baltimore Sun, 226
Barkley, Dean, 235, 243
Barnes, Ben, 258
Barnes, Roy, 24, 26, 44–45, 51, 61, 177, 178, 182; 2002 campaign of, 179–81
Barr, Bob, 71
Bartlett, Jeff, 52
Barton, Joe, 170
Baselice, Mike, 258
Beckwith, Dave, 171–72
BeneCard, 108
Bentsen, Ken, 171
Bentsen, Lloyd, 171
Berman, Hy, 49
Blagojevich, Rod, 26, 209–17
blame game, for poor Democratic showing, 40–43

Blanton, Ray, 157, 161
Blodgett, Jeff, 90
Blue, Dan, 139, 140
Bond, Kit, 98, 101, 103
Bonilla, Henry, 76, 169, 170
Bonior, David, 40, 70
Boschwitz, Rudy, 89
Boston Globe, 47
Boston Herald, 47
Bowles, Crandall, 140
Bowles, Erskine, 37, 138–43
Bowles, Harlan "Skipper", 139
Boxer, Barbara, 173
Brabender, John, 249
Bradley, Bill, 110
Branstad, Terry, 78, 220–21
Braun, Carol Moseley, 216
Breaux, John, 19
Bredesen, Phil, 159, 161, 162, 165
Broder, David, 54
Brown, Anthony, 228
Brown, George H., Jr., 164
Brown, Sherrod, 69
Bryant, Ed, 156, 158, 160–61
Buchanan, Pat, 156
Burns, Max, 184–85
Burris, Roland, 210
Bush, Barbara, 100
Bush, George H. W., 5–6, 9, 19, 96, 149, 156, 171
Bush, George W.: agenda-setting by, 8; and beginning of term, 1; and California politics, 189; campaigning for candidates by, 8–10, 15, 19, 39, 50, 74, 82, 93, 96, 109, 126, 131–32, 139, 143, 165, 179, 203; and D.U.I. charge, 35; and foreign policy, 9; future prospects of, 42–43, 144; and midterm elections, xi, 8, 11; New Hampshire vote count for, 126; popularity of, 1–2, 37–38, 50, 96; and risking of political capital, 9–10; in "Social Insecurity" video, 62–63; and South Dakota politics, 145, 146, 148, 150–51; states carried by, 36;

and Texas politics, 167–68, 169, 170, 172, 174–75, 255, 256, 257, 258; and 2000 election, 2, 156
Bush, Jeb, 24, 27, 61, 195, 198; 2002 campaign of, 199–206
Bush, Laura, 93, 150, 174
Bush, Noelle, 201–2
Bush v. Gore, 112
Butcher, C. H., 163
Butcher, Jake, 159, 163
Butler, Carol, 168

California: governor's race in, 27–28, 187–93; voter turnout in, 14
Camarena, Enrique "Kiki", 259
campaign contributions, 59–60. *See also* election spending; fundraising
Capito, Shelley Moore, 70, 75
Capitol Broadcasting, 54
Carcieri, Don, 24
Carnahan, Jean, 15, 19, 41, 91; 2002 campaign of, 95–103
Carnahan, Mel, 91, 95, 96
Carolina Panthers (football team), 140
Carter, Jimmy, 5, 9, 42, 43, 91
cartoons, 62–63
Carville, James, 151
Castañon, Ricardo, 258
Cato Institute, 235, 239
Cayetano, Benjamin, 26
Census Bureau, U.S., 69
Center for Media and Public Affairs (CMPA), 48, 49
Center for Responsive Politics, 59–60
Center for the Study of Elections and Democracy (CSED), 50, 53, 54
Centerforpolitics.org, 59
Central Intelligence Agency (CIA), 109
Chambliss, Saxby, 14, 51, 70, 178; 2002 campaign of, 182–83
Chang, David, 106, 108, 109
Cheney, Dick, 86, 234; campaigning for candidates by, 19, 74, 82, 93, 96, 143, 150, 174, 179; and Halliburton, 38

Cheney, Lynne, 96, 99, 150
Chiles, Lawton, 202
Christian Coalition, 182
Christian right, 133, 139, 160, 211
CIA. *See* Central Intelligence Agency
City and County Bank of Knox County, 163
Cleland, Max, 14, 19, 41, 44, 51, 178; 2002 campaign of, 182–83
Clement, Bob, 159
Clement, Frank, 159–65
Cleveland, Clyde, 222
Clinton, Bill, 91, 203; and foreign policy, 9; impeachment of, 7, 32, 35, 158; and midterm elections, 2, 6; and Monica Lewinsky scandal, 2, 7; and North Carolina, 140, 143; role in party of, 42; and rural appeal, 42; and sexual scandals, 15; and South Dakota, 151
Clinton, Hillary, 42, 47, 173, 183
Club for Growth, 131
CMPA. *See* Center for Media and Public Affairs
coattail elections, 3–8, 39, 177, 205
Cochran, Barbara, 53, 54
Cohen, Rich, 100
Cole, Tom, 74
Coleman, Norm, 14, 49, 234; background of, 86–87; 2002 campaign of, 87–93
Commercial Appeal, 164
Concealed Carry Reform Now, 237
Concord Monitor (New Hampshire), 128
Condit, Gary, 71
Confederate flag, 45, 179–80
Congress, voting record reporting on Internet, 64. *See also* House of Representatives; Senate
Congressional Quarterly, 64, 161
Connecticut, Internet campaigns in, 63–64
Constitution Party, 235
contributions, campaign. *See* campaign contributions

Cook, Charlie, 99
Cook, Rhodes, 177
Cooper, Jim, 155
Cornyn, John, 167–75
corporate scandals, 8, 38, 89, 163, 192
corruption, political. *See* political corruption
Corzine, Jon, 107, 110, 120, 151
Coverdell, Paul, 181, 182
Cox Television, 54
Crawford, Craig, 48
Crespo, Henry, 203
CSED. *See* Center for the Study of Elections and Democracy
Cuban Missile Crisis, 3
cultural wars, 78, 133

Daley, Richard J., 209, 216
Daley, Richard M., 216
Daniels, Lee, 212
Darden, Buddy, 185
Daschle, Tom, 15, 41, 42, 97, 99, 111, 167; and South Dakota politics, 145, 147, 148, 151, 153
Davis, Arthur, 76
Davis, Gray, 14, 24, 27–28, 62; 2002 campaign of, 187–93
Day, Darrel, 96
Dean, Howard, 82
Dean, Tony, 149–50
debates: in Florida, 198, 200–201; in Georgia, 185; in Illinois, 215; in Massachusetts, 52; in Minnesota, 236; in Minnesota, 92; in North Carolina, 141–42; in Tennessee, 163–64
"Defenders, The" (television show), 158
Delisi, Ted, 170
Democratic Congressional Campaign Committee, 68, 185
Democratic National Committee (DNC), 62–63
Democratic party: blame game for poor showing, 40–43; and "Dream Team" slate in Texas, 168, 171–72, 174–75, 257; leadership of party, 41–42; strength in Maryland of, 225–26

Democratic Senatorial Campaign Committee (DSCC), 115, 159, 165
Dewey, Thomas E., 255
DiFrancesco, Don, 107
DNC. *See* Democratic National Committee
Dole, Bob, 7, 35, 156
Dole, Elizabeth, 15, 37, 55; 2002 campaign of, 137–44
Domenici, Pete, 90
Douglas, Jim, 28
Doyle, Jim, 26
Drudge, Matt, 62
DSCC. *See* Democratic Senatorial Campaign Committee
Duncan, Douglas, 226
Durbin, Dick, 213
Dutcher, Judi, 234, 235

e-gray.org, 62
E. W. Scripps, 54
Ebensteiner, Ron, 91
economy, 38–39
Edgar, Jim, 209
Education Networks of America (ENA), 163
Edwards, John, 37, 82, 137, 196
Ehrlich, Robert, 27; and gun control, 10; 2002 campaign of, 225–32
Eisenhower, Dwight D., 3, 65
election spending: in Florida, 204–5; in Minnesota, 237, 238; in New Hampshire, 131; in New Jersey, 114–15; in North Carolina, 142; in Pennsylvania, 249–50; in South Dakota, 148; in Texas, 255–56, 260–61; 2002 midterms, 20. *See also* campaign contributions; fundraising
elections, presidential party gain or loss in, 4t
Emanuel, Rahm, 74
Emily's List, 131
ENA. *See* Education Networks of America (ENA)
Engler, John, 26

Enron, 8, 38, 141, 167, 172
Ervin, Sam, 137
Evans, Don, 96
Everglades, Florida, 128
Ewing, Hickman, 158
exit polls, 10–11, 45, 48, 55, 115

Faircloth, Lauch, 37, 137
Farmers Insurance, 260
FEA. *See* Florida Education Association
Federal Bureau of Investigation (FBI), 106
FedEx, 162
Feinstein, Dianne, 173
Feldman, Ted, 100
Fenwick, Millicent, 113
Fernald, Mark, 131
First Union, 140
Fisher, Jimmie Lou, 26
Fisher, Mike, 26, 65, 248–51
Fitzgerald, Peter, 216
Fleischmann, Alan, 228
Fletcher, Bill, 162, 163, 165
Fletcher, Lee, 68
Florida: governor's race in, 27, 195–207; Republican control of, 205; 2004 politics of, 206–7; 2000 presidential election, 195
Florida Education Association (FEA), 196–97, 198, 204
Florida Elections Commission, 197
Forbes, Steve, 51
Ford, Gerald, 5
Ford, Harold, Jr., 159, 165
Ford, Harold, Sr., 158, 165
Ford, John, 159
foreign policy, 8–9
Forrester, Doug, 15, 105–9, 112–19
Forstmann Little, 142
Fort Worth Star-Telegram, 175
Foster, Mike, 19
Fowler, Wyche, 183
Fox, Michael J., 81
Fox News, 61
Franks, Bob, 107

free airtime, 54–55
Frew, John, 80
Frist, Bill, 155, 156, 160, 165
Frost, Martin, 185
fundraising: in California, 192; in Maryland, 226, 227, 230; in Minnesota, 89, 92, 243; in Texas, 175. *See also* campaign contributions; election spending

Gallardo, Miguel Felix, 259
Gallego, Pete, 256
Ganier, Al, 163
Gannett newspaper chain, 162
Ganske, Greg, 77–84
Garza, Tony, 169
Gates, Kent, 250
Gejdenson, Sam, 75
Gekas, George, 75
geography, and distribution of party preference, 36–37
George, Walter, 181
George Washington University Institute for Politics, Democracy, and the Internet, 60
Georgia: congressional elections in, 184–85; Democratic control of, 177, 186; governor's race in, 179–81; journalism role in, 51; Republican success in, 178, 186; Senate race in, 181–83; state flag issue in, 45, 179–80; 2002 midterms, 44–45, 177–86
Gephardt, Dick, 40, 68
gerrymandering. *See* redistricting
get-out-the-vote (GOTV) efforts, xii, 12; in Florida, 202–4; in Georgia, 51; via Internet, 61; in Iowa, 79, 83–84, 219, 222–23; in Missouri, 100, 101–2; in New Hampshire, 52, 129; in Texas, 256. *See also* voter turnout
Gibbons, Bill, 165
Gilman, Rhoda, 242
Gingrey, Phil, 185
Gingrich, Newt, 7, 91

Giuliani, Rudy, 150, 179, 191, 203
Glendening, Parris, 27, 226, 229, 230, 231
Global Crossing, 8
Goldwater, Barry, 62, 177
González, Antonio, 258, 259
Gonzalez, Elian, 128
Gordon, Bart, 159
Gordon, Houston, 155
Gore, Al, 75, 84, 91, 126, 129, 189, 203, 249; and Tennessee politics, 159, 161, 164, 165; and 2000 election, 2
Gore, Tipper, 159
GOTV. *See* get-out-the-vote (GOTV) efforts
government: reorganization of, 43; shutdown of (1995), 2
governorships: California race, 187–93; Florida race, 195–207; Illinois race, 209–17; Iowa race, 219–23; Maryland race, 225–32; Minnesota race, 233–45; Pennsylvania race, 247–52; Texas race, 255–61; 2002 midterms, 21–29, 43–45
Graham, Bob, 205
Gramm, Phil, 168–69, 170–71, 183, 256
Granholm, Jennifer, 26
Granite Broadcasting, 54
Grassley, Charles, 222
Green Party, 233, 234, 235, 241–42, 243, 245
Gregg, Judd, 133
Gross, Doug, 220–22
Guinn, Kenny, 24, 27
gun control, 10, 99–100, 149–50, 230, 236–37

Hagan, Tim, 61–62
Halliburton, 8, 38
Hancock, John, 101–2
Hanna, Jack, 252
Hanson, Al, 96–97
Harkin, Tom, 90, 92, 219; 2002 campaign of, 77–84, 222, 223

Harris, Katherine, 74
Hartford Courant, 49
Hartigan, Neil, 209
Harvard University, 139
Hastert, Dennis, 128
Hearst-Argyle Television, 54
Helms, Jesse, 137, 138, 139
Henry, Brad, 28, 44
Henry, Jim, 161
Hensarling, Jeb, 74
Herenton, Rodney, 164
Herenton, Willie, 164
Hernandez, Andy, 258
Heston, Charlton, 149, 174
Hildebrand, Steve, 146
Hilleary, Van, 156, 159, 161, 165
Hirono, Mazie, 26
Hispanics: and Florida politics, 202–3;
    as governors, 27; racism and, 259;
    and Texas politics, 168, 169, 170,
    175, 257–58; voter turnout by, 11,
    12
Hodges, Booker T., IV, 235
Hodges, Jim, 24, 26, 221
Hoeffel, Joe, 75
Holbrook, Hal, 156
Holden, Bob, 103
Holden, Tim, 75
Homeland Security Department, 41, 43,
    150
Horton, Willie, 239
House Mexican American Legislative
    Caucus, 256
House of Representatives: former strate-
    gists as members of, 74; midterm
    elections for, 3–8; political divisions
    on Opening Day, 7t; 2002 midterms,
    19–21, 67–76. *See also* Congress;
    redistricting
House Race Hotline, 67
Houston Chronicle, 169
Huckabee, Mike, 24
Hughes, Karen, 96, 99, 174
Hume, Brit, 55
humor, 61–63

Humphrey, Hubert, 87
Hunt, James B., 137
Hutchinson, Tim, 15, 19

Illinois, governor's race in, 209–17
Illinois Medical Society, 213
ImClone, 8
impeachment, of Clinton, 7, 32, 35, 158
incumbents: defeated in 2002, 73t; los-
    ers among, 75; matchups of, 72;
    redistricting as benefitting, 69;
    returned to office, 19, 20, 21
Independence Party, 233, 234, 238, 239,
    243, 245
Independents, as governors, 28–29
Inouye, Daniel, 151
interest groups, 242
International Bank of Commerce, 260
Internet: advantages of, 58; campaign
    future of, 65–66; campaign humor
    on, 61–63; and campaign websites,
    58–60; changing nature of, 57; polit-
    ical effectiveness of, 58–61; substan-
    tive coverage on, 63–65; and use for
    campaigning, 60; and user character-
    istics, 59; and voter behavior, 61
Iowa: caucuses of, 82; governor's race
    in, 219–23; Senate race in, 77–84
Iowa Farm Bureau Federation, 79
Iraq, war with. *See* war with Iraq
IssuesPA.net, 65

Jackson, Rev. Jesse, 203
Janensch, Paul, 49
Janklow, Bill, 24
Jeffords, Jim, 1, 14, 41, 42, 134, 151
Johanns, Mike, 24
Johnson, Eric, 179
Johnson, Lyndon, 4–5, 9, 62, 169
Johnson, Nancy, 64, 72
Johnson, Tim, 15, 17, 145–54
Jones, Alex, 53
Jones, Bill, 188, 189
Jones, Daryl, 196, 197, 198, 203
journalism. *See* media coverage

Kahn, Rick, 92
Kahn, Roger, 185
Kansas City Star, 98
Kanzler, Jay, 96
Kaplan, Martin, 50, 54
KARE-TV (Minneapolis), 49
Kean, Thomas, 106
Kempthorne, Dirk, 24
Kennedy, Ethel, 27
Kennedy, John F., 3
Kennedy, Robert, 27, 225
Kennedy, Ted, 183
Kerrey, Bob, 113, 151
Kerry, John, 82, 151, 196
King, Angus, 28
King, Martin Luther, Jr., 164
Kirk, Ron, 167–75, 257
Kitzhaber, John, 24
Kline, John, 76
Knoxville Journal, 162, 163
Kulongoski, Ted, 24
Kurtz, Howard, 51
Kustoff, David, 163

Landrieu, Mary, 17, 19
Laney, Pete, 171
Lapic, Tom, 91
Largent, Steve, 28, 44
Larson, Charles, 228, 229, 231
Larson, Chuck, Jr., 80
Lautenberg, Frank, 15, 105, 120; 2002
    campaign of, 110–19
Leach, Jim, 39
League of Conservation Voters, 148–49
Lear Center Local News Archive, 50,
    53, 54
Lee, Barbara, 173, 190
Lewinsky, Monica, 2, 7, 158
Libertarians, 132, 235, 239
Liberty Corporation, 54
Lichter, S. Robert, 48, 49–50
Lieberman, Joseph, 196, 203
Lightfoot, Jim Ross, 77, 219–20
Lillehaug, David, 90
Limbaugh, Rush, 61

Lindsey, Larry, 19
Lingle, Linda, 26
Link, Jeff, 80, 83
Lockheed Martin, 162
Lott, Trent, 91, 109, 128, 140
Louisiana, Democratic success in, 68
Lourey, Beckey, 234
Lublin, David, 184
Lucio, Eddie, 256
Lungren, Dan, 188–89

MacEvoy, Mary, 91
Madigan, Michael, 214–15
Maine, voter turnout in, 14
Maloney, Jim, 64, 72
marginal voters, 36, 79
Marie (movie), 161
Marshall, Elaine, 139, 140
Martin Marietta, 162
Maryland, governor's race in, 225–32
Maslin, Paul, 187
Massachusetts: governor's race in, 47;
    television advertising in, 52
Matalin, Mary, 96, 99, 149
Matheson, Jim, 75
Matheussen, John, 106–7
Mattingly, Mack, 177
McAuliffe, Terry, 195
McBride, Bill, 27, 61, 195–206
McCain, John, 47, 126, 189; and
    Internet campaign, 60, 65
McCall, Carl, 27
McCallum, Scott, 26
McDermott, Jim, 40
McGovern, George, 145
McGreevey, Jim, 105, 107, 110, 111,
    119, 120
McKinney, Cynthia, 71, 179
McLaughlin, Will, 91
media coverage: of Bush campaigning,
    50; cable news, 49; decline in, 49–50;
    free airtime and, 54–55; of Iraqi war
    issue, 38; local stations, 50; network
    news, 49; poor quality of 2002,
    48–49; public opinion of, 53; reform

of, 53–55; relation to advertising of, 53; of sniper shootings, 49; of Wellstone story, 49; and winner predictions, 55. *See also* Internet
Mehlman, Kenneth, 125
Menendez, Robert, 110
Merck, 140
Merrill Lynch, 8
Miami-Dade Democratic Black Caucus, 203
Midterm Election Map, 265m
midterm elections: history of post-WWII, 2–8; influence of, 2; predictions concerning, 2
Miller, Zell, 182–83
Minge, David, 75
Minneapolis Star Tribune, 90
Minnesota: future politics of, 245; governor's race in, 28, 233–45; Senate race in, 85–93; voter turnout in, 14
Minnesota Citizens Concerned for Life (MCCL), 242
Missouri: as bellwether state, 103; Senate race in, 95–103
Missouri Ethics Commission, 99
Moe, Roger, 28, 234–44
Mondale, Walter F., 14–15, 48, 49, 61; background of, 86; 2002 campaign of, 90–93
Moore, Dennis, 75
Morales, Dan, 258
Morales, Victor, 170–71
Morella, Connie, 75, 231
Moscow theater siege, 49
Moussaoui, Zacarias, 239
MoveOn.org, 60
Mundt, Karl, 17
Murkowski, Frank, 28
Murkowski, Lisa, 28
Murphy, Tom, 178

NAB. *See* National Association of Broadcasters
Nader, Ralph, 126, 233
NAFTA, 140

Napolitano, Janet, 26
NARAL. *See* National Abortion Rights Action League
NASCAR, 42
National Abortion Rights Action League (NARAL), 131
National Association of Broadcasters (NAB), 53, 54
National League of Conservation Voters, 131
National Republican Congressional Committee, 39
National Republican Senatorial Committee (NRSC), 80, 115, 142
National Rifle Association (NRA), 131, 139, 149–50
National Right to Life organization, 131
national security, 1–2, 32, 41
negative campaigning. *See* attack ads
Nelson, Bill, 205
nepotism, 28
Net. *See* Internet
Neustadt, Richard, 8
New Hampshire: party preference in, 125–26; Senate race in, 125–34; and state income tax, 126, 131; television advertising in, 51–52
New Hampshire State Democratic Committee, 131
New Hampshire State Republican Committee, 131
New Jersey: party preference in, 119; Senate race in, 105–20
New Jersey State Republican Committee, 115
New Jersey Supreme Court, 15, 111–12
New York Times Broadcasting, 54
New Yorker, 172
News & Observer (Raleigh, North Carolina), 140
Nine Sundays plan, 55
Nissan, 157
Nixon, Richard, 5, 9
Noonan, Peggy, 92
North Carolina, Senate race in, 137–44

North Carolina State Board of Election, 139
Northrup, Anne, 75
Norton, Gale, 96, 99, 150
Novak, Alan, 249
NRA. *See* National Rifle Association
NRSC. *See* National Republican Senatorial Committee
Nunn, Sam, 181
Nussle, Jim, 75

O'Brien, Shannon, 26, 47, 52
obstructionism, 41
October Surprises, 3–4
Oklahoma, governor's race in, 28, 44
Oliver, Jack, 63
O'Malley, Martin, 226
O'Malley, Patrick, 211, 212
O'Neal, Joe, 27
O'Neill, Paul, 19
Opensecrets.org, 59–60
Oracle, 131
Owens, Bill, 24

PACs. *See* political action committees
Paige, Rod, 150, 260
Pallone, Frank, 111
Panici, Elizabeth, 157
parties. *See* political parties *and specific parties*
Pataki, George, 24, 27
Pawlenty, Tim, 28, 86, 234–45
Peirce, Neal, 65
Pelosi, Nancy, 42, 173, 185
Pennsylvania: governor's race in, 247–52; Internet campaign influence in, 65
Pennsylvania Economy League, 65
Penny, Tim, 28, 233–45
Pentel, Ken, 233–34, 235, 236, 239, 240, 241, 243
People for the American Way, 131
Perdue, Sonny, 24, 26, 44, 51, 61, 178, 179, 181, 186
Perot, Ross, 6

Perry, Rick, 24, 27, 169; 2002 campaign of, 255–61
"Perry Mason" (television show), 158
Petty, Richard, 139
Phelps, David, 73
Pickering, Chip, 73
Planned Parenthood, 242
Polinard, Jerry, 260
political action committees (PACs), 60, 89
political corruption, in New Jersey, 120. *See also* Torricelli, Robert
political parties, gain or loss in elections, 4t
Politicalweb.info, 58
"Politics in Minnesota" (newsletter), 239
polling: exit, 10–11, 45, 48, 55, 115; methodology, 82; in Minnesota governor's race, 241t; of New Jersey voters, 116t—17t; online, 61
Poshard, Glenn, 210
Posthumus, Dick, 26
prescription drugs, 88
presidents: party gain or loss in elections, 4t; re-election and party control of Congress, 43
Pressler, Larry, 17, 147, 148
primary runoffs, 140
Pryor, Mark, 15

Qwest, 8

race, 171–75. *See also* African Americans; Hispanics
Racicot, Mark, 62
Racine, Doug, 28
Ragghianti, Marie, 161
Ramstad, Jim, 90
Ray, Bob, 78, 221
Reagan, Ronald, 5, 9, 21, 164
redistricting, 20, 67, 69–71; in Georgia, 177, 178, 180, 184, 186; political factors in, 69–70; and technology, 69; in Texas, 264; in 2004, 71
Reeve, Christopher, 81

Rendell, Ed, 26, 65, 247–52
Reno, Janet, 27, 196–99, 203
reorganization of government, 43
Republican National Committee
   (RNC), 62–63, 115, 138
Republican party: 1994 midterms, 2, 6;
   and one-party rule, 42; right wing of,
   133, 211; 2002 midterms, 14, 15,
   36–39; 2002 state legislature seats,
   29
Republican Party of Minnesota, 239
Richards, Ann, 170, 171
Richardson, Bill, 27
Richardson, Gary, 28
Ridge, Tom, 250, 251
Right to Life. See National Right to Life
   organization; Right to Life Party
   (South Dakota)
Right to Life Party (South Dakota), 152
Riley, Bob, 26
Riordan, Richard, 187–88, 189–90, 191
Rite-Aid, 8
RNC. See Republican National Com-
   mittee
Robinson, Jay, 222
Romney, Mitt, 24, 47, 52
Roosevelt, Franklin D., xi, 2, 3, 8, 65
Rossin, Tom, 204
Rounds, Mike, 24
Rove, Karl, 8, 150, 167, 258
Rowland, John, 24
Ruppersberger, C. A. "Dutch", 226, 231
rural America: Democrats and, 42; Iowa
   Senate race, 77–84
Russell, Richard, 181
Russert, Tim, 52, 200–201
Russo, Sal, 191
Ryan, George, 26, 210–11, 214, 215
Ryan, Jim, 26, 211–16

Sabato, Larry, 59
Sachs, Kari, 235
Salier, Bill, 78
Sanchez, John, 27
Sanchez, Tony, 27, 170, 171; 2002 cam-
   paign of, 255–61

Sanford, Mark, 26
Saturn (automobile manufacturer), 157
Sauerbrey, Ellen R., 226, 227, 228, 231
Schaefer, William Donald, 227, 229,
   230
Schundler, Bret, 105, 107, 119
Schurick, Paul, 227
Schwarzenegger, Arnold, 44
Schweiker, Mark, 251
Scott, Alexis, 180
Sebelius, Kathleen, 26
security. See national security
Senate: Iowa race, 77–84; midterm elec-
   tions for, 3–8; Minnesota race,
   85–93; Missouri race, 95–103; New
   Hampshire race, 125–34; New Jersey
   race, 105–20; North Carolina race,
   137–44; political divisions on Open-
   ing Day, 6t; South Dakota race,
   145–54; Tennessee race, 155–65;
   Texas race, 167–75; 2002 midterms,
   14–19. See also Congress
Senate Ethics Committee, 106, 108, 109
September 11, 2001 terrorist attacks, 1
sexism, 47, 99
Shaheen, Jeanne, 52, 125–34
Sharp, John, 257
Sharpton, Al, 203
Shea, Gwyn, 256
Shields, Mark, 149
Shipp, Bill, 178
Shorenstein Center (Harvard Univer-
   sity), 55
Shows, Ronnie, 73
Siegelman, Don, 24
Sierra Club, 131
silent majority, 5
Simon, Bill, Jr., 14, 27–28, 61–62; 2002
   campaign of, 188–92
sixth-year itch, 3, 5, 35
Smith, Andrew, 52
Smith, Bob, 19, 125, 127, 128, 129–30,
   131–32, 133
Smith, Chris, 203–4
Smith, Frederick W., 162

Smith, Jim, 198
Smith, Neal, 77
sniper shootings, 10, 39, 48, 49, 230
"Social Insecurity" Internet video, 62–63
Social Security, 62–63, 88, 97
Socialist Workers Party, 235
soft money: in Florida, 204; in New Jersey, 115
South: Democrats and, 42; 2002 state legislature races, 29–31
South, Garry, 187–88
South Dakota: Senate race in, 145–54; voter turnout in, 14
Southwest Voter Registration Education Project, 258
Spacek, Sissy, 161
spending, election. See election spending
Spring Industries, 140
St. Paul Pioneer Press, 239
St. Petersburg Times, 197, 203
Star Tribune (Minneapolis), 239
Starr, Ken, 158
Starr Report, 65
state legislatures, 2002 midterms, 29–31
statehouses. See governorships
states: electoral preference of, 36; fiscal problems of, 43; significance of, in midterms, 264–66
Steele, Michael, 228
Steinberg, Arnold, 191
Stewart, Martha, 8
Sukup, Steve, 220, 221
Sullivan, Brian, 235
Sullivan, John, 76
Sundquist, Don, 156, 158, 163, 164
Sununu, John, 19, 39, 52; 2002 campaign of, 125–34
Supreme Court. See New Jersey Supreme Court; U.S. Supreme Court
Sweet, David, 250
swing voters, 36

Taft, Bob, 24, 69
taftquack.com, 62

Talent, Jim, 15, 95–103
Talmadge, Herman, 177, 181
Tanner, John, 158, 159
tape-gate, 80–81
targeting, campaign, 76
Taylor, Paul, 54
television advertising: in California, 187–88, 190; in Florida, 197, 199–201, 204; in Georgia, 181; House candidates with Bush and, 74; in Illinois, 211; in Iowa, 78, 80; in Maryland, 229; in Massachusetts, 52; in Minnesota, 86–87, 236, 238, 239, 241–42; in Missouri, 100–101; in New Hampshire, 51–52; in North Carolina, 141–42; in Pennsylvania, 248; and quality of media coverage, 53; quantity of, 50, 51–52, 53, 54; in South Dakota, 147–50, 151–52; as subject of media coverage, 48; in Tennessee, 162. See also attack ads
Tennessee, and South Dakota politics, 155–65
Terrell, Suzanne Haik, 17, 19
Tesoro Savings and Loan of Laredo, 259
Texas: governor's race in, 255–61; Senate race in, 167–75
third-party candidates, 233–45
Thompson, Bennie, 76
Thompson, Ed, 26
Thompson, Fred, 155–56, 157, 161, 165
Thompson, Mike, 40
Thompson, Tommy, 26
Thune, John, 15, 145–54
Thurman, Karen, 75
Time, 172, 189
Toomey, Pat, 75
Torricelli, Robert, 15, 105–10, 119
Townsend, Kathleen Kennedy, 26, 27; and gun control, 10; 2002 campaign of, 225–32
Traficant, James, 71, 72
Trans World Airlines, 98

Treffinger, Jim, 106
Trinchitella, "Trinchi", 204
Truman, Harry S., 3, 255
Tyco International, 8, 130
Tyndall, Andrew, 49, 50
Tyndall Report, 49

Ulmer, Fran, 26, 28
Umphrey, Walter, 171
unemployment, 19
unilateralism, 38
Union Leader (Manchester, New Hampshire), 52, 127, 128
United Seniors Association, 131
University of Wisconsin, 50
U.S. Chamber of Commerce, 131
U.S. Supreme Court, 112
USC Annenberg School, 50

Vallas, Paul, 210
Van Hollen, Chris, 231
Vander Plaats, Bob, 220, 221
Veneman, Ann, 150
Ventura, Jesse, 15, 28, 65, 90, 233, 234, 240, 244
Vermont: governor's race in, 28; voter turnout in, 14
Vietnam War, 4–5
Vilsack, Tom, 24, 78, 84; 2002 campaign of, 219–23
Vinroot, Richard, 138
VNS. See Voter News Service
Voter News Service (VNS), 10–11, 45, 48, 55, 115
Voter Reform Project, 131
voter turnout, 11–14, 32t; in Maryland, 231; in New Hampshire, 132; in North Carolina, 143; as Republican advantage in 2002, 37. See also get-out-the-vote (GOTV) efforts
voting patterns, 10–14; in Florida, 205; in Georgia, 178–79; in Minnesota, 244

Waffleman, 239
Walker, Champ, 184–85
Walker, Charles, 178
Walker, Dan, 209
Wallace, George, 158
Wamp, Zach, 156
war with Iraq: and Baghdad 3, 40; as focal point of midterm elections, 8–9, 38, 48, 49; fundraising against, 60; Wellstone on, 88
Washington Post, 184, 228, 230, 231
Watts, J. C., 150
Weber, Vin, 90–91
websites. See Internet
Webster, Bill, 103
Wellstone, David, 90
Wellstone, Paul, 14–15, 28, 48, 84, 86, 96, 237; death of, 90, 240, 242; and Internet campaign, 61; liberalism of, 85; memorial service for, 49, 91–92; political success of, 87; 2002 campaign of, 87–90
Wharton, A. C., 165
Wilder, L. Douglas, 27
Wilkinson, Bud, 44
William C. Velásquez Institute, 257–58
Williams, Carl, 231
Wilson, Rilya, 201
WMUR-TV (Manchester, New Hampshire), 51–52, 131
women: as governors, 26–27; in Senate, 134
Wood, Corrine, 211, 212
WorldCom, 8, 73
WRAL-TV (Raleigh, North Carolina), 138
WTOC-TV (Savannah), 51–52

York, Myrth, 26–27
Yost, Berwood, 251
Yu, Audrey, 109

About the Contributors

Mark Z. Barabak is a political writer for the *Los Angeles Times*.

James W. Brosnan has been the Washington reporter for *The Memphis Commercial Appeal* since 1983.

Charles S. Bullock III is a professor in the School of Public and International Affairs at the University of Georgia.

Michael Cornfield is an associate research professor at the Graduate School of Political Management at George Washington University and the director of the Institute for Politics, Democracy, and the Internet.

Peggy Fikac is the Austin bureau chief of the *San Antonio Express-News*.

Thomas Fitzgerald is a staff writer for the *Philadelphia Inquirer*.

Linda L. Fowler is the director of the Nelson A. Rockefeller Center at Dartmouth College and is a professor in the Government Department.

Mike Glover is the Iowa statehouse reporter and chief political writer for the Des Moines bureau of The Associated Press.

Paul Green is the director of the School of Policy Studies and Arthur Rubloff Professor of Policy Studies at Roosevelt University in Chicago. He is also known for his political commentary on WGN.

Holly A. Heyser is the state government editor for the *St. Paul Pioneer Press* and president of the Association of Capitol Reporters and Editors, a national organization of statehouse journalists.

Daniel J. B. Hofrenning is an associate professor at St. Olaf College. He has contributed works to several journals and newspapers including the *Star Tribune* and the *St. Paul Pioneer Press*.

Mark Jurkowitz is a columnist with the *Boston Globe*, where he focuses on media coverage of political news.

David Kranz is a columnist for the *Sioux Falls Argus Leader* and has covered South Dakota politics for thirty years.

Steve Kraske is a political correspondent for the *Kansas City Star*.

Bruce A. Larson is an assistant professor at Fairleigh Dickinson University, specializing in the American electoral process.

Daniel LeDuc is the deputy national editor for *The Washington Post*.

Susan A. MacManus is the Distinguished University Professor of Public Administration and Political Science at the University of South Florida and a frequent media commentator and political analyst.

Jay Root is Austin bureau chief of the *Fort Worth Star-Telegram*.

According to *The Wall Street Journal*, **Larry J. Sabato** is "probably the most quoted college professor in the land," and *The Washington Post* calls him "the Mark McGwire of political analysts." Dr. Sabato is director of the University of Virginia's Center for Politics, and is the Robert Kent Gooch Professor of Politics. Sabato has authored over twenty-five books, including *Overtime! The Election 2000 Thriller* (2001), *Peepshow: Media and Politics in an Age of Scandal* (2000), *Dirty Little Secrets: The Persistence of Corruption in American Politics* (1996), and *Feeding Frenzy: How Attack Journalism Has Transformed American Politics* (1991).

Maureen Schweers is the editor of *The House Race Hotline*, a twice-weekly news briefing that "covers the coverage" of the most competitive House races, with an emphasis on special elections, open seats, and endangered incumbents.

Ryan Thornburg has recently returned to washingtonpost.com's OnPolitics page. He formerly served as the editor and publisher of *The Carolina Political Report.*

Chuck Todd is editor-in-chief of *The Hotline*, Washington's premier daily briefing on American politics.

David Yepsen is a political columnist for the *Des Moines Register* and has covered Iowa politics for twenty-five years.